Changing Fathers?

Fatherhood and Family Life in Modern Ireland

Kieran McKeown

Harry Ferguson

Dermot Rooney

GW00542547

The Collins Press

Published by the Collins Press, Carey's Lane, The Huguenot
Quarter, Cork

British Library Cataloguing in Publication data.

Editing and layout by Stephanie Dagg, Virtually Perfect Editing
Services
Index by Kate Duffy
Printed in Ireland by Sci Print, Shannon
Jacket design by Upper Case Ltd, Cork

ISBN: 1-898256-55-1

'He didn't speak to us much. It was that typical Irish thing, a father and son not really speaking to each other, not really knowing each other ... But was I close to him? No. I loved him and I admired him, but I didn't really know him. He didn't have that much to say ... Irish family life has many virtues, but emotional openness is not among them. It is, I believe, a curse of our culture that we find ourselves unable to tell those closest to us how much we care; expressions of love, gratitude and admiration, which should flow naturally between us, rather than make us squirm. My father was as much a victim of this syndrome as any other of his generation: he was content to show rather than to express. But expression is important too, as I know too well, having failed miserably and repeatedly to put it into practice down through the years. In the case of my father, though, I did find that kind of maturity which overcame my foolish fears. He did not die in doubt. I am glad of that.'

David Hanley

We honour our fathers by dedicating this work to them:

James McKeown
Tom Ferguson (1931–1993)
Cha Rooney

Contents

The authors

Kieran McKeown
Kieran McKeown is the father of three children and has written about his own experience of fathering and being a father. He has been involved in social and economic research for about twenty years and his work has been widely published.

Harry Ferguson
Harry Ferguson works as a senior lecturer in the Department of Applied Social Studies, University College, Cork (UCC). His books include co-authorship of *Taking Child Abuse Seriously* (with the Violence Against Children Study Group), London: Routledge, 1990; *On Behalf of the Child: Child Welfare, Child Protection and the Child Care Act 1991* (with Pat Kenny), Dublin: A and A Farmar, 1991; *Protecting Irish Children: Investigation, Protection and Welfare* (with Tony McNamara), Dublin: IPA, 1996.

Dermot Rooney
Dermot Rooney is a clinical psychotherapist and lecturer. He has taught and designed an extensive range of courses in counselling, psychotherapy and psychology.

Acknowledgements

We wish to acknowledge the help received from a number of people in writing this book.

We are grateful to the Commission on the Family (1995–1998) for funding the research on which the book is based. We are particularly grateful to Catherine Hazlett, the secretary of the Commission, for allowing us access to the literature and for her advice at different stages of the research.

We are grateful to Con Collins for his enthusiastic support in ensuring that this book was published and for his keen interest in advancing understanding of men's issues.

The National Children's Resource Centre, based in Barnardo's, carried out literature searches for us and its librarian, Martina Tumbleton, sourced a wide variety of materials.

Parental Equality: the Shared Parenting and Joint Custody Support Group has been helpful throughout the research. We particularly want to thank Liam O'Gogáin, Alain Beirne, and Norman Newell for their openness and generosity in sharing their experiences and expertise.

Margot Doherty and Margaret Dromey of Treoir: Federation of Services for Unmarried Parents and their Children were helpful in sending us relevant documentation and in discussing some of the key issues.

Margaret Burns of the Council for Social Welfare: a Committee of the Catholic Bishops' Conferences sent us some documentary material which we found useful.

Charlie Delap, who is preparing a doctorate on fathers at University College Dublin, was generous in giving us access to his well-endowed archive of articles on this subject and for his comments on an earlier draft.

We are also grateful for the comments and support received from Hugh Arthurs, Paula Clancy, Grace

Fitzgerald, Edmond Grace, Fergus Hogan, Tom Hyde, Peter Kieran, Peadar King, Susie King, Claire MacKinnon, Brendan Murphy, Orla O'Donovan, Alan O'Neill and Sean Reynolds.

Maire Leane, Lecturer in the Department of Applied Social Studies, University College Cork, provided many helpful references and posed some important questions about parenting, power and gender relations. Questions raised by students in the Department of Applied Social Studies, University College Cork and dialogue with them over the years has also proved challenging and helpful.

The special tabulations of the 1996 Labour Force Survey reported in chapter five were carried out by Anthony Murphy of University College, Dublin.

To all of the above we offer our thanks while absolving them of any responsibility for the use which we made of their help.

Foreword

by Professor Anthony Clare

Fatherhood in the late twentieth century is an emotional minefield into which modern men stumble, grappling with a riot of confusing feelings and uncertain responses, dimly aware that within the reawakened memories of their own fathers can be identified the ghostly signposts to how they might survive and prosper as fathers themselves. Contemporary images of fatherhood are neither positive nor encouraging. Today's dad is likely to be portrayed as foolish and antiquated when he is not being abusive or feckless.

In this book, three Irish social researchers examine the changing role of men in Irish family life and challenge many traditional assumptions about men's capacity to love, relate to, inspire and engage with their children. Kieran McKeown, Harry Ferguson and Dermot Rooney explore the paradox whereby while the day-to-day work of private and of public child care is undertaken, for the most part, by women, it is bureaucratic men, whose paternal authority lies in organisational rationality and authority, who are the public administrators of family life.

In a keenly articulated argument for a concerted and sustained effort to support those fathers, and there are many, who wish to be more involved with their children, Kieran McKeown, Harry Ferguson and Dermot Rooney acknowledge that traditional marital and family structures have not been in the best interests of women but provide convincing evidence that they have not been in the best interests of men either. This is a formidable, honest and long awaited contribution to the growing analysis of men by men. It draws extensively on the expanding literature on fathers, in psychology, sociology, social policy, legal studies and psychoanalysis. Throughout, it endorses a vision of fatherhood at once committed, involved, responsible and intimate and it constantly reminds us that in exploring the core and the shaping of fatherhood we are touching on the most basic structures – political, legal, social and educational – of society itself. If we can arrive at a more emotionally stable, psychologically integrated and socially valued idea of fatherhood, this book argues, much of what is corrosive and abusive in modern society could well be eliminated.

Preface

We live in a time of change for men, women and children as traditional expectations about gender roles and family relationships are changing dramatically. The male role and masculinity no longer match the reality of the circumstances in which many men live and work. After some three decades of feminism and other social changes, the meanings of work and intimacy in men's lives are under revision. The tendency for men to find their identity and fulfilment exclusively in the world of work and to have their role as fathers valued because of the income they bring to the family is increasingly challenged. This is because some men face persistent long-term unemployment and have no work identity or income; a minority of young men never even make the successful transition to the world of work. There are increasing numbers of men in dual earner families who are no longer the sole breadwinners and who expect – and are expected – to play non-traditional fathering roles. The growth of lone parent families, usually headed by mothers, is practically and symbolically important in showing the viability of 'fatherless' families and raises questions as to whether men have a dispensable role in the rearing of children.

All men are affected by these developments. Some are slowly coming to an awareness of the need to reflect on what it is to be a good man and a good father. Others are beginning to examine the attitudes and structures that shape how men are expected to be in society. This book is intended as a contribution to such a project. While much attention has rightly been given over the past twenty-five years to the position of women in society, systematic attention to the place of men has been relatively ignored. The twentieth century has seen significant changes in the status of women and in their consciousness. We agree with those men and women who believe that more needs to be done to change social attitudes and structures which limit women's opportunities to live a full and fulfilling life of their choice. However, we also believe that, as we enter the twenty-first century, a period of reflection and development is needed so that the structures of our thought as much as our institutions can facilitate active fatherhood and support those men who wish to respond positively to the changing circumstances of their lives. The emergence of men's groups and father's groups is just one indicator of such organised change.

We live, then, at a time when issues surrounding men are now routinely subjects for debate in the media, academia, and everyday life. Men have even become an explicit subject for political debate as when, in January 1998, Fine Gael TD Brian Hayes called on the government to establish a Commission on the Status of Men to investigate the well-being of men in Irish society from the vantage point of the risks that are known to exist from such things as male suicide, crime, unemployment, changing family structures and the marginalisation of fatherhood. Public awareness of fathers' roles and rights has also been raised by the work of Parental Equality: The Shared Parenting and Joint Custody Support Group, and the writings of *Irish Times* columnist John Waters, who both strongly advocate a much greater role for men in their lives of their children.

At a cultural level, indicators of the new interest in men's lives and curiosity about 'masculinity' include the explosion of men's magazines – of which the first Irish version, *Himself*, was published in 1998 – and the profusion of images about the so-called 'new man' of the 1980s and the 'new lad' of the 1990s. Then there is the extraordinary success of *The Full Monty* – a film about a group of disaffected, unemployed men who find some meaning in their lives through becoming male strippers – which became the biggest earning British movie of all time. A centre-piece of the film was the struggle of one man to be an active, 'good' father by keeping up his maintenance payments to his estranged wife and maintaining contact with his son.

Thus, through it all, while there are many parts to men's lives, their role as fathers has become more and more a public issue. Yet, despite the new-found interest in the changing roles of men, little has been produced on the nature of fatherhood in Irish society. The aim of this book is to contribute to filling this gap in our understanding of fathers and the changing role of men in Irish family life. It is our intention not only to chronicle recent social changes as they have impacted on fatherhood and men more generally, but also to contribute to change by advancing the case for men to become more actively involved in parenting. As we show in what follows, such an objective requires us to rethink some of the taken-for-granted assumptions about the nature of being men and women and constitutes a real challenge to the structures of thought and power that inhibit men from becoming more active fathers and carers. We believe that fatherhood is an opportunity and a gift which no man should let pass by. While our primary focus is on men and fatherhood, our analysis takes us into considering key aspects of the lives and roles of women and children and, more generally, what constitutes a good society.

Writing this book has itself been a challenging process for the three of us as men; we have had to struggle to reach a working consensus on where we stand on many of the key issues. We have been helped in this by participating in a men's group since 1992 and by organising a number of men's gatherings. While we speak in a collective voice, it is important to recognise the division of labour and creative process that was involved in producing this book. Each chapter was drafted by one of us and commented on by the other two. Kieran McKeown wrote chapters one, three and five; Harry Ferguson wrote chapters four and seven, and chapter two was written by Dermot Rooney. Chapter six was co-written by Kieran McKeown and Harry Ferguson. Each chapter bears the unmistakable marks of its author but also carries the indelible traces of our shared discussions and reflections.

Kieran McKeown, Harry Ferguson, Dermot Rooney
August 1998

Introduction

'Fathers and families need new images of what a father can be, images that go beyond the idea of father as outsider, father as provider, or father as intruder in the home. There is a need for images that acknowledge father as a potent nurturant force within the family as well as a creative liaison with the world outside the family.'

Colman and Colman (1988)

Everyone has a father and everyone knows what a father is. This makes fatherhood – like motherhood – one of the most universal human experiences. No one lives without some sense, however vague, of the individual and collective meanings of fatherhood and its personal significance. This book is about the meanings and practices associated with fatherhood and the changes affecting it – and Irish society – as we move into the twenty-first century.

Fatherhood is constituted not only through the biological act of procreation but also, and more significantly, through the ideas and beliefs that define how men play this role. One of the defining features of our time is that ideas and beliefs about the role of fathers – and men generally – are undergoing considerable change and debate and the reasons for this are explored in the book. In particular, we endeavour to provide answers to the following key questions:

- what changes are affecting the role of fathers?
- what is the function of a father?
- what is the meaning of fatherhood and its relation to 'masculinity'?
- what differences do fathers make to the development of children?
- what do fathers do at home?
- how does work impact on the fathering role?

- are the rights and responsibilities of fathers adequately enshrined in law?
- what services and supports facilitate good fathering?

A central theme in the book is the relationship between fathers and their children. Relationships between fathers and mothers and between mothers and children are also explored because they are inseparable from the relationship between fathers and children. The book is grounded in the soil of Irish experience from where we draw many examples and to which we offer suggestions on ways of promoting and supporting the role of fathers.

The word 'father' has many different meanings. It means the biological father, the symbolic father and the person who engages in the practical act of fathering. These are usually one person: the biological father. But they may also be different people, such as a step-father, adoptive father, foster father or other father figures. 'Father' also has many different images. There is the image of the 'traditional' father who is a hard working breadwinner but often absent, both physically and emotionally, from his children. There is the 'modern' father who pushes prams and changes nappies, takes his children to school and plays with them in the park, reads to them at night and discusses the events of the day. There is the 'non-resident' father – whether single, separated or married – who may see his children regularly, or he may make an appearance only once or twice a year, or he may lose contact with his children completely.

There are also images of the father that depict particular qualities. There are loving fathers, dependable fathers, involved fathers, committed fathers, strong fathers, adoring fathers. Equally, there are images that depict negative qualities. There are disinterested fathers, unreliable fathers, workaholic fathers, abusive fathers, weak fathers, violent fathers. These different images are also part of the way in which men are seen in society.

Expectations are changing about what it is to be a good father. Good fathers are increasingly expected to be emotionally involved with their children. They are expected to share housework and take an interest in the children's schooling. It is no longer presumed that the father is the sole breadwinner or that his role is simply to supply the weekly wage packet. There is a presumption that fathers will want to be at the birth of their children and that they will have the same practical skills of child rearing – apart from breast-feeding – as the mother. However, it appears that few contemporary fathers have actually experienced this type of fathering themselves (Hyde, 1996). As a result, many of them cannot rely on their own fathers as models of good fathers, even if they were good fathers by the standards of their time (Daly, 1995).

All of the contemporary images of the father – both the positive and the negative – are true in the sense that they reflect some aspect of how fathers are experienced. Just as there are many different ways of being a man, so there are many different ways of being a father (see Connell, 1995; Ferguson, 1997a). The public imagery associated with fatherhood tends to be contradictory and involve both positive and negative aspects. These contradictory images are, in our view, a reflection of the change and uncertainty affecting the cultural meaning of men and fatherhood. By contrast, the public imagery associated with motherhood tends to be consistent and positive – sometimes to the point of veneration – although some feminist writers have usefully drawn attention to ambiguities within the role of mother, its difficulties, as well as the positive rewards it can bring to women's lives (see for example, Byrne and Leonard, 1997; Featherstone and Holloway, 1997; Hooper, 1992).

One commentator has attributed this change and uncertainty to the 'demise of cultural consensus on the meaning of manhood [which] has left men in a no man's land, searching for new meanings and definitions of maturity' (Gerson, 1993, p. 5). The contemporary experience of fatherhood in the United States, as described by one writer, is probably not very different from that in Ireland: 'fatherhood in recent decades has become a kaleidoscope of images and trends, a sure sign that it has

3

lost cultural coherence ... Buffeted by powerful demographic, economic, and political changes, fatherhood in American culture is now fraught with ambiguity and confusion. Not surprisingly, so, too, are fathers themselves' (Griswold, 1993, p. 244). We believe that the writing of this book is itself a sign of change and uncertainty and of the need to take stock of the position of fathers in families and in society generally.

The public imagery of fatherhood and the private experiences of individual fathers mutually influence each other. Contemporary images of fatherhood often have a strong negative hue. This can be seen by looking at how some commentators have depicted the contemporary image of the father. A Jungian analyst in the United States, for instance, has observed that: 'when we watch Dad on TV sitcoms and the accompanying ads, he's a rather foolish man. He's not quite with it; a piece of him is astray. Commentators on contemporary fatherhood complain that he is being deliberately made to look foolish and antiquated, because this weakened image helps take down the stuffed-shirt power of the patriarchy, makes more equal the relations between the genders, and blurs the hierarchical differences between fathers and children. Therefore wives are shown to be more practical and connected, children to be more with it and savvy. Even if he's a good guy, Dad is a little dumb' (Hillman, 1996, p. 80). In Britain, another commentator has written about the negative image of fathers: 'many of the images we have of fatherhood today are negative. Fathers are seen as absurd, pitiable, marginal, violent, abusive, uncaring and delinquent ... As it has become more difficult to give emotional meaning to paternal absence, the image of the absent father has gathered force and negativity, and father-absence associated with the rising tide of out-of-wedlock births has become a symbol of moral degeneration' (Burgess, 1997, pp. 19–20). Some of the literature compounds these negative stereotypes by characterising men's motivations as rational and selfish in contrast to women's motivations which are seen as selfless and altruistic: 'male individualism is counterbalanced by female altruism ... rational economic man is taken care of by irrational altruistic woman' (Folbre, 1994, p. 119).

The negative imagery we have just described associated with men and fatherhood also appears in discussions about how to involve men in childcare. For example, a seminar on Men as Carers for Children which was organised by the European Commission Network on Childcare in 1990, raised a number of concerns about the prospect of greater involvement by men in childcare: 'The prospect [of men being more involved in the care of children] raised a number of anxieties and concerns – for example, about child abuse, about men invading "women's space" and being too dominant, about fathers taking over the more rewarding and pleasant childcare tasks' (European Commission Network on Childcare, 1990). At the same conference, one commentator even suggested, as a reason why men should participate in the care of children, that 'closer contact with children will help men to express themselves in less aggressive and abusive ways' (*Ibid*, p. 5). Does this imply that men normally express themselves in aggressive and abusive ways? And if it does, then who is responsible for advancing such imbalanced images?

The fact that such imbalanced images of fathers can exist can be explained to some extent by the fact that traditional constructions of 'masculinity' have not required men to make themselves the subjects of critical reflection and dialogue. Manhood has been heavily based on rationality, competition and action in the world; it is something that just 'gets done'. In western industrial countries like Ireland, the dominant construction of 'masculinity' has meant the triumph of reason over nature; of mind over body (Seidler, 1997). The effect of this is that even when men have been (and are) actively involved fathers, this experience has not been articulated by them in public discourse and the 'private' dimensions to men's lives have remained largely hidden. Thus, in facing the challenge of articulating our experience in the context of recent social changes, men in general are only beginning to find the language and skills to communicate about such personal issues. We regard this book as a contribution to this important project.

The negative imagery we have just described is not just bad publicity for men and fathers, although it is certainly that. It has a base in the experiences of men and women and, in turn, helps to mould that experience. The imagery, even if it is truly representative of the lives of only a small minority of men and fathers (who knows?), is now part of our collective consciousness and seems to 'go with the territory' of being a man and a father in our time.

The negative imagery we have just described is both dismaying and challenging to men because it asks questions of every man and father: Is this a true image of me? Am I a good man and a good father? For society generally, it raises questions that are just as serious: Does society want men and fathers to be characterised in this negative way? What images of men and role models of fathers does society wish to promote and facilitate? What impact is this negative imagery having on men and fathers or on mothers and children? By what ideals and values are boys to grow into men and fathers? These questions cannot be avoided, either individually or collectively. Indeed, the negative imagery may become even more negative if these questions are ignored and the consequences for men and society may become even more negative. Accordingly, the theme of fatherhood touches deeply on matters that are personal as well as political, private as well as public. They concern men first, and fathers second, since no one can become a father without first becoming a man. In other words, a 'good father' must first become a 'good man' and must search for the meaning of those terms in his life (McKeown, 1997b).

In attempting to illuminate these issues, this book brings together evidence from a range of sources. It draws upon an extensive review of the growing literature on fathers, particularly in the areas of psychology and sociology, but also in psychoanalysis, social policy and legal studies. It analyses new data on the amount of time Irish fathers spend at work, at home and what they actually do with their children, as well as mapping out and examining the implications of recent legislative changes for fathers and the relationship between fathers and social supports. Our analysis is also informed by our experience of working with men in men's groups and larger gatherings over a number of years. While this is obviously more subjective 'evidence', we believe that what we have learnt from the experiences of many Irish men has a real value in shaping our understandings of men's lives and fatherhood and this is reflected in the arguments we make here.

In reviewing the evidence, we have come to the view that promoting the active involvement of fathers in the care and upbringing of their children is an ideal worth aspiring to, irrespective of whether the father is married or not, separated or not, resident with his child or not, heterosexual or not. We agree with the Commission on the Family on the importance of joint parenting: 'Joint parenting should be encouraged with a view to ensuring as far as possible that children have the opportunity of developing close relationships with both parents which is in the interests both of children and their parents. The option of joint parenting may not always be available or indeed optimal (for example, when violence, abuse or extremes of conflict are involved). In cases where children's interest is best served by joint parenting, public policy has a key role in promoting this interest' (Commission on the Family, 1996, p. 14).

In forming this perspective, we have sought to understand the significance that fathers can play in the lives of children, as well as the different factors – in the home, in work, in law, in social services, in cultural expectations – which have inhibited fathers from being more involved in the care and upbringing of their children. While the specific focus of the book is on the caring relationship between fathers and children, itself a major issue, we see this as part of the broader issue of what it is to be a man and to care for others. Men, like women, have obligations to care for others throughout their adult lives, including care for frail parents and older relatives, care for older children as well as for grandchildren. In our view, men need to actively negotiate these caring responsibilities and share them with women at each of the different stages over the course of a life.

The kernel of our analysis is that the ideal of greater involvement by fathers in the care and upbringing of their children – increasingly presented as the ideal and standard towards which the modern father should aspire – is either opposed or not supported by many of the structures, policies and practices that have a direct impact on fathers. Our analysis shows this in many spheres of public and private life:

- in the symbolic sphere, where the father-child relationship is treated as secondary to the mother-child relationship, and the crucial role of the father, as seen in the psychoanalytic perspective of Freud, Lacan and others, is ignored. In this perspective, the father's role is crucial in drawing attention to the fact that mother and child must desire and connect with a world outside each other if they are to live and grow as separate independent persons;
- in the sphere surrounding the birth of children, including preparation for parenthood, where the father is treated, often unwittingly, as a secondary, supporting parent;
- in the sphere of work, where some fathers work very long hours thereby reducing the time and energy available for involvement with the children but also, at a deeper level, sustaining the self-image of father as the principal breadwinner;
- in the legal sphere, which confers greater parental rights on mothers than fathers, particularly pronounced in the case of separated and unmarried fathers;
- in the sphere of State services and supports which often treat parenting as synonymous with mothering and ignores fathers or fails to make the necessary contact with them.

The net effect of these forces is that the overall involvement of men in the care and upbringing of children may actually be declining precisely at a time when a growing number of fathers appear interested in having closer emotional involvement with their children. This is so for a number reasons. First, a growing number of children are placed in childcare facilities each working day, where virtually all the staff are women, thereby reducing their contact with men and fathers. Second, a growing number of children are in lone parent families under the sole custody of the mother and the amount of access by fathers to these children may be on the decline, either because the mothers restrict access or because the fathers do not wish to have more access (see Table 1.2 on page 21).

In this scenario, it is hardly surprising that children learn to perceive caring as women's rather than men's work and, out of these experiences, form the attitudes that sustain the distancing of men from children for the coming generation. In our view, this pattern will not change unless there is a concerted and sustained effort to support those fathers who wish to be more involved with their children as well as supporting those men who wish to work with children in the caring professions.

It is possible to advance four different reasons or perspectives for promoting the greater involvement of fathers in the lives of their children:

- benefits to children's development as a result of being emotionally close to both parents;
- benefits to families in supporting the interdependent relationships – economic, social and emotional – that hold its members together, including members of the extended family;
- benefits to women in the form of greater equality in the labour market and in the domestic division of labour;
- benefits to men in the form of greater involvement as fathers with their children which can lead to their

own and their children's personal development and growth.

Many of the arguments, both in Ireland and elsewhere, tend to cite the benefits for women and children of greater involvement by fathers (see for example, Second Commission on the Status of Women, 1993, chapter three; Employment Equality Agency, 1996; Moss, 1993). However, there are fewer arguments citing the benefits for fathers from being more involved with their children, although there is plenty of criticism for their failing to do so, and there are fewer arguments still from the perspective of the needs of the family as an interdependent unit of relationships (Hawkins et al., 1995). Our book endeavours to broaden the agenda about fathers' involvement with children by including all these perspectives as ways of looking at relationships within families.

The book comprises seven chapters which can be read as individual essays on particular themes, or as part of the whole:

- in chapter one we discuss the traditional definition of father and observe some of the changes that have occurred in the institution of fatherhood in recent years, and how men and women are responding to those changes;
- in chapter two we summarise the psychoanalytic perspective on fathers which tries to explain, at a deep level within the psyche, the importance of the role of fathers in establishing meaning and identity for the child;
- in chapter three, we review a number of empirical studies that examine the impact of fathers on child development;
- in chapter four, we describe what fathers do in the home, drawing on a range of empirical studies and teasing out the underlying theoretical perspectives which inform those studies;

- in chapter five, we explore the impact of work on fathers and draw upon the results of a special analysis of the 1996 Labour Force Survey in order to throw light on the specific labour market characteristics of fathers with young children;
- in chapter six, we review how the law and the legal system impacts on different types of father, most notably married, separated and unmarried fathers as well as abusive fathers;
- in chapter seven, we review and comment on research which has examined the way in which State services and other supports interact with fathers.

Finally, it has to be said that the scale and scope of the agenda involved in promoting men's greater involvement in caring for children and others should not be underestimated. The traditional division of labour between men as providers and women as carers has deep roots in our values and attitudes about the nature of men and women, and in the structures of society which express and support those values. These structures have created inequalities in power, property and other resources between men and women; but we would also argue that it has not been in the best interests of many men or children either. It is our belief that men and women have a shared interest in working for change and developing relationships – personal, social, economic, legal etc – that allow the full potential of each person to be discovered and expressed.

Chapter 1: Fathers in a Time of Change

Introduction

'The information necessary to create a male is encoded in our DNA, but it takes all the institutions of a culture to produce a man. The male body is the biologically given "hardware", the myth of manhood is the "software" inserted by society through a series of formal and informal rites of passage.'

Sandor McNab

The concept of father, in its most basic form, involves a relationship with a child that is both biological and psycho-social. That is the normal meaning and usage of the term 'father'. In exceptional circumstances, there are fathers (such as adoptive fathers and step-fathers) who do not have a biological relationship with the child, just as there are biological fathers (who have never seen their child) who do not have a psycho-social relationship with the child. In the main, however, a man's standing as a father, notwithstanding the law (see chapter six), rests on both his biological and psycho-social links with the child. Whether the father is the biological father or not, the vital issue, as we argue in chapter two, is that the father takes up his symbolic role in the family.

It is true that the father's relationship with the child's mother is often used, particularly in the Irish Constitution and its laws, to define and differentiate fathers. Thus married fathers are treated differently from separated fathers and both are treated differently from unmarried fathers. This procedure can create enormous legal complexities but, more importantly, as we will see in chapter six, it effectively undermines the status and standing of fathers (since some fathers are more equal than others) and can cause hardship and injustice to men who find themselves in one of the legally unprotected categories of father.

Our purpose in this chapter is to explore the roots of our present understanding of fathers and the underlying structures and values that inform that understanding. We begin this process by describing the traditional image of father and the structures that have supported it. We then discuss how the role of father has been affected by general changes in family structures and by a range of more specific developments. This is followed by some reflections on the growing number of men's groups and gatherings that have been organised in Ireland in recent years which is, we believe, symptomatic of the changes affecting men and fathers. The process by which a man becomes a father is not straightforward and we examine this process to throw light on why fathers often see themselves – and are seen by others – as the secondary parent. The question is then addressed of how to define a good father. Our answer to this question acknowledges that there are many ways to be a good father, although some core principles seem to inform all types of good fathering.

Changes in the Role and Image of Father

One of the most influential images of fatherhood for many centuries has been the patriarch which literally means 'father and ruler'. In the hands of medieval Church and State, the image of the patriarch became the over-arching image of patriarchy in both heaven and earth, with one layer of fatherhood resting upon another. In this imagery, God is the father and ruler of heaven and earth; the king is the father and ruler of his people; the priest is the father of his flock and the man is the father and head of his family. Throughout the generations, this imagery and, more particularly, the structures which support it, has conferred power and status on men, or at least on some men, in the public spheres of work, politics and religion. At the same time, it has also allowed women, or at least some women, to exercise considerable power in the home, particularly in terms of rearing and influencing children, preparing them for life outside the home, and forming bonds of emotional attachment with them.

This patriarchal structure suited well the needs of the industrial and post-industrial society, as men worked outside the home and assumed the role of the main provider in the family; gradually, the patriarch became the provider and the roles of father and mother became increasingly segregated, even polarised. Men were, and often still are, seen as naturally de-skilled in the art of child rearing and care-giving. As we noted in the introduction to this book, both men and women suffer the consequences of patriarchy. Despite the fact that men have benefited a lot more than women, many theorists are arguing that the present social structure is having a destructive effect on both sexes. Neither men nor women are able to adequately express themselves within these confines, and there is a great need for this to be researched, particularly for men in their role as fathers.

In the Christian tradition, the father is a central image of God. The unseen father God in the New Testament is incomprehensible but intimately involved with human affairs. It is symptomatic of the esteem in which fathers were once held that the image of the father should be used to express the power and goodness of God in the 'other world'. Conversely, since God cannot be separated from the images of God, the decline of belief in God – and, within Ireland, the tendency for believers to shift from believing in God as a person to God as some sort of spirit or life force (Hornsby-Smith and Whelan, 1994, p. 34) – may itself be symptomatic of the decline in the symbolism of the father, and possibly vice versa. It is as though the father figure has lost its power to signify the world of goodness and desire that the human heart seeks. How the human desire for 'otherness' and the 'other world' gets symbolised and mythologised in the wake of the declining potency of Christian and patriarchal imagery is a major challenge of our time. We address it further in chapter two where the role of the symbolic father in establishing meaning and identity for the child is seen as a central theme of psychoanalysis.

In the incarnate world of real fathers, the Bible has many stories of fathers, and particularly fathers and sons, from Abraham who was prepared to sacrifice his son, to the figurative prodigal son who is reconciled with his father, the latter indicating, according to one commentator, that 'reconciliation between father and child is one of the fundamental projects in a person's life' (Abramovitch, 1997, p. 32). Joseph, the adoptive or foster father of Jesus, is presented as a decent, hard-working carpenter but does not come across as an effective father in the symbolic sense (see chapter two). Some of the early paintings depict Joseph as caring in practical ways for the baby Jesus but, by the seventeenth and eighteenth centuries, his position, like that of fathers generally, is presented as more remote from the child and his domestic involvement vanishes (Burgess, 1997, p. 11). However, it is the relationship between Jesus and his father in heaven that captures some abiding themes in father-child relationships: Jesus is called or sent to do his father's business – which he is happy to do – and is crucified for it; he also feels abandoned on the cross by an apparently absent father, an experience that is not uncommon in father-child relationships. Thus the Christian tradition, like the tradition of Greek mythology, reflects the different aspects of fathering, with its shades of brightness and darkness, joyfulness and sadness, that are an inescapable part of how fathers are imagined, symbolised and lived. In recent times, God the father has shared with his incarnate fathers a decline in status and esteem and both seem to have lost their potency as images of power, goodness and desire.

Moving from religion to myth, one finds a parallel decline in the standing of heroes who have traditionally been male or, at least, the embodiment of masculine energy. Heroes have an uneasy position in contemporary culture and society, waiting precariously for their weaknesses to be exposed and their characters brought low (McNeely, 1996). Women have not escaped this trend, but men, because they are more numerous in public positions of power, have had greater exposure to its biting and levelling influence. This pattern reflects a rejection of the traditional male hero as unassailably strong and invulnerable in favour of an antihero who is ordinary and fallible (see Silber, 1990). Indeed, one writer has described the notion of hero as 'male pathology' that should be 'relegated to the historical scrap heap' (Keen, 1991, p. 153; see also Bateson, 1990). The vacuum left by these developments has been described by one Jungian analyst in the following terms: 'The Greek idea of the hero, or today's antihero, may have done much to put men into relationship problems, perhaps more than any other set of myths. How many men, in today's socio-economic climate of dog-eat-dog competition, can achieve something heroic in the eyes of women?' (Ryce-Menuhin, 1996, p. 64).

Fatherhood, like motherhood, is a social construct which, in Western society, has traditionally been built around marriage. The social contract between fathers and mothers, which was solemnised in marriage, required the father to work as the breadwinner outside the home and the mother to work as the carer inside the home. In an economic sense, mothers and children became dependent on fathers as the source of family income just as, in an emotional sense, fathers and children became dependent on women as the source of caring within the family home.

This social contract, whose ideal is embodied in the Irish Constitution, implied a strict, almost polarised division of labour between men and women, both inside and outside the home. The social contract had paradoxical consequences for fathers as one sociologist has observed: 'In this golden age [sic] of the modern conjugal family, paternity appears to be characterised by an ambiguous and ambivalent social status: on the one hand, the father's role was completely central and powerful, given that he retained the near monopoly of the access to the family's subsistence resources, and on the other, his role as breadwinner for the family distanced him from it physically because of the distance between place of work and the family home, and symbolically because he is relatively marginalised in daily life' (Schultheis, 1993, p. 232).

The traditional social contract also had a number of consequences for mothers whose lack of economic and political power outside the home contrasted with their power and influence inside it, particularly in matters affecting the rearing and education of children and the inculcation of moral and religious values. One sociologist has documented the influence that Irish mothers have exercised on the education of their children, particularly in farming families; these mothers see education as a form of human capital which, unlike the physical capital of the farm, is not under male control and not subject to inheritance by the eldest son (O'Hara, 1997). She writes: 'Women embraced the challenge of preparing children for the wider society, not just because it gave them power and authority in a social form constructed on patriarchal lines, but as a way of resisting patriarchal dominance and creating a separate sphere of influence' (*Ibid*, p. 153). Another sociologist has drawn attention to the crucial role of mothers in the inculcation of moral and religious values: 'The Irish mother has, then, been responsible for the moral training and discipline of children within the home. She is the last but vital link in the Catholic formation of each new generation. It is often because of her, and an interest in maintaining the solidarity and prestige of the family, that children maintain their adherence to the Church in later life (Inglis, 1987, p. 69).

It is clear from this, therefore, that fatherhood is never simply the product of individual decisions by men and women about child rearing. Fatherhood is a social practice which is shaped by its social context. Thus, just as the Irish Constitution accords primacy to the role of the mother in the home, it simultaneously implies that the father's role lies elsewhere. As Articles 41.2.1 and 41.2.2 state: 'In particular, the State recognises that by her life within the home, woman gives to the State a support without which the common good cannot be achieved' and 'The State shall, therefore, endeavour to ensure that mothers shall not be obliged by economic necessity to engage in labour to the neglect of their duties in the home'.

Traditional fathers were not expected to be directly involved in childcare and housework. To say this does not mean that traditional fathers did not love their children. Nor does it mean that fathers were never intimate with, and present for, their children. Recently published reflections by Irish men on their fathers reveal that while many were indeed largely absent, this was a matter of degree and a variety of fathering practices went on (Hyde, 1996). The point rather is to draw attention to the fact that the norms of the time dictated that a father's love was expressed in one dominant way: by going out to work and providing. The 'good provider' model (Bernard, 1983) was the defining core of fatherhood and masculinity. Women became the 'specialists in love and the emotions' as men, in playing out the idealised male breadwinner role, lost touch with the emotional basis of their lives and of society generally (Giddens, 1992; Ferguson, 1997a). Good fathers were, inter alia, good breadwinners; conversely, as one commentary has suggested, failure as a breadwinner has always been a significant feature of the bad dad' (Pleck and Pleck, 1997, p. 48).

This traditional model of the family, and its related roles of father and mother, remains strong in Ireland but is changing, as the analysis in the next section reveals.

Changes in Family Structures

In order to throw light on the overall structure of families in Ireland, a special analysis of the 1996 Labour Force Survey was carried out. Table 1.1 is derived from this analysis and shows the proportion of adults who were parents in Ireland in 1996. It reveals that half the adult population (49%) – defined in this instance as persons aged 20 and over – in Ireland in 1996 were parents. Correspondingly, the proportion of adults who were not parents was 51%. It is also worth noting that the number of mothers exceeds the number of fathers. The reason for this is that a parent is defined as someone who lives with her or his child and mothers are more likely to live with their children; the reasons for this, in turn, are discussed later in this chapter and elsewhere in the book (see notably chapter six).

Table 1.1 Proportion of adults (20 years and older) who were parents in Ireland in 1996

Parent / Not a parent (1)	Men (4) %	Women (5) %	Total %
Parent (2)	47	51	49
Not a parent (3)	53	49	51
Total	100	100	100

Source: 1996 Labour Force Survey, Special Tabulations by Anthony Murphy at University College, Dublin.
(1) The Labour Force Survey defines parents as those adults who are living with their children of any age. This has three limitations. First it includes children over the age of 18 and who, while living with a parent or parents, are not children in the legal sense of the term. Second, it excludes a number of men who are fathers but are not living with their children. Third, it excludes men who are step-fathers or boyfriends but not fathers, but who play fathering roles within the family. In our analysis, we have added a fourth limitation by defining as adult any person aged 20 or over; this will exclude a very small number of fathers but was necessary since the next available statistical cut-off point, at 15 years, includes too many children. It also includes a relatively small number of parents (83,000 comprising 43,000 women and 40,000 men), equivalent to less than 1% of all parents, who are 65 years or over and who are unlikely to be active parents.
(2) The total number of adults who are parents is approximately 1.2 million.
(3) The total number of adults who are not parents is approximately 1.2 million.
(4) The total number of men aged 20 and over in Ireland in 1996 was 1.1 million.
(5) The total number of women aged 20 and over in Ireland in 1996 was 1.2 million.

In order to find out more about parents, a more detailed analysis was undertaken of the distribution of parents between different household types. The results are

summarised in Table 1.2 which distinguishes between
older families (where none of the children are under 15)
and younger families (where at least one of the children is
under 15) and, within these categories, between one and
two parent families. From this it emerges that in 1996,
two-thirds of parents (68%) lived in younger families and
one-third (32%) lived in older families. Most parents live in
two parent families (90%); one parent families are much
more common among older families because many of
them involve widows or widowers living with an adult
child.

Table 1.2 Distribution of adults by type of household in Ireland in 1996

Type of family (1)	N ('000)	%	One earner %	Two earner %	No earner %	Total %
Older families (2)	370	100	45	17	38	100
Two parent families	304	82	50 (6)	20	30	100
One parent families	66 (4)	18	23	-	77	100
Younger families (3)	786	100	49	36	15	100
Two parent families	734	93	50 (6)	39	11	100
One parent families	52 (5)	7	36	-	64	100
Total N	1,156	100	550	345 (7)	260	-
%	100	100	48	30	22	

Source: 1996 Labour Force Survey, Special Tabulations by Anthony
Murphy at University College Dublin.
(1) The Labour Force Survey defines parents as those adults who are
living with their children of any age. This has three limitations. First it
includes children over the age of 18 and who, while living with a
parent(s), are not children in the legal sense of the term. Second, it
excludes a number of men who are fathers but are not living with their
children. Third, it excludes men who are stepfathers or boyfriends but
not fathers but who play fathering roles within the family. In our
analysis, we have added a fourth limitation by defining as adult any

person aged 20 or over; this will exclude a very small number of fathers but was necessary since the next available statistical cut-off point, at 15 years, includes too many children. It also includes a relatively small number of parents (83,000 comprising 43,000 women and 40,000 men) - equivalent to less than 1% of all parents - who are 65 years or over and who are unlikely to be active parents.
(2) In this analysis, an older family is defined as a family which has no children under the age of 15 years.
(3) In this analysis, a younger family is defined as a family which has any child under the age of 15 years.
(4) This comprises 53,000 mothers (80% of older lone parents) of whom 19% are earners and 13,000 fathers (20% of older lone parents) of whom 31% are earners.
(5) This comprises 47,000 mothers (90% of younger lone parents) of whom 36% are earners and 5,000 fathers (10% of younger lone parents) of whom 60% are earners.
(6) In the vast majority of cases (93%), the one earner in two parent families is the father.
(7) The proportion of dual earners where the partner is employed part-time is 18%.

Table 1.2 also distinguishes between the number of earners within each family type. Both older and younger families were similar in that approximately half of each type were one-earner families. However, they differed dramatically in that younger families were twice as likely to have two earners (39%) compared to older families: one in three of younger families (36%) are dual earners compared to one in six of older families (17%). They also differed dramatically in that older families were twice as likely to have no earners compared to younger families: more than one in three of older families (39%) had no earners compared to nearly one in six of younger families (15%).

These results are significant because they reveal that only half of all families, and irrespective of whether they are younger or older, conform to the traditional image of having one breadwinner. In younger two parent families, a very substantial proportion (39%) are in fact two-earner families. At the same time, it is also worth noting that a significant minority of younger two parent families (11%) are no-earner families and are therefore likely to be living at or below the poverty line. The same applies to the majority of one parent families (64%) which are also no-earner families. These families and their children are likely to be living in poverty; it has been estimated that between 26% and 39% of all children in Ireland in 1987 were living in households below the poverty line, defined as either 50% or 60% of average household income respectively (Nolan and Callan, 1990).

The various types of families depicted in Table 1.2 also highlight the emergence of a polarisation between 'work rich' and 'work poor' families which has been observed in other EU countries. In Britain, for example, it has been found that the proportion of dual-earner and no-earner families has grown at the expense of one-earner families (Gregg and Wassworth, 1995). No comparable data exists in Ireland on the trend over time. It has also been found that dual-earner families in Britain tend to be better qualified and to have higher status and higher paid jobs while those with no earner tended to be the opposite (Ferri and Smith, 1996). This is also the case in Ireland, particularly among younger families. Table 1.3 reveals that two parent, dual-earner families tend to be of higher socio-economic status than one-earner families and higher still than no-earner families. As regards one parent families, Table 1.3 reveals that those with one earner tend to be of higher socio-economic status than those with no earner.

It is interesting to observe that the growth of dual-earner families is largely a by-product of women's increased participation in the labour force, itself inspired by the ideal of gender equality in the distribution of paid work outside the home. Paradoxically, the achievement of greater gender equality has resulted in growing inequalities between families in the distribution of paid work (McRae, 1997, p. 399). This indicates how gender and class are quite independent dimensions which impact on families in separate and sometimes opposite ways.

Table 1.3 Distribution of one, two and no-earner families by socio-economic status in Ireland in 1996

Type of family (1)	Two parent families			One parent families	
Older families (2)	One earner %	Two earner %	No earner %	One earner %	No earner %
Farmers, relatives assisting etc.	19	10	19	16	20
Professionals, employers, managers	21	33	12	21	13
Non-manual employees	29	37	29	42	34
Manual employees	31	20	40	21	33
Total (%)	100 (50)	100 (20)	100 (30)	100 (23)	100 (77)
Younger families (3)	One earner %	Two earner 5	No earner %	One earner %	No earner %
Farmers, relatives assisting etc.	13	8	7	5	4
Professionals, employers, managers	21	31	4	24	8
Non-manual employees	30	41	24	53	50
Manual employees	36	20	65	18	38
Total (%)	100 (50)	100 (40)	100 (10)	100 (36)	100 (64)

Source: 1996 Labour Force Survey, Special Tabulations by Anthony Murphy at University College Dublin.

(1) The Labour Force Survey defines parents as those adults who are living with their children of any age. This has three limitations. First it includes children over the age of 18 and who, while living with a parent(s), are not children in the legal sense of the term. Second, it excludes a number of men who are fathers but are not living with their children. Third, it excludes men who are stepfathers or boyfriends but not fathers but who play fathering roles within the family. In our analysis, we have added a fourth limitation by defining as adult any person aged 20 or over; this will exclude a very small number of fathers but was necessary since the next available statistical cut-off point, at 15 years, includes too many children. It also includes a relatively small number of parents (83,000 comprising 43,000 women and 40,000 men) - equivalent to less than 1% of all parents - who are 65 years or over and who are unlikely to be active parents.

(2) In this analysis, an older family is defined as a family which has no children under the age of 15 years.
(3) In this analysis, a younger family is defined as a family which has any child under the age of 15 years.

From the perspective of fathers, the changing family structure in Ireland has a two-fold significance. First, more than half of all families do not rely on fathers as the exclusive breadwinner; many of these rely on income earned by both parents, or on income transfers from the State in the form of social welfare payments. In other words, breadwinning is no longer the monopoly of fathers and this clearly signals a change in their power and status within families. Second, a significant minority of families live without a father since the vast majority of one parent families are, in fact, 'fatherless' families. These families are symbolically important in showing that families can exist without fathers thereby making fathers appear dispensable, at least for this type of family.

It is worth teasing out in more detail the factors that have contributed to the changing significance of fathers within families since they are central to understanding the present situation in which fathers find themselves.

Changes Affecting the Role of Fathers

In our view, there are four main factors that have affected fathering in recent decades. The first is the growth in the number of women, especially married women, working outside the home. In the twenty-five years between 1971 and 1996, the proportion of women in the Irish labour force (the labour force participation rate) increased from 28% to 36%; in the same period, the labour force participation rate of men fell from 81% to 69% (Department of Enterprise and Employment, 1996, p. 28). In 1996, just under half (47%) of all women in the labour force were married compared to just over half (58%) for men. The projection is that these trends will continue: 'Male labour force growth is forecast to be about half the female forecast trend, due in part to the dramatic increase in the participation of married women in the labour force' (*Ibid*, p. 29). These developments are helping to break the mould that sustains the gendered division of labour in the workplace and thereby reduces – perhaps more symbolically than practically – the role of father as the sole breadwinner by showing that women can be both breadwinners and care givers. This development contains a challenge to fathers, at least implicitly, to combine breadwinning with care giving.

The second factor is that the breadwinning role of many men is severely threatened by the persistence of high levels of unemployment in Ireland, particularly since the 1980s. Unemployment makes it difficult for young men to make the transition to adulthood and fatherhood (Hannan and O'Riain, 1993) and there is evidence that some women may prefer the prospect of lone parenthood to sharing child rearing responsibilities with a young unemployed father (Wilson and Neckerman, 1986; Roberts, 1996). Older established fathers have also seen their breadwinning role wiped out through unemployment and the prospects of returning to that role diminish with each passing year of long-term unemployment, since the prospects of employment diminish rapidly with each additional year of long-term unemployment (see Department of Enterprise and Employment, 1996, pp. 42–43). One study of the psychological impact of unemployment in Ireland found that unemployment causes a higher level of psychological distress among men than among women, and higher still among married men than among single men due, essentially, to the erosion of their role as breadwinners, itself undermining their self image as men (see Whelan, Hannan and Creighton, 1991, pp. 41–4).

The third factor is the growth in the number of one parent families. In the fifteen years between 1981 and 1996, lone parent families as a percentage of all families with children under the age of 15 years increased from 7% in 1981, to 11% in 1991, to 18% in 1996 (Census of Population, 1981, 1991 and 1996, Volume 3). This is due mainly to marital breakdown and births outside marriage.

In a narrow economic sense, the welfare state, through the One Parent Family Payment and other measures, may have helped replace the breadwinning role of the traditional father and made these families economically viable, even if only barely so (see McCashin, 1993; 1996). For the mothers concerned, the dynamics of the social welfare system are such as to make the father's absence a condition of receiving payment thereby helping to compound the separation of fathers from their children. As already indicated, some young women, particularly in disadvantaged areas, may be choosing to bring up their children with the support of the One Parent Family Payment because the fathers of those children are unable or unwilling to play the breadwinner role of husband and father. Moreover, since most one parent families (87%) are headed by a mother, this is sometimes taken to prove – both symbolically and practically – that families can exist without fathers. Our review of the evidence in chapter three suggests that children can grow up normally without their biological fathers, although the memory of the biological father may never be totally erased; more importantly, as we argue in chapter two, we believe that every child needs a 'father figure' in its life to grow into a normal adult.

The growth of one parent families has also served to break the link, at least conceptually, between marriage and parenthood by showing that marriage is not a necessary condition of parenthood, even if many people enter marriage with a view to parenthood (Millar and Warman, 1996, p. 48; Bjornberg, 1992). The severing of parenthood from marriage also serves to crystallise the definition of mother and father as involving a relationship with their child rather than with each other. The implications of this for fathers – particularly for separated and unmarried fathers – are still being worked out and, as the analysis in chapter six indicates, the legal implications have still not been addressed.

The fourth factor is less quantifiable but no less real and involves changes in expectations about what constitutes a 'good father'. Parenting can be seen as having two interrelated aspects: the provider or 'investment' role and the caring or 'involvement' role. Traditionally, the father's role was defined by investment while the mother's role was defined by involvement. However, involvement is increasingly perceived much more highly than investment, particularly by children, but often by both fathers and mothers themselves (see, for example, O'Brien and Jones, 1996). The rising status of children within families – and the corresponding changes in norms about good parenting – have made it less easy for fathers to be exclusively preoccupied with investment at the expense of involvement (see Ferguson, 1996a). Indeed, according to a 1993 European-wide survey of 13,000 men and women aged 15 and over, the vast majority (87%) of Europeans believe that fathers should take a hand in bringing up their children right from birth while three quarters (75%) believe that both parents should share all aspects of the childcare work (Eurobarometer 39.0, 1993, pp. 89, 93; see also Social Europe, 1994, p. 24). Other research suggests that Irish attitudes on these matters are 'not consistently more traditional than those of the economically more advanced countries' (Whelan and Fahey, 1994, p. 79).

These developments place fathers, particularly those who are sole breadwinners, in an awkward psychological position because investment without involvement no longer carries the esteem that it once did. Ironically, the father's investment role may be esteemed by the mother but not the children and its effect, however unintentional, may be to strengthen the mother's relationship with the children while weakening the father's relationship with his children. Many fathers are experiencing the stress of having to combine both investment with involvement roles and, being unable to rely on the role model of their own father, are having to learn new ways of being a father. At the same time, there appears to be a growing receptivity to the idea that the breadwinner role should not be the sole defining characteristic of a man's worth as a man and a father (Marsiglio, 1995).

These changes have caused confusion about the role of fathers in a wide variety of situations. For men in employment, there is a growing expectation that they will become more involved with their children, even if the demands of work can make that difficult. For men who are unemployed, there is an enforced loss of the traditional provider role which challenges their self-image as both men and fathers. For men who are separated or divorced, there can be a loss of contact with children which threatens to undermine if not erase their role as fathers. For fathers who neither marry nor cohabit with the mother of their child, the practical role of father is often non-existent.

Men and fathers are responding to these changes in a variety of ways. The extent of change is examined in other chapters of the book. One of the changes worth noting in the present context is the growth of men's groups which have been formed in Ireland in recent years to discuss and share experiences of being men and fathers.

Men's Groups

The emergence of men's groups and men's gatherings in Ireland in recent years is evidence that some men are responding to the changed circumstances in which men find themselves and this too is likely to have its impact on the practice of fathering. In the 1980s, men began to meet together in Ireland to discuss their lives in groups such as 'Merlin'. In the 1990s, one of the first men's gatherings in Ireland was held at the Marino Institute of Education in Dublin in September 1992; it was facilitated by Michael Meade and James Hillman and attended by around one hundred men. A second gathering attended by a similar number of men, this time facilitated by Michael Meade and Maladoma Somé, was held in Bellinter House in Navan, County Meath in October 1994. In February 1997, a major conference on the theme of Men and Intimacy was held in Carlow and attended by nearly two hundred men and women (Saint Catherine's Community Services Centre and Accord, 1997). Another men's gathering was held in Marino Institute of Education in Dublin in April 1997. These are just some of the one and two day events that have been happening in Ireland in recent years which, in turn, have had a ripple effect in terms of the formation of men's groups throughout the country consisting of between eight and fifteen men which meet weekly or fortnightly.

Parallel with these developments, the Second Commission on the Status of Women recommended in 1993 that funding, which had been made available through the Department of Social Welfare (which became the Department of Social, Community and Family Affairs in June 1997) to women's groups since 1990 should be extended to men's groups. The rationale for the recommendation was that 'there is a real problem for men at the bottom of the social and economic pyramid, because the positive incentives that have encouraged their wives to seek change, have in many cases passed them by. Yet their traditional role no longer exists. The automatic assumption that they controlled family finances and decision-making is gone. While children may benefit from seeing their mothers behaving more independently and confidently, men can feel threatened' (Second Commission on the Status of Women, 1993, pp. 86–87). The recommendation was implemented in 1994 and the Department of Social, Community and Family Affairs now funds both men's and women's groups.

As Table 1.4 reveals, women's groups received IR£1.17 million in 1996 compared to IR£0.15 million for men's groups. This reflects the fact that there are eight times more women's groups than men's groups throughout the country since the average grant to each group is broadly similar at IR£1,400 each. In both categories, only two-thirds of the groups were successful in their applications. From these developments, networks of men's groups have been established in disadvantaged areas, with the South East Men's Network having the first full-time co-ordinator. The Men's Network Resource Centre of Ireland, launched in Ballymun, Dublin, provides advice and support for men as well as co-ordinating information on men's groups nationally. An evaluation of the men's groups funded by the Department of Social, Community and Family Affairs was carried out in 1997 and found them to be 'a limited success' (Cousins, 1997, p. 45).

Table 1.4 Funding for men's and women's groups by the Department of Social, Community and Family Affairs in 1996

Category	Women's groups	Men's groups
Number of applications from groups	1,177	152
Number of groups funded	792	103
% of applications funded	67	68
Average amount received by each group	IR£1,476	IR£1,438
Total amount received by all groups	IR£1,168,930	IR£148,135

Source: Department of Social, Community and Family Affairs, 1997.

There is some debate on the purpose of men's groups and the merits of men meeting separately from women in this manner (for a heated review of perspectives on men's groups, see Kimmel, 1995). Our experience is that men can find support and togetherness in these groups – a space where they can be open and vulnerable without feeling threatened – and can explore issues of concern to their lives such as fathering, loving, working, health, grief and celebration. In many ways, these groups offer men an opportunity to critically reflect on their lives and to explore the broader issues affecting the roles which men and women play in society. We explore the importance of these issues at greater length in chapter seven.

In 1993, Parental Equality: the Shared Parenting and Joint Custody Support Group was formed in response to the problems experienced by fathers of obtaining shared custody of their children. In essence, the problem is that many fathers are not given equal parenting rights to their children, usually in the wake of separation/divorce or where the father is not married to the mother of his children; in some instances, fathers are given virtually no parenting rights at all. The legal context that gives rise to these problems is explored in chapter six.

Becoming a Father

'I became a father for the first time in 1978 when I was 36. In my case it became a decisive event in my life, and that includes my professional life. By then, I had acquired considerable experience as a specialist in gynaecology and childbirth ... It struck me that in my encounters with all those couples, I had spontaneously turned to the women, since they were clearly the most "important" persons. I had only occasionally focused directly on the men, and this also applied to emotional questions, fear, expectations and anxiety or happiness prior to birth and parenthood. And yet I am a man myself. Why wasn't it natural for me to also be able t "see" men on their own terms? Eventually, I began to understand that there were several aspects to these difficulties and inner obstacles. As a man – despite my profession – I did not have the words or language for men's feelings and experiences in connection with childbirth and fatherhood'.

Goran Swedin, 1995

It is hard to state precisely where the process of becoming a father begins: At the moment of the child's conception? At the birth of the child? When the baby is first planned? The vagueness of the father's relationship to the child, and of his rights to the child while in the womb, mirrors the vagueness of the father's role in general. It is only in relatively recent times that a father could be said to have a desire and a right to be at the birth of his child.

By comparison with the process of becoming a mother, which is clearly signalled in the woman's pregnancy and the physical changes in her body over nine months before giving birth, the process of becoming a father normally has no outward signs for a man. 'Women do have the bio-logical edge with infants', according to some psychologists (Colman and Colman, 1988, p. xvii). 'They have wombs, they create the milk, they have a great abundance of attachment hormones rushing through their bodies after birth' (*Ibid*). A woman's motherhood is never in doubt once she has given birth, whereas a man's fatherhood is always a matter of presumption. The psychological consequences of this are explained by one Jungian analyst as follows: 'The male's lack of any physical experience, beyond copulation, in the bearing and delivering of the child, leaves his psychic relationship at a primitive, almost magical level. Fatherhood seems to be more about the acceptance of paternity than the impregnation of the female. The father's acceptance of paternity demonstrates the emergence of the generations within history' (Ryce-Menuhin, 1996, p. 74).

Until recently, men did not attend the birth of their children. Pregnancy, therefore, is the period when women prepare and, through ante-natal visits and classes as well as reading books and leaflets, are prepared for motherhood. Moreover, while men cannot get pregnant, it has been assumed, at least until recently, that men do not need to be involved in the ante-natal process of preparing for fatherhood. Even books on pregnancy, childbirth and child rearing tend to be directed at women rather than men. Indeed, as one researcher has pointed out: 'Structural disincentives for male involvement in pregnancy are legion ... Ante-natal classes are given by women, are overwhelmingly directed at women and, to accommodate hospital and tutors' schedules, are generally held during the day, with, at the most, one 'father's evening' and one hospital tour scheduled. Ante-natal appointments are also held in the daytime, and there is no awareness among professionals of any need to improve upon a casual invitation to fathers ... The average expectant father is killed off through lack of interest, his concern tolerated at best (and discouraged at worst) by health professionals completely out of touch with paternal experience' (Burgess, 1997, pp. 112–113).

The process of becoming a father both before and after the child's birth is heavily laced with signals to indicate

33

that the primary parent is the mother and the secondary parent is the father. The father's main role is seen to support the mother whose views on how to look after the child are treated as paramount. Even the existence of maternity but not paternity leave from work reinforces the social image of the mother as the primary carer of the child; it is recognised, of course, that maternity leave is also important to allow the mother time to recover physically from the birth of the child. In addition, official statistics on births contain information on the characteristics of the mother but nothing on the father (see, for example, Department of Health, 1993). These observations, which are not intended to undermine the role of the mother, simply indicate that the journey to parenthood is quite different for mothers and fathers, and the process does little or nothing to prepare fathers for involvement with the child.

If, as we believe, that fathers are equal parents of the child and should be encouraged to be more actively involved in child rearing, then some of the existing conventions surrounding pregnancy, childbirth and child rearing need re-examination. For example, are ante-natal classes sufficiently inclusive of, and sympathetic to, men? Does the information provided through text, pictures and videos portray a full and positive role for fathers? Is it appropriate that there is no paternity leave for fathers which would facilitate bonding with their new-born child just as there is maternity leave for mothers in recognition of the physical demands of childbearing and breast-feeding? Much of the research evidence suggests that, with better preparation for fatherhood and parenthood, the attachment between father and child, as well as between father and mother, can be greatly strengthened; in addition, fathers become more involved with the child after its birth (Jackson, 1984; Nickel and Kocher, 1987; Cowan, 1988; Brazelton and Cramer, 1991).

What is a Good Father?

Every generation blames the one before
And all of their frustrations come knocking on your door.
I know that I'm a prisoner to all my father held so dear.
I know that I'm a hostage to all his hopes and fears.
I just wish I could have told him in the living years.

I wasn't sure there that morning when my father passed away.
I didn't get to tell him all the things I had to say.
I think I caught his spirit later that same year.
I'm sure I heard his echo in my baby's new born tears.
I just wish I could have told him in the living years.
Mike and the Mechanics (1988, *The Living Years*, WEA Records)

All fathers are not the same. As one commentator has pointed out, 'fathers are not a uniform group of people. They range from the few men who produce sperm but have no contact with their offspring through to another small minority who take sole charge of their children. Within those extremes, men perform such a variety of familial roles that an analysis of them as a group is not easy' (Lewis, 1993, p. 89). The way in which men play the role of father varies according to a wide range of variables including their own personal experience of being men and of being fathered, their marital and residential status, the number and ages of their children, their social class and employment status, and the relative importance which they attribute – consciously or unconsciously – to work, to fathering and to seeing fathering as valuable work. Inevitably, in view of such complexity, there are many ways to be a good father just as there are many ways to be a good mother. Conversely, as one commentator has pointed out, 'there is nothing intrinsically good about family values or about the father as one of the embodiments of these values. A good father is a good thing, a bad father is a bad thing' (French, 1995, p. 5).

The task of defining the good father must also address the apparent paradox that every father – indeed every parent – is destined to face: the child will be disappointed

35

by their limitations, no matter how good they are. As one writer has observed: 'we are always disappointed by our fathers. If we don't learn that lesson we never grow up – we never mature or become our "own persons"' (Wilmer, 1990, p. 177). If such disappointment is inevitable, is there any point in trying to be a good father?

A powerful explanation of this paradox has been put forward by Meade: 'If children were simply satisfied with what the parents offered to them, they would remain children forever. It's not simply that parents don't try to give enough to the child, rather it's that whatever the parents give is never enough for the child. The child has a destiny outside the imagination of the parents. The child has an origin that is not simply made of the understanding of its parents. There is a mysterious occurrence when the child is born. It's stunning to the son to realise that his own father doesn't feel the delicate uncertainty with which he walks into life. The father and son are both shocked by the great longing they feel for each other and the way that they clash when they come close to each other. Between fathers and sons, a long distance grows easily, silences spread from something small to something wide and seemingly unending. Something mysterious connects them and something awkward and painful drives them apart' (Meade, 1993, p. 67).

It is worth teasing out this explanation in a little more detail by looking at the expectations that both father and son – and parents and children generally – bring to this relationship. For fathers, the appeal of the call to be a 'good father' rests not with the rewards which it brings in terms of the child's gratitude or approval, but with the intrinsic rewards of engaging with life as the father of a child. In this engagement, the father enters the archetypal world of fatherhood, as Jung termed it, and connects – sometimes consciously, sometimes unconsciously – to the common if highly diverse stream of experiences that all fathers have experienced. At its core, the fatherhood experience is grounded in taking responsibility for the child which one has created. Its appeal comes from within the father, not the child. Indeed, it could be said that the appeal to be a good father is essentially a derivative of the call to be a 'good man'.

Each man is called, by virtue of his existence, to be a good man in a way that is unique to each, and to take the journey of discovering his purpose (McKeown, 1997b). A good man, in this sense, will always be a good father. The reverse process – of presenting fathering as the raison d'être of a man's existence – carries the danger that a father's purpose in life becomes substituted for his child's purpose. As Hillman has pointed out: 'I have learned, through years of work with patients and in men's retreats, and from listening to what cautions me, that when a child substitutes for your daimon you will resent that child, even grow to hate it, despite good will and high ethics ... When your child becomes the reason for your life, you have abandoned the invisible reason *you* are here ... Any father who has abandoned the small voice of his unique genius, turning it over to the small child he has fathered, cannot bear reminders of what he has neglected ... Result: a child-dominated fatherless culture with dysfunctional children' (Hillman, 1996, pp. 83–85).

For the child, the experience of disappointment seems to have a fundamental significance. There is a tendency to see disappointment in negative terms as if it were a sign of failure for which parents were to blame. That is only part of the picture, however. Disappointment is also a normal experience associated with the growth of wisdom and the loss of innocence; indeed, there can be no wisdom without the loss of innocence. No one can grow as a person without experiencing disappointment and shedding expectations or behaviours that are no longer appropriate. To learn about life is to listen to the promptings of disappointment and to be tutored by them. Disappointment, therefore, has two faces – one face we call 'imposed disappointment', the other we call 'invited disappointment'. In life, disappointments are not always easy to classify in this way but retrospection and awareness can help to place them in their true context.

Many children, especially sons, have spoken about the imposed disappointment which they have with their fathers (see, for example, Hyde, 1996; Wilmer, 1990). This disappointment arises from two extremes: from fathers who have been too remote, silent, disinterested and absent on the one hand, and from fathers who have been too controlling, dominating, violent and devouring on the other. These imposed disappointments are typically experienced as avoidable suffering that children have to live with as best they can. Their extent is difficult to quantify, but writers on men's issues who have been involved in leading retreats for men over many years suggest that many men have been deeply wounded by their fathers (Bly, 1990; Keen, 1991; Meade, 1993; Hillman, 1996). The experience of imposed disappointment seems to be felt most acutely by that generation of sons who, having become fathers, wish to respond to a different, more caring and respectful type of fathering; to become 'earth fathers' rather than 'sky fathers' as some writers have called it (Coleman and Coleman, 1988). The issue of what constitutes a good father, therefore, is about avoiding the imposed disappointments of previous forms of fathering.

Invited disappointments, by contrast, are those experiences, stemming from a deep desire within the psyche, which are 'invited' precisely because of the wisdom they can bring. The story of Adam and Eve is particularly instructive in this regard. Eve ate the forbidden fruit – and therefore invited disappointment – because, in the words of the story, 'it was enticing for the wisdom it could give'. Still drawing upon Biblical sources, the story of the prodigal son is also about disappointment because it was only by leaving home, and therefore disappointing his father, that the son was able to learn the full extent of his father's love; indeed, the story suggests that the alternative to disappointment is staying at 'home' and becoming the resentful son. In both stories, the 'father' takes no responsibility for the disappointment which his children invited upon themselves and this is an important signal as to the limits of the father and of parents in general. The writer W. H. Auden captured this quality of invited disappointment when he wrote: 'The so-called traumatic experience is not an accident, but the opportunity for which the child has been patiently waiting – had it not occurred, it would have found another, equally trivial – in order to find a necessity and direction for its existence, in order that its life may become a serious matter' (Auden, 1996).

These considerations suggest that the issue of being a 'good father' is not just about effective parenting, although hopefully that will be an outcome; it is also about the transformation which follows when a man grows in awareness of what fatherhood entails. It is precisely because fatherhood is irreversible, and therefore a rite of passage, that no man can ignore the invitation which the birth of his child brings. Men become good fathers by recognising the invitation and by responding to the needs of their child as best they can.

In our endeavours to define what is a 'good enough' father, we have come to the somewhat minimalist conclusion that the good enough father must:

- be physically present on a reasonably regular basis to his child, and
- have a positive and not a negative influence on his child.

A reasonably regular basis, even for a separated father, according to one psychologist, 'probably means at least once a week' (Andrews, 1994). Resident fathers will normally see their children at least once a day.

A positive rather than a negative influence is less easy to define but it involves protecting the child from harm through a bond of attachment between the parents and the child. Beyond that, as one psychiatrist at the Tavistock Clinic in London has pointed out: 'we need to be careful not to be too certain about what we think is right for children ... the truth is that there are no rules about childcare but there are some principles that we can be fairly confident are universal' (Kraemer, 1995, p. 14). The most important of these principles, according to the same psychiatrist, is attachment which is taken to mean protection from physical and emotional harm: 'A secure attachment is like an invisible elastic which can stretch and contract depending on the need for protection. So when you are ill or in pain, tired or afraid, you move towards the person with whom you feel secure and when all is well you can move away to explore the world around. Clearly this applies to all of us, but most of all to small children' (*Ibid*).

The importance of attachment, and the associated flexibility that allows both closeness and distance, has been emphasised by other commentators: 'A father who is too close or too remote will not be good enough ... In contrast, the good father is able to successfully maintain the golden mean. Such a father is close but not too close, strong but not overwhelming, loving but not seductive, supportive but able to discipline, caring but encouraging autonomy' (Abramovitch, 1997, p. 31).

The practical application of these principles has been used to inform a government-backed publicity campaign in Southern Australia called 'Six ways to be a better Dad!'. The six ways are summarised in Table 1.5.

Table 1.5 Six ways to be a better Dad

---

1. BEING A ROLE MODEL

As a dad, you are a role model whether you realise it or not. *How you act teaches your kids how to act when they grow up.* For example, if you talk problems through, your kids will probably grow up to do the same. If you lose your temper, get abusive or become violent, your kids will probably grow up to do the same.

Kids learn mainly from what you do, not what you say.

Treat your daughter with love and respect so she grows up expecting to be treated the same by boys and men.

Teach your son that a man is caring, fair, a mate to his kids and treats women with respect.

---

2. SHOW THEM YOU CARE

Getting involved in your kids' lives is a terrific way to show your kids you care.

Do things that they want you to do.

Give them a hug and tell them they're great.

Help out with their homework.

Play footy or basketball.

Go to a school function, go to parent/teacher interviews, watch them play sport.

Learn their friends' and teachers' names.

3. WORK AND FAMILY

Let's face it, work can be tiring, stressful, and creates worries. No doubt these worries are for real, but it isn't fair or useful to pass them on to your kids.

Put aside some time just for you to recharge your batteries.

Look after your health through diet and exercise.

Try and leave your work hassles at work.

4. WHAT TO DO WHEN YOUR KID'S BEHAVIOUR IS NOT OK

As hard as it is, try and *stay calm*!

When you feel stressed and feel that you might lash out – walk away.

Leave the room and do something to distract yourself.

Don't act in anger or you will probably regret what you do.

Kids need to learn right from wrong. Set rules and stick to them. Be clear about what will happen when the rules are broken. This could include not letting your kids watch their favourite TV program. If they break the rules, do what you said would happen.

5. PARENTING AND PARTNERSHIPS

Being a parent is a partnership – whether you and your children's mother are together or not.

Respect your kid's mother.

Don't argue in front of the kids.

Do something about relationship problems.

Get professional advice if you can't sort out problems together.

Kids can't cope with their parents putting each other down.

> **6. SPEND TIME WITH YOUR KIDS**
> The time you spend with your kids is a good investment in
> *their* future. Show your love by getting involved with their
> sports or hobbies or involving them in your interests. Kids
> grow up so quickly, so don't miss out!
> Share a regular meal.
> Talk to your kids.
> Listen to their views without criticising.
> Praise their efforts.
> Encourage them and help them make decisions.

Source: The Office for Families and Children, Southern Australia

Conclusion

The analysis in this chapter revealed that the concept of
father, in its most basic form, involves a relationship with
a child that is both biological and psycho-social. Fatherhood, like motherhood, is a social construct which, in
Western society, has traditionally been built around
marriage. Traditionally, this social contract has involved a
division of labour between fathers and mothers, such that
fathers worked as the breadwinner outside the home
while mothers worked as carers inside the home. This
arrangement, whose ideal is embodied in the Irish
Constitution, gave fathers control over the family's
subsistence resources while distancing them physically
and emotionally from their children. In this way, men
expressed their masculinity and their love for wife and
children by going out to work and providing. In this value
system, 'good fathers' were essentially 'good providers'
and they were esteemed accordingly; their role was more
about 'investment' than 'involvement'.

This traditional model of fatherhood, and the related
model of motherhood, is still popular but is declining as
new family forms are emerging. In 1996, only half of all
families in Ireland fitted the traditional model of having two
parents with one earner, typically the father. Two-earner
families constituted 30% of all families while no-earner

families comprised 20% of the total. These changes crystallise a number of other trends in society, including:

- the growth in the number of women, especially married women, working outside the home. In the years between 1971 and 1996, the proportion of women in the Irish labour force more than doubled from 14% in 1971 to 39% in 1996. This development helped to break the mould which sustained the gendered division of labour in the workplace and thereby reduced, perhaps more symbolically than practically, the role of the father as the sole breadwinner by showing that women could be both breadwinners and care givers.
- the breadwinning role of many men is severely threatened by the persistence of high levels of unemployment in Ireland, particularly since the 1980s. For example, older established fathers have seen their breadwinning role wiped out through long-term unemployment while some younger men in very disadvantaged circumstances fail to make the transition to involved fatherhood.
- a steady growth in the number of one parent families which now constitute more than a tenth of all families. This is due to both marital breakdown and births outside marriage and the role of the welfare state in financially supporting these 'fatherless' families. Moreover, since most one parent families (87%) are headed by a mother, this is sometimes taken to prove, both symbolically and practically, that families can exist without fathers.
- a shift in attitudes about what constitutes a 'good father'. The shift involves a growing expectation, possibly associated with the rising status of children, that fathers should combine 'involvement' with their children along with their more traditional 'investment' role. In this sense, modern fathers are expected to give more than traditional fathers and it is becoming less easy for fathers to be exclusively preoccupied with investment at the expense of involvement.

> Ironically, the father's investment role may be esteemed by the mother but not the children, and its effect, however unintentional, may be to strengthen the mother's relationship with the children while weakening the father's relationship with the children.

Many fathers are experiencing the stress of having to combine both investment with involvement roles and, being unable to rely on the role model of their own father, are having to learn new ways of being a father. At the same time, there appears to be a growing receptivity to the idea that the breadwinner role should not be the sole defining characteristic of a man's worth as a man and a father. The emergence of men's groups and men's gatherings in Ireland in recent years is evidence that some men are responding to the changed circumstances in which men find themselves. For example, the Department of Social, Community and Family Affairs offered funding to over one hundred men's groups in 1996. Our experience is that these groups offer men an opportunity to critically reflect on their lives and to explore the broader issues affecting the roles which men and women play in society.

Our analysis of the process by which men become fathers, both before and after the child's birth, suggests that it is heavily laced with signals to indicate that the primary parent is the mother and the secondary parent is the father. If, as we believe, fathers are equal parents of the child and should be encouraged to be more actively involved in child rearing, then some of the existing conventions surrounding pregnancy, childbirth and child rearing need re-examination. For example, are ante-natal classes sufficiently inclusive of, and sympathetic, to men? Does the information provided through text, pictures, videos, etc., portray a full and positive role for fathers? How can men see themselves as equal parents if Irish society grants maternity leave to mothers but not paternity leave for fathers? Much of the research evidence suggests that, with better preparation for fatherhood through counselling, education and encouragement, the attachment between father and child – as well as between father and mother – can be greatly strengthened; in addition, fathers become more involved with the child after its birth.

The way in which men play the role of father varies according to a wide range of variables, including their own personal experience of being men and of being fathered, their marital and residential status, the number and ages of their children, their social class and employment status, and the relative importance which they attribute – consciously or unconsciously – to the investment and involvement aspects of fathering, etc. Inevitably, in view of such complexity, there are many ways to be a good father just as there are many ways to be a good mother.

In trying to define what constitutes a good father, we first wish to state that being a good father is essentially a derivative of being a good man. A good man, as we understand it, endeavours to be true to his own purpose in life, with all that that entails. A good man, in this sense, will always be a good father. The reverse process – of presenting fathering as the raison d'être of a man's existence – carries the danger that a father's purpose in life becomes substituted for his child's purpose, with all the resentment and frustration that this is likely to cause.

In our endeavours to define what is a 'good father' or a 'good enough father', we have come to the somewhat minimalist conclusion that the good enough father must:

- be physically present on a reasonably regular basis to his child, and
- have a positive rather than a negative influence on his child.

We do not wish to be too certain or too prescriptive about what constitutes good enough fathering because doctrinaire approaches can be dangerous and do more harm than good. However, in the course of our reading, we came across some very practical guidelines on how to become a good father which could be useful, such as the six ways to be a good father that are being used by the government in Southern Australia to develop awareness of good fathering. This could be adapted to Irish circumstances as an aid to promoting discussion and debate about what constitutes a 'good father'.

The analysis in this chapter suggests four implications for public policy. First, the ideals of 'good fathering' and 'good enough fathering' need to become matters of public and private debate and discussion. The objective of such debates should be:

- to help elevate the status and importance of fatherhood in society;
- to give men, women and children an opportunity to talk about their ideals of fatherhood;
- to allow fathers and potential fathers an opportunity to reflect on their experiences of fathering and the issues that arise for fathers in trying to meet the competing demands of work and family, of being a carer as well as a breadwinner.

We see this objective being pursued in these ways:

- through education, both second level and second-chance, in the form of fathering and relationship courses; appropriate resource materials would need to be prepared to service these courses;
- through the media, both electronic and print, where informed and constructive comment meets with the recorded experiences of fathering by men, women and children in different situations;
- through research on fathering ideals and practices in differing settings, taking into account differences in family types, stage in the family cycle, social class, employment, marital status, geographical location, etc.

Second, we believe that support for men's groups by the Department of Social, Community and Family Affairs should continue and be expanded. We see men's groups as important areas where men and fathers can meet to discuss their experiences. It is our experience that men will only engage in discussion about their role as men and fathers if their vulnerabilities are respected and if they are given a safe space to be heard without being automatically criticised for not being good enough. We agree with the existing concentration of support for men's groups in disadvantaged areas. It should also include financial support for groups of men who are endeavouring to address specific issues such as parenting alone or separation from their children.

Third, it needs to be acknowledged that the process leading up to, and following, the birth of a child should be more inclusive of fathers. In order to achieve this objective, we recommend that an examination of the conventions and practices that take place before, during and after childbirth to identify areas where fathers could be more involved in the preparation for fatherhood. We recommend, subject to the outcome of detailed examination, that these conventions and practices should be modified where they do not promote the objective of joint parenting. This examination should be wide ranging and should include pregnancy, ante-natal classes, childbirth, child rearing and home visitation, as well as information and publicity materials about these topics in the form of text, pictures, videos, etc.

Fourth, we recognise that young men and young fathers who are unemployed or otherwise disadvantaged have special needs which require urgent attention. We recommend that services are developed to help them overcome the obstacles that currently hinder their transition to adulthood and fatherhood. This will require increased investment in a range of services for disadvantaged adolescents and young people covering education, training, personal development and parenting education. These services need to be delivered with skill and sensitivity in each local area so that young men can value the importance of being a role model in their child's life.

Chapter 2

The Symbolic Father: a Psychoanalytic Perspective

Introduction

'In the majority of neuroses of our time we can designate the principal determinant in the personality of the father who is always lacking in some way or another, absent or humiliated, divided or sham.'

Jacques Lacan

This chapter is a brief introduction to a psychoanalytic understanding of the role of the father in child development. We begin by highlighting how eclipsed the father-child relationship has been by the mother-child relationship in the social sciences, including psychoanalysis. Today many psychoanalysts are, once again, emphasising the destructive effects of ignoring the function of the father in the child's psychological and emotional development. The decline of the paternal image and the marginalisation of the father are sometimes cited as one of the possible bases for the huge increase in neurosis and pathologies in individuals, families and society. Some of these illnesses can be traced back to the relationship and separation process between mother and child, and the role of the father in this transition.

In this chapter we return to earlier psychoanalytic writings to discover a very useful model for displaying the crucial role of the father in this necessary separation of the child from the mother. We document this model in detail, stressing the importance of the mother-child-father dynamic. This in turn displays the complex psychological drama that the child undergoes in order to individuate and separate from the mother, and the role of the father in this process. We recognise some of the key problems with this model and re-frame it in light of the work that has subsequently been done in this area. Once again, the father, albeit the symbolic father, is shown to be the key figure in the crucial separation process between the mother and the child. It is this process that allows the child to take up his/her own unique position in the socio-symbolic culture which, we argue, the symbolic father represents. We conclude with a critique and a discussion of this material.

Psychoanalysis Today – the Absent Father

Contemporary psychoanalysis, like the majority of the human sciences, has primarily emphasised the importance of the mother-child relationship for the healthy development of the child. This has largely been to the virtual exclusion of any discussion or debate on the father-child relationship (Frosh, 1994). We are going to display how detrimental it is to ignore the father-child relationship. This is not to undervalue the importance of the research and findings regarding the mother-child relationship. John Bowlby's writings on 'attachment theory' have popularised, and effectively revolutionised, our understanding of the mother's relationship with the infant (Bowlby, 1969, 1973, 1980). The 'holding environment' that the mother provides for the helpless and dependent infant is crucial in allowing the infant to develop a bonding process, which in turn is the foundation of his/her future ability to trust and to relate (Winnicott, 1964; Bowlby, Ibid). These clinicians rightly argue that this early bonding process with the mother is of great significance to the child's psycho-social and emotional development, as it is at this stage that the child inter-nalises a working model of safety, security, and trust – the bedrock of selfhood and independence. The model of the 'mother-child relationship' is the paradigm that dominates contemporary social science, child psychology and psychoanalysis.

While we fully agree with the crucial importance of the mother-child relationship, it is significant that the father is almost completely absent in this description of child development. The most obvious question, and the one underlying this chapter, is: how are fathers necessary for the emotional and psychological development of children? Some writers seriously question whether fathers are necessary at all for the psychological development of the child (Belsey and Moore, 1989). At the same time as these questions are emerging, so too is a much greater awareness of the contemporary breakdown of family and community life, the growth of dependency (in children and adults) and neurosis, and the massive increases in all sorts of therapies and promises of cures. No doubt there are many possible explanations for these phenomena, but a number of social theorists are claiming that there is a connection between these massive problems and the definite decline of the paternal role and image (Lacan, 1977; Hillman, 1994; Frosh, 1994). It is important to observe that these theorists are not solely concerned with the contemporary debate on the mother-child relationship, but are also captivated by what was once a primary question for psychoanalysis, namely: what is the role or function of the father in the psycho-sexual and emotional development of the child (Frosh, 1994).

In the five major case histories published by Sigmund Freud, the founder of psychoanalysis, all of the patients presented with illnesses that had their origins in how the patient perceived the role or position of the father in their lives. Jacques Lacan, the eminent French psychiatrist and psychoanalyst, states categorically that the present day failure of the father in his symbolic role in the family is central to the increase in individual psychopathology (violence, addiction and neurotic behaviour), and the problems facing family life, particularly the personal identity of the child. Lacan goes so far as to suggest that it is this very failure that is perpetuating across generations a fundamental breakdown in meaning and having a destructive effect on individuals, families, communities and, in turn, societies and cultures (Ecrits, 1977). In an

Irish context, a considerable number of psychologists, sociologists and social researchers are expressing a similar viewpoint. Some examples of this can be found in the writings and teachings of Dr Cormac Gallagher, the Director of the School of Psychotherapy, St Vincent's Hospital, and Dr Paul Andrews SJ, author and founder of St Declans School, both highly respected clinicians (Gallagher, 1986; Andrews, 1994; 1997).

Today many different disciplines, such as feminism, psychology, sociology, psychotherapy and theology, are turning to psychoanalysis and to re-reading Freud. All these schools of thought are particularly concerned with the contemporary issue of personal/sexual identity – how a child becomes a desiring man or woman and what it is that they desire. Psychoanalysis, as we shall see, postulates that the formation of desire – of a person's fundamental identity – is primarily to do with the role and position of the father.

Psychoanalysis and Mythology – the Paternal Mystery

'Every new arrival on this planet is faced with the task of mastering the Oedipus complex; anyone who fails to do so falls victim to neuroses.'

Sigmund Freud

In order to understand the position of the father from a psychoanalytic viewpoint, it is necessary to quickly grasp some of the basic tenets of psychoanalysis. Freud revolutionised human psychology when he unearthed and named the two key tenets of psychoanalysis – the unconscious and the Oedipus complex.

Psychoanalytic ideas (like slips of the tongue, wishes in dreams, fantasies, sexual identity, father/mother complex, etc.) are now used readily by lay people as well as psychologists. So too is the idea of the unconscious. Freud emphasised the notion of the 'unconscious' in order to display that there exists mental activity of which the person is unaware, but which nonetheless exerts a profound effect on his/her behaviour. The word unconscious can be used metaphorically: an entity influencing a person unbeknownst to that person. Thus in psychoanalytic practice, and most psychotherapies, there is a particular emphasis upon the phenomena of the unconscious and on bringing out the unconscious meanings of the words, stories, actions, repetitions and the products of the imagination of an individual person. As we shall see, in making the unconscious 'conscious', one picture that invariably emerges for a person is his/her family drama. This involves uncovering where you are situated in relationship to your father and mother, and the influences that this has on your present relationships, including the one that you have with yourself.

One of the most valuable ways of working with the unconscious is through mythology. Mythology is the tool that Freud, a physician and scientist, was to place on the centre stage of his inquiry into the human 'psyche' (psyche is from the Greek meaning soul). Myth, quite simply, is a way of telling a story that has a universal appeal. It has been defined as something that never was but always is. There is something in it that transcends race and culture and touches what is essentially human in each of us (Deane, 1994). Myths are about life, the gods, morality, relationships, men, women, fathers, mothers and children. The famous mythologist Joseph Campbell contends that myths contain truths – truths that are disguised but express the unconscious desires, fears and tensions that underlie the conscious pattern of human behaviour. It is thus of great significance that the role of the father in psychoanalysis is typically understood through a Greek myth, as told by Sophocles in his play *Oedipus Rex*. (See the note at the end of the chapter for a synopsis of the Oedipus myth.) Freud chose this myth as the metaphor for psychoanalysis and the central tool for analysing the human psyche. This famous myth places *both* father and mother as key players, each holding positions and having desires, in the psychological and emotional drama of child development.

What the Oedipus Rex myth promoted for Freud, and many others after him, is the crucial significance of the triangular relationship that every infant finds themselves in: father-child-mother. It was through Freud's self-analysis, significantly at the time of his father's death, and listening to his patients that led him to the myth of Oedipus Rex and the momentous discovery of what he came to call the 'Oedipus complex'. In a letter to a very close friend, he writes: 'I have found, in my own case too, falling in love with the mother and jealousy of the father, and I now regard it as a universal event of early childhood ... If that is so we can understand the riveting power of *Oedipus Rex* ... the Greek myth seizes on a compulsion which everyone recognises because he feels its existence within himself' (Laplanche and Pontalis, 1988, p. 283). In this one statement, Freud changed the way many people, particularly psychoanalysts, understand childhood development and the role that both parents play in this development (Wolheim, 1971). Freud realised that the child is born into a pre-existing structure, namely a symbolic and historical culture with mores and laws that directly effect the child. The Oedipus myth is a wonderful example of this cultural inheritance. The child is also born into a very complex relationship (of hopes, fears, love and hate) where he or she holds many different meanings for the mother and the father. The child also brings an added complexity to this relationship; not only does the child take on a particular significance for both parents, but the father and the mother (be they absent or present, dead or alive) take on a very complex significance for the child. This rite of passage into the world, which every child must go through, is founded on the structure of mother-child-father. This is what Freud set out to explore and, in doing so, offered the first mapping of the Oedipus complex.

Psychological Puberty – the Child's First Love Affair

The Oedipus complex can be seen as referring to a group of largely unconscious ideas and feelings expressing both the loving and hostile wishes that the child experiences towards each of its parents. Freud discovered, through his own analysis and in listening to patients, that the child has a psychological puberty (a love and hate relationship, albeit unconscious) long before teenage physical puberty. Freud, and many others after him, saw the evidence of childhood sexuality in infant and child observation, and in the dreams and fantasies of adults. Freud also commented on the way men and women play and act out their child-like relationships with their mother and father in their relationship with their present partner. Freud saw this psychological puberty as the interplay of emotions and desires that takes place for the child as he or she moves from loving and desiring one parent to a situation of rivalry and wanting rid of the other parent. Freud writes that 'in the very earliest years of childhood, approximately between the ages of two and five, a coming together of the sexual impulses occurs of which, in the case of boys, the object (a psychoanalytic term) is the mother. This choice of object, in conjunction with a corresponding attitude of rivalry and hostility towards the father, provides the content of what is known as the Oedipus complex which in every human being is of the greatest importance in determining the final shape of his erotic life' (Freud, 18, 1923, p. 247)[1]. Thus the child is both a desired *and* a

---

[1] This is what has become known as the positive or simple form of the Oedipus complex. Freud, no doubt prompted by this early clinical work, and his other case histories, soon became more aware of the manifold incestuous desires of the child and later postulated 'that in the little boy the Oedipus complex has a double orientation, active and passive, in accordance with their bisexual constitution; a boy also wants to take his mother's place as the love-object of his father' (Freud, PFL 7, 1925, p. 333) (see also 1924, p. 318). In displaying this 'feminine attitude' to his father, there appears a corresponding jealousy and hostility towards his mother. This process radically shifted the concept of identification and became known as the negative form of the Oedipus complex. The description of the complex in its complete form allows

desiring human being from a very early stage of life and, despite the fact that this is happening unconsciously (although any parent will tell you about the tell-tale signs of these first 'love-affairs' with either parent), it has, as we shall see, profound importance in the child's personality development. One can already see the importance of the father emerging in the interplay of the triangular relationship: mother-child-father.

Mother-Child-Father

'She never cared for fashion's style,
Nor jewels and treasures
She found them in her baby's eyes ...'
From the song: *My Yiddish Mama*

Freud first described the Oedipus complex in 1897. Despite the fact that it was such a radical concept, Freud was naturally influenced in his findings and theories by the pervading ethos and social structures of the time which were both very patriarchal and conservative. Freud has been criticised at length, particularly for his understanding of female development. Nonetheless, it is generally acknowledged, that not only did he open the gate to further questioning and debate on the whole area of gender development, but he also raised questions that continue to challenge and resonate today. Thus, it is important to try and suspend judgement while reading Freud's understanding of the Oedipus complex, keeping in mind that it is a description of largely unconscious processes, and that it was written one hundred years ago. It is important to understand the original Oedipus complex

---

Freud 'to elucidate ambivalence towards the father, in the case of the boy child, in terms of the play of heterosexual and homosexual components, instead of making it simply the result of a situation of rivalry' (Laplanche and Pontalis; Freud, S. E. 19, p. 31). This allows for the many different sexual identities that a person can develop. It also de-pathologises homosexuality and allows this to be a normal, if different, consequence to the Oedipal drama.

(Freud's version) so as to grasp the way it has been used by later theorists. It is a central argument to show how the Oedipus complex offers a different understanding of the position and function of the mother, and particularly the father, in the development of the child.

The mother-child relationship is described by Freud as the 'first relationship' and the prototype of all other relationships that the child will have. Nonetheless, he noted very early in his clinical work the importance of the child's need to separate from the mother. He emphasised how the child's independence and the development of his/her unique personality depends on this process. Freud discovered in his clinical work that failure to separate, or a frustration of this process, can lead to serious personality and emotional problems later in life. Hence, the key questions that emerged for Freud, and which he spent the next forty years trying to answer, were: How, when and why does the child detach itself from the mother? What is the role of the father in this process? In what ways is this process different for boys and girls?

In his clinical work, Freud found that the Oedipus complex was a very different experience for boys and girls. The little boy, in order to enter the social world, must give up his unconscious desire and attachment to the mother. The boy does this as he realises that his father stands in that place. The boy, in his child-like imagination, sees the father as being much bigger and stronger. The father represents something different that is at once frightening and exciting. In other words, he sees the father as prohibiting his desire for the mother. Freud controversially called this prohibition the 'castration complex'. Put simply, the boy develops an unconscious narcissistic interest in his penis and feels that this may be taken away from him by the father as a punishment for his desires for the mother. This fantasy is confirmed for him by the fact that there are those without a penis, namely little girls. Thus the best course of action for the little boy is to repress his frustrated desire for the mother and his hostile wishes for the father. The boy then replaces these unsociable desires by an identification with the father, so that one day he too will be able to attract someone like his mother. This leads to the creation of the super-ego, similar to conscience, and initiates the processes that are designed to make the boy find his place in the cultural community. Thus, the father's role and position are crucial in this process of initiation into the social world – the world of inter-dependence rather than complete dependence.

Freud had much greater difficulty when it came to describing the Oedipus complex of the little girl. In fact, Freud was never clear in his writings regarding female sexuality and he ultimately referred to this as 'the dark continent' from which he could gather little information. Nonetheless, he attempted to document his clinical practice with women. For Freud, the little girl has a much 'stranger' rite of passage than the little boy. While the boy must give up the first object of his desire – the mother – it is, generally speaking, for another woman, whereas the girl must manage the same renunciation for the sake of the opposite sex (Freud, 1931). The girl, then, has to change her love/sexual object – from the woman (mother) to the man (father). How does this complex process take place?

We saw that for the boy the castration complex leads to the end or repression of the Oedipus complex (the love and hostile wishes the child harbours for the parents). By contrast, the castration complex begins the Oedipus complex for the girl. Freud claimed that the castration complex for the girl child include an unconscious feeling of deprivation in relation to the boy and a wish to possess a penis as he does. He saw this simply as an anatomical (bodily) difference between the sexes and one that leads the girl child into a series of new relationships with both the mother and the father. The girl sees the mother as wanting or loving something outside of herself; the father. The little girl may feel a resentment towards the mother who failed to provide her with a penis. Thus the mother depreciates in the child's eyes and the incestuous tie to the mother may be loosened. In setting out to redress the balance, the girl looks to her father and 'her desire slips into a new position along the line of the symbolic equation "penis-child'" (Freud, PFL 7, 1925, p. 40). Having a baby takes on the symbolic significance of having a penis. For the purpose of getting a child, she now takes her father as love object and the mother becomes the object of jealousy. The mother also becomes the object with which the girl identifies, so that she too may, one day, get a man like her father.[2] Again, one observes the importance of the role of the father in allowing the separation process for the child from the mother to begin.

This was the first documenting of the Oedipus complex, and numerous viewpoints have subsequently emerged. The reason we have documented Freud's thesis is because it is the only systematic study of child development to date that includes a detailed description of the role and place of the father in this complex process. Early feminist schools constantly debated Freud's understanding of child development, seeing it as patriarchal, 'penis-centred' and, in some cases, misogynistic. Other theorists tried to re-write Freud's thesis, placing the emphasis on various aspects of his work. But regardless of what stance people took, they kept finding themselves reading and arguing with Freud; this interestingly includes contemporary feminism. This return to Freud was largely prompted by Jacques Lacan (1901–1981) who offers a very interesting and contemporary reading of Freud's Oedipal narrative – one that again places both father and mother at the forefront of family and individual development.

---

[2] Freud emphasised the precariousness of the girl's Oedipal complex, and wrote that the girl never totally abandons her attachment to the mother (or woman) as love object, nor does she abandon her hostility towards her. At the same time, the attachment to the father is equally problematic: 'girls remain in the Oedipus complex for an indeterminate length of time; they demolish it late and even so, incompletely' (Freud, PFL 7, 1925, p. 340).

The Symbolic Father

'Do not swallow yourself up Mother,
Do not swallow me down in that which flows
from you to me.
I'd like it so much if we could be there,
Both of us,
So that one does not disappear into the other,
Or the other into the one'.

Luce Irigaray

Freud had tried to understand femininity and masculinity by anatomical (bodily) differences. He claimed that the lack of a penis is what unconsciously separates the girl from the mother as she turns to the father so as to receive a baby from him or a representative of him. He saw the boy as repressing his attachment and desire for the mother due to the father's presence and the boy's own attachment to his penis. Despite the obvious biological and cultural reductionism in these claims, one can see that, for Freud, sexuality and personal identity are founded in difference; this means separation from the mother and an identification with or movement towards the father. Nonetheless, Freud's account of how this process occurs, particularly his viewpoint that women 'lack' a penis, has rightly been criticised. Lacan puts a very different slant on Freud's rather archaic model. For Lacan, all human beings are 'lacking' – each of us is in a continual state of need and want. Nothing ever fully satisfies, and we passionately hold onto anything that satisfies for any length of time, but eventually this too is not enough. Lacan calls this constant state of need and want, characterised in our need to know, advance, believe and addict, the human search for the 'phallus'. The phallus is not the penis – it is a signifier, a bearer of meaning around which the child's identity is constituted. It ultimately represents desire and loss, separation and difference (or otherness). The child's entry to the symbolic order of language and culture is dependent on an awareness of this mystery. Lacan deliberately chose an image that conjures up strength, mystery and maleness. The present structure that underlies the family configuration places the father in a key position, as the one who initiates the child into the world of difference, of otherness – represented by the phallus. But at the outset, it is important to emphasise the phallus is something that every human being lacks.

Despite the obvious crudeness of some of Freud's writings, Lacan highlights the significance that Freud gave to all three parties in the family – father, mother, and child. For Lacan the child/infant is born in a premature and uncoordinated state and finds itself totally dependent on its given environment for survival. This has profound consequences for the infant and leaves the infant trying to adapt and conform to its surroundings in a way that will maximise survival. Now, as we know, the primary relationship at this time is the mother-child dyad (or twosome). Lacan calls this very important and necessary stage the 'imaginary order', in which the infant sees or imagines itself as the focus of the mother's desire, and sees her as the all-enveloping object of his/her desire. 'Lacan sees as the gateway to this world those moments in the first eighteen months of life when the child comes to delight in his (sic) own image as reflected in the mirror and in the loving gaze of those who care for him, especially the mother. A failure to enter this world of the captivating image would leave the child sunk in the miseries of motor incoordination characteristic of the infant in the early weeks and months after birth ... as a "fragmented body" vulnerable to dislocation and death' (Gallagher, 1986, p. 134). In order to maximise survival at this early stage, the infant/child unconsciously tries to imagine and identify himself or herself with what he or she thinks the mother desires, so that the infant can become that object of desire, thus guaranteeing immediate survival and complete dependence. It is important to remember that the child also has unconscious desires for the mother herself (the Oedipus complex). So the child tries to become everything for the mother and sees the mother as having everything it needs.

For her part, the mother tries to provide the complex and necessary caring, feeding and satisfaction of the infant's needs. At the same time, because she was a child herself, there also remains within her the desire for something other than satisfying the infant's needs. All human beings are lacking and are constantly trying to fill this lack. Unconsciously the mother may come to see the child as potentially filling this lack for her, and hence the child can take on a meaning for the mother which has nothing to do with the child itself. So the mother can get trapped into unconsciously trying to fulfil her 'lack', which echoes the painful separation from her own mother and the oftentimes frustrated relationship with her father (her Oedipus complex), and indeed the simple loneliness of being alive. This is what Lacan calls the human search and longing for 'the phallus': 'the mother lacks the phallus, and desires in the infant something other than himself – the phallus she lacks, the basis of the relationship with her parents, and of her own Oedipus complex' (Benvenuto and Kennedy, 1986, p. 132). The infant and mother are thus caught in this imaginary relationship: the infant unconsciously trying to become everything for the mother while having desires for the mother herself, and the mother unconsciously seeing the infant as an extension of herself and something that will fulfil her desire. For many psychoanalysts, this dual relationship does not provide the child with an appropriate structure or healthy environment for the development of personality; rather 'it opens up a number of potentially alienating and crippling identifications (mother-child- mother) situating the child in a line of fiction subjected to the mother's desire' (*Ibid*, p. 132). The child can become lost in its mother's desire and risks constantly trying to be what she wants, hence negating its own personality. This obviously has major consequences for the child later in life – for example identity crises, separation issues, dependence, co-dependency and much more. In fact, for Lacan, complete failure to move beyond this imaginary identification means to remain in a potentially psychotic state, and partial failure leaves the child more prone to a neurotic state of existence.[3] In other words, unless this 'imaginary' relationship between mother and child is punctuated, and a process of symbolic separation begins, the child will not be able to adequately develop his/her personality. This, as we shall see, is where the father becomes crucially important as the symbolic figure who ignites this separation process for both mother and child.

The unconscious desire of the mother has received little or no commentary outside mythology, until very recently. 'In one of his most illuminating case histories, "Little Hans", Freud has shown how the desire of the mother for the child, which in its origin draws the child away from his early misery into a sense of life and joy, can, when excessive, become death-bearing and prevent the child from moving beyond this phase of imaginary captivation into the symbolic ordering of human affairs within which s/he must eventually find his/her place. So great was the need of the mother of Little Hans for the child that she imposed onto the fantasies of her son none of the limits normally set by a mother. She not only had him in her bed all the time – against the remonstrances of a physically present but totally ineffectual father – but also encouraged him as a spectator to all her most intimate physical activities, dressing and undressing, using the toilet and so on. So that without any of the traumas that are supposed to be necessary for the production of a neurosis, Little Hans found himself at the age of five in the grip of an overwhelming set of phobias and anxieties that, without intervention, might well have perverted the whole subsequent course of his existence' (Gallagher, 1986, pp. 134–135). An Irish version of the Oedipus myth can be found in Frank O'Connor's *My Oedipus Complex*. Gallagher offers a very interesting reading of this, highlighting the fact that the father must at some level intervene in the mother-child relationship 'to allow the

---

[3] Psychosis is where there is a complete loss of connection with what we call reality, for example, hallucinations. Neuroses are psychological illnesses like obsessions, paranoia, phobias and addictions.

child a new access to his own originality, creativity and truth' (*Ibid*, p. 135).

Lacan, building on Freud's insights, including the 'Little Hans' case history, saw the need for symbolic separation between mother and child as being paramount to the psychological survival and development of the child. In order to escape the all-powerful, imaginary relationship that the child and mother find themselves in, it is essential to have acquired what Lacan calls 'Le Nom' or 'Le Non-du-Père' – 'The Name' or 'No-of-the-Father'. This is crucial if the child is to separate from the mother. This exists beyond the imaginary order of the mother-child relationship, and it is what Lacan calls the 'Symbolic Order'. The father represents the symbolic order, which is the order of culture, language and law. This is the world of 'difference' beyond the imaginary order. In representing the symbolic order, the father is the one who metaphorically says 'no' to both the child's desires and the mother's desires. He says, as it were, to the child: 'No you won't sleep with your mother, and your survival is not dependent on conforming to what you think her desire is'; and to the mother: 'No, the child is not going to fulfil all your desires, it is not your phallus, that is elsewhere' (Benvenuto and Kennedy, 1986). This symbolic 'no' of the father begins the separation process from the mother. The child realises that there is something 'other' to the mother (the father) and that the mother is not completely fixated on him/her. The mother's desire is elsewhere; this for the child means that the mother is somehow lacking (she does not have everything) and the child turns to see what it is that the mother desires.

The father's position in our present family structure represents the 'other' to the mother. The father introduces otherness or difference to the child. Simply, one can see it as a three stage separation process. Firstly, the mother's desire must be directed or focused outside herself; something other than the child must be in her life. As we have seen, this is to break a potential symbiotic and destructive dependency emerging between the mother and the child. Secondly, the father stands in the crucial position of this 'other', and he must be significant enough so as to capture the desire of the mother. The father must somehow represent the 'phallus'. Thirdly, the child follows the mother's desire outside herself, thus moving towards otherness. It is crucial that the mother has desires outside herself. Thus the father must be 'present', at the very least metaphorically, so as to symbolically engage both the child's and the mother's desire. Lacan, importantly building on Freud's insights, sees the father as exercising his function and role in a twofold operation – prohibition and promise. 'The purpose of *prohibition* is to complete the detachment begun with the weaning of the child from his mother, and, more specifically, to repress the desire for the mother which reaches a high point during childhood.' (*Ibid*, p. 136). The *promise* allows the child to move beyond the dual imaginary relationship with the mother, to a process of identification (with both father and mother) that offers new possibilities of existence. Lacan remained adamant that 'for both sexes it is the imago, the unconscious image of the father, that allows this identification and sublimation to take place' (*Ibid*, p. 137). The child thus begins the painful process of separation from the cosy and insular relationship with the mother. In turning to the father, the child is turning to the world of difference – the world of symbols and culture. Lacan is not as naïve as Freud, and is quick to point out that the child soon discovers that the father is 'lacking' and does not have all the answers (the 'phallus') and that his desire is also elsewhere. This, too, is part of the process of separation and individuation for the child and, painful as it may be, initiates the child to the world of questioning and mystery outside itself: a world that is paradoxically frightening and wonderful. Ultimately, and most importantly, it allows the child to begin the journey of discovering his/her own unique desire and place in the world.[4]

---

[4] Kristeva interestingly calls the separation of the child from the mother 'symbolic castration' and writes that it is the debt to be paid if one is to take up one's structured position as a desiring sexual subject and have

Conclusion

'We are the sons of our father,
To whom only can we speak out
The strange, dark burden of our heart and spirit,
We are the sons of our father,
And we shall follow the print of his foot forever'.

Thomas Wolfe

This chapter has set out the psychoanalytic understanding of the role of the father in child development. Psychoanalysis highlights how detrimental it is to ignore the symbolic function of the father in the development of the child's identity. The decline of the paternal image and the marginalisation of the father are cited as the bases of a number of neurotic dispositions that are commonplace today. These neuroses can often be traced back to the relationship and separation process between mother and child, and the role of the father in this transition. The mother's relationship with the child is seen as fundamental to the child's survival; it allows the child to internalise a model of safety and trust which is the basis of healthy development and of future relationships. This, we argue, includes mother-child 'bonding' as a basic survival need. Despite the importance and intensity of this relation-ship, it needs to enter a process of separation. This is necessary for both the child and the mother, so

---

access to the order of socio-symbolic culture and language. For Kristeva 'the fear of castration is precisely symbolic – the fear of the loss of presence, totality, pleasure, which is consequent upon the acquisition of language, the paternal metaphor, as separation from nature (mother). This separation – the entry into the Symbolic order – a world of difference and so of power and meaning is the socio-symbolic contract which is the basis of identity and it is common to both men and women' (Kristeva, p. 34). To bring home the significance of the Oedipus complex, Kristeva concludes 'together with the organising role of the Oedipus complex in relation to desire, the Symbolic castration, the separation of the child from the mother and the father, governs the position of each person in the triangle of the Father-Mother-Child, in the way it does this it embodies the law that founds the human order itself.'

that they can move away from the potentially destructive closeness of their relationship. One could say that it gives them both a new freedom. For the child, it allows new identifications and new possibilities in the world. For the mother, it gives her back her sense of self, separateness and independence. Failure to move beyond the mother-child dyad can leave the child and mother prone to severe neurotic dispositions.

The father, in the vast majority of cases, is the key player in this process of separation, acting as the 'other' or the third person to the mother. He moves the two person (mother-child) dependency based relationship into the complex inter-relational based triangulation of mother-child-father. This allows the child to move away from a potentially alienating imaginary world (mother-child) and to enter the social and cultural symbolic order (mother-child-father). The father is seen as fundamental to the child letting go of the mother: he symbolically prohibits the potentially incestuous closeness and attachment of the child to the mother; he also symbolically promises and represents new and more exciting ways of being in the world. The father is also fundamental to the mother letting go of the child: he is the person who sustains part of the mother's desire and meets this desire, not the child. Psychoanalysis teaches that unless the father takes up his position representing the symbolic order for the child and the mother, the separation process can become frustrated resulting in various neuroses and disturbances for the child and, indeed, for the relationship, the family and society.

What is being described here is an extraordinarily subtle process that takes place largely unconsciously for all human beings. The three key questions that are normally asked of this viewpoint are:

1. is the psychoanalytic understanding of the father, with its emphasis on the phallus, not still a patriarchal construct perpetuating an ideology that further undermines and marginalises women?

2. what about all the families that do not have fathers or traditional family structures?
3. can the father be shown how to take up his symbolic role in the family?

We now address each of these questions in turn.

Is the psychoanalytic understanding of the father, with its emphasis on the phallus, not still a patriarchal construct perpetuating an ideology that further undermines and marginalises women?

'Is Lacan an arch phallocrat ... or is he the prick who dares to speak its name to reveal the self-deception behind the masculine aspiration to phallic status? Does his work affirm or undermine phallocentrism? Or does it do both?'

E. Grosz

Psychoanalysis is often criticised or even ignored due its presentation of women and gender development. This is largely due to Freud's chauvinistic and conservative representation of female sexual development. Criticisms of his work often make his entire writings synonymous with phrases like 'penis envy' and 'female castration'. While fully agreeing with the need to re-think and criticise some of Freud's concepts, as we have done in this chapter, we have shown that his ideas are a lot more complex and important and cannot be reduced to one single idea in order to legitimate a position or reject his entire work. We have shown how contemporary psychoanalysis, in re-writing Freud's Oedipal narrative, offers an extremely useful model of the family dynamic and highlights the significance of the father's symbolic position.

Despite the complex re-writing of Freud's chauvinistic Oedipal model by contemporary psychoanalysis, it might be legitimately asked if it still remains a patriarchal and phallocentric paradigm? This is a major question and one to which there are no certain answers. However, it is a question that calls for discussion and debate. It also calls for a dialogue which is open rather than dogmatic, poetic rather than literal, and which recognises the intrinsic limitations of this, as all, theoretical models.

Contemporary psychoanalysis, primarily the work of Lacan, reiterates that the central tenet of psychoanalysis is the Oedipus complex. It is largely founded on the question of how does a person – a child – become a desiring sexual being, what is it that he or she desires, and what shapes this desire? It places an emphasis on the crucial role of the father in this complex formation of sexual identity. It argues that the separation of the mother-child dyad is crucial in order to break both the incestuous Oedipal bond, and the mother's potentially unhealthy desire which can situate the child in an alienating identification in the imaginary order. It is essential to acquire this symbolic castration – that is, the separation of the child from the mother and their desire for each other. As noted above, this is called 'No-of-the-Father' and is crucial if the child is to take up its structured place as a sexed being and have access to the socio-symbolic order of language and culture. Within our contemporary social structures – and particularly our family structures – the father stands in the position of the third term that must break the asocial dyadic unity of mother and child.

In Lacan's account, the father represents the phallus in ways that we do not fully understand. The phallus is the key symbol of lack and desire in the human condition. It is not the penis but stands for the lack which all children, regardless of their sex, experience when they cannot be what they want to be in relation to the mother and, indeed, the father. In other words, 'lack' is the structural lack in the symbolic order around which every human being has to construct an answer, since this ongoing answer is the basis of personal identity. In the context of the mother-child relationship, the father represents the phallus and, in turn, the symbolic world of interdependence and exchange. The status of the phallus, therefore, is ultimately unknowable and remains a mystery around which human desire and the search for its fulfilment is constituted. As one commentator has observed: 'One wonders [why] it has not yet become clear from Lacan's own texts that his concept of a phallus refers to a signifier for the language imposed on any subject with the purpose of giving that subject an identity? The resulting identity is paradoxically one of mental alienation. And insofar as identity is gendered and erotic (heterosexual, homosexual, bisexual, transsexual) the effect of the phallic signifier does link up with sexual organs ... but the primary functions of the phallic signifier involves the learning of separation where the demand links up to the drive to create limits and boundaries: the acquisition of a place within the Symbolic (cultural) order' (David-Menard, p. 77).

What Lacan recognised is that the cultural order itself contains the lack or malaise that feminists have equated with patriarchy. In other words, to be human is to lack. Thus psychoanalysis does shift the ground of our understanding of patriarchal power relations and their social reproduction. The father's role in drawing attention to the lack, both within the child and the mother and indeed within himself, is clearly shaped by the fact that men are physically and sexually different to women. Just how the physical gender differences between men and women shape the symbolic order, and how men and women are socially constituted as different from each other on the basis of these physical gender differences, is poorly understood but is, and needs to be, debated. Thus, what is needed is a further consideration of the relation between gender and representation, between the effect of gender on symbolic expression and the effect of a pre-existing system of representation on the emergence of gender. We believe that the psychoanalytic understanding of the role of fathers contains insights about otherness, lack, desire and meaning that are central to all human experience; it is not just a patriarchal construct offering only a male perspective.[5]

---

[5] Nonetheless, many feminists argue that, while taking this into consideration, the psychoanalytic discourse is still conservative in its

And what about all the families that do not have fathers or traditional family structures?

The answer to this question is in the psychoanalytic model we describe. Lacan clearly states that it must be someone 'other' than the mother who initiates the process of separation. Within the present structure of the nuclear family in the Western world, the father generally – and psychoanalysis would claim importantly – takes up the position of the 'other'. But that is not to say that the 'other' has to be either the father or a man. 'While there may be disagreements about the form that the symbolic father takes it has been affirmed that it must be someone other than the mother who introduces the symbolic law to the child, severing it from these alienating identifications and enabling it to take up a position outside of her desire' (Benvenuto and Kennedy, 1986, p. 123). The 'other' must be the person (or deity in some rare cases) who engages the mother's desire enough to create a sense of 'otherness' and difference for the child. So all sorts of triangulations are possible; for example, gay or lesbian couples (as noted the primary care giver does not have to be female) or single parent families where there is either a real sense of the father or some other father figure. So what actually constitutes an 'other' to the mother is extremely open-ended, but the father is given a priority for a specific reason. The reason why the father is given such a prominent role is due to the socio-cultural structures that the child is presently born into. In order for the child to have a sense of identity, the child must in some way be initiated into these structures. In this culture, the present structures prioritise the nuclear family – mother-child-father – and there is an entire system of societal organisation set up around this structure. The family is

---

virtual closure to women of a relation to the Symbolic and to themselves, which is not mediated or dominated by the symbolic law of the father. In Lacan's formulation of this structure as an inevitable law, patriarchal dominance with its inherent phallocentrism is not so much challenged as displaced from biology to the equally unchangeable socio-linguistic law of the father.

seen as the most valuable unit that best protects and helps the child develop. Hence it is crucial that the child experiences, at the deepest level of its being, an awareness of these structures. It is argued that this will give the child a sense of identity and of belonging. The initiation process for the child into the nuclear family, the movement away from the safe world of sameness (mother-child) and into the world of difference (mother-child-father), is largely dependent on the desire of the mother and the symbolic position that the father takes up in the family.

Can fathers be shown how to take up their symbolic position in the family?

A symbol is not something that can be reduced to one literal meaning, or indeed to a blueprint. A symbol, like a metaphor, is a way of representing something else – something that often has more than one meaning. Thus the symbolic position that the father takes up in a family can have many different meanings. Fathers stand for very different things, and stand for them in very different ways.

In the majority of families in our society, the symbolic position of the father is largely dependent on the character and desire of the person, and the circumstances that prevail, including the circumstances of his own fathering and mothering. It is also, as we have seen, dependent on the character and desire of the mother. Overlapping both of these is the cultural status and standing of fatherhood and manhood. If a society places a high value on fatherhood, then individual fathers are more likely to respond positively to those values and to desire them. A man must first desire to be a good father, whether consciously or unconsciously, before he can be one. It may seem strange, but every father and aspirant father needs to ask: 'Do I want to be a father?' This prompts a further question: 'Where can a man ask this question and hear his answer and the answers of other men?' If fatherhood is not valued – especially by men themselves – then it will not be desired and its symbolic importance is thereby undermined.

In the symbolic sphere, there are no quick-fix solutions. Our understanding of the psychoanalytic process leads us to the view that a man cannot be shown or taught how to be a good father, any more than he can be taught how to be a good person; this can only be educated – in the sense of being brought or led out of the person. Likewise, no father can be shown how to take up his symbolic position in the family since no one fully understands the inscrutable processes of the unconscious. However, he can be supported and encouraged in his desire to be a good father and in trying to understand the symbolic position that fatherhood confers on him within the family. We think such support and encouragement can happen in two ways. First, through increasing self-awareness among men and fathers, and secondly through increasing the symbolic importance that society attaches to fatherhood.

Increasing self-awareness takes place over the course of a lifetime and is an integral part of the process by which men and women grow as persons. Understandably, psychoanalysis places a high value upon self-awareness because it helps people understand why they are the way they are; in turn, this can empower people to embrace life and meet its challenges. Equally, self-awareness can help men understand the socially constructed roles that they play both inside and outside the family. This can throw light on the choices that are available to men – as fathers, partners, sons, workers, carers, etc. – thus increasing their strength and independence. Self-awareness can help in breaking some of the more destructive patterns in which men are engaged; some of these have been internalised from their relationships with their parents, be it an over-dependency on their mother (and continued with their partner), or working through their inevitably imperfect relationship with their father. A person unconsciously does this, because it is what he or she knows best (it's what is famil-y-ar!). When a man becomes a father, he is very likely to act in a similar or an opposite way to his experience of being fathered. He either identifies with his father or else a process of 'reaction formation' occurs and he sets out to do things differently (although they often turn out the same). Either way we can see the massive impact of the father on the father-son relationship, and how this repeats itself across the generations. In view of this, it can be very helpful for a man to look at these relationships to avoid the same patterns being played out again, and left for another generation to deal with.[6]

In our view, fathers can be supported and encouraged to take up the symbolic role within their families by becoming more self-aware of their relationships with significant others – such as their own fathers and mothers, their partners and other men – and how these shape their understanding of the fathering role. Self-awareness also includes awareness of one's own character which is unique and cannot be reduced solely to the influence of parents and environment. We are not suggesting that every man should undergo psychoanalysis or therapy before becoming a father! However, we do argue that men could benefit from participating in groups, such as men's groups, that provide a safe environment for exploring matters, both vulnerable and intimate, that are extremely important in the journey towards self-awareness and the understanding of what it is to be a man. As indicated in chapter one, this is now an option for men which did not exist before, and it is one which increasing numbers of men are availing of.

The symbolic importance of fatherhood in society generally is a matter that deserves widespread public debate. We are struck by the fact that many public debates on matters such as childcare, one parent

---

[6] This needs to be qualified: firstly it does not mean that a person only internalises destructive patterns in their childhood; and secondly it is not a blame game – the majority of parents genuinely do their very best (they too are dealing with their pasts); thirdly, the child does not come into the world a blank sheet but arrives with a character and this interacts with the environment; in other words, they are not simply the products of their parents.

families, family-friendly measures in the workplace etc., make no reference to fathers, presumably because fathers are seen as having no role to play. This is powerful testimony to the demise of the father figure in public life and in the symbolic sphere generally. In this chapter, we have noted the detrimental consequences that follow from undervaluing the symbolic role of the father in family life.

We believe that the demise of the symbolic father figure needs to be addressed in a number of ways:

- First, the imagery associated with fathers, as described in the introduction to this book, needs to be more supportive of an ideal that men can desire and towards which fathers can aspire. As we recommend later in chapter six, our Constitution needs to make a clear statement regarding the value that Irish society places equally on fatherhood and motherhood. We also recommend public discussion and debate on gender roles and the importance of fathers in forming the identity of each child. This includes raising consciousness about what it means to be a man and a father in today's society.
- Second, men need to be included and encouraged to participate in debates and discussions about families and children so that fathers are recognised as an integral part of our paradigm of family life in all its various forms.
- Third, the educational system, particularly at second level, has an important role to play for both boys and girls in promoting the value of manhood and fatherhood.
- Fourth, support groups for men can allow men to discover in other men the depth and meaning of manhood and the wisdom to be a good father.

Note to chapter: synopsis of the Oedipus myth

The following is a brief summary of the myth based on Robert Graves' translation: "Laius, the King and ruler of Thebes, was married to Jocasta but they were childless. Laius, no doubt stung by the fact that this publicly called into question his virility, went to consult the Delphi oracle as to the cause. There he was told that this was a blessing as any son of his would murder him and marry his wife.

In fear of being deposed Laius refuses to have a sexual relationship with Jocasta. Jocasta is angry with this situation, claiming that 'she would fly in the face of the gods to conceive'. Thus she connives to get her husband drunk and then manages to seduce him and conceives. She bears a son but Laius is terrified of the power of the prophecy and takes the baby and abandons him on the side of Mount Cithaeron. Before abandoning the baby Laius, pierces his feet with a spike so that when he is found by a passing shepherd he is named Oedipus ('swollen feet'). The shepherd brings the child to the King and Queen of Corinth and as they are childless they see him as a blessing from the gods and raise him as their own. One day a close companion told Oedipus in a teasing way that he was not really King Polybus's son. This strikes a deep chord in Oedipus and not knowing what to believe, he becomes determined to consult the Delphi oracle in order to learn the truth. After completing his mission he is stunned when he discovers that he is destined to murder his father and marry his mother, and warned not to go to the land where he was born.

Oedipus decides to set out for Thebes, the opposite direction from Corinth. En route to Thebes he meets a chariot whose passenger unceremoniously forces him off the road. Oedipus retaliates to this indignity, and in violently attempting to stop the chariot, overturns it killing all. The passenger, unbeknownst to Oedipus, is Laius, his father.

On arrival in Thebes, he finds the city terrorised by the sphinx, a lioness with a woman's head who kills everyone who fails to answer her riddle. Oedipus succeeds where those before him had failed and solves the riddle of the Sphinx. The Sphinx, in anger and hatred, kills herself. The inhabitants of Thebes are overjoyed at being at last free of the power of the Sphinx and welcome Oedipus as their new King. He marries the recently widowed Queen Jocasta, who is his mother.

The play *Oedipus Rex* opens with the city of Thebes ravaged by plague and King Oedipus sending his wife's brother Creon to the oracle to ascertain the cause of such devastation. Creon returns with the frightening news that the plague is the revenge of the gods on Thebes for harbouring King Laius' murderer. Oedipus sets up a public investigation and passionately seeks the truth. Even when the evidence is mounting and slowly the full story is becoming clearer, Oedipus insists that the truth be revealed. Despite pleas from Jocasta, lies from the shepherd and the wise advice of the seer, Oedipus continues to put the pieces into place. Finally Oedipus tragically discovers who he is but also what he has done – murdered his father and married his mother.

Queen Jocasta hangs herself unable to live with the truth that she is mother, lover and wife to her son. Oedipus, in a moment of moving passion and despair in the play, blinds himself and begs for exile.

Chapter 3
Fathers and Children

Introduction

'When I look back on my childhood I wonder how I survived at all. It was, of course, a miserable childhood: the happy childhood is hardly worth your while. Worse than the ordinary miserable childhood is the miserable Irish childhood, and worse yet is the miserable Irish Catholic childhood. People everywhere brag and whimper about the woes of early childhood, but nothing can compare with the Irish version: the poverty; the shiftless loquacious alcoholic father; the pious defeated mother moaning by the fire; the pompous priests; bullying schoolmasters; the English and the terrible things they did to us for eight hundred long years'

Frank McCourt, *Angela's Ashes: Memoir of Childhood*

'It's never too late to have a happy childhood'

Anonymous

This chapter addresses two questions. The first concerns the amount of involvement that fathers have with children in the home. The second concerns the impact that fathers have on the development of their children. Clearly the two questions are related. In answering the first question, we examine whether the division of labour within families – particularly regarding the care of children – has changed significantly from the traditional pattern where almost all of the care was undertaken by the mother. This question is raised again in chapter four with particular emphasis on the perspectives that inform research in this area. In answering the second question, we look at some of the impacts that fathers have – or can have – on their children.

Before addressing these questions, it is useful to draw attention to some core beliefs about parenting which shape contemporary practice since, unless undetected, these beliefs become part of the answer, rather than part of the question. One writer has suggested that three beliefs have dominated our understanding of parenting over the past three hundred years which, although they may be true, have little in the form of scientific evidence to prove that they are true. 'One is that what happens in the family sets the course of a child's development early in life and what is done cannot be undone. The second is that love for the child is the most critical ingredient and, in our century, that love should be physical and involve embracing and kissing the child. Third, the mother is seen as the central figure in the child's development' (Kagan, 1990, p. 71).

The main consequences of these beliefs are to inflate the importance of both the nuclear family and the parents, possibly beyond the point of realistic expectations. The nuclear family is the idealised home where couples seek the all-satisfying goal of private companionable love and where each is expected to be the other's lover, best friend, colleague, adviser, etc. In a way, the modern nuclear family is expected to be both a family and a community all in one (McKeown, 1997a). So carefully packaged is this ideal that the burden beneath its surface is often difficult to see. Into this fragile crucible of great expectations is added the belief that the life of a child is fundamentally determined by its parents. This belief gives parents a sense of responsibility which is disproportionate to their power or capabilities. Moreover, the constant stream of advice on how to be a good parent which flows from this belief may be more effective in producing guilt feelings within parents than increasing their capabilities to care for their children. One writer has variously described this vision of parenting as 'the parental fallacy' and a fantasy which 'holds our contemporary civilisation in an unyielding grip' (Hillman, 1996, p. 63).

At its core, the fallacy in this vision of parenting lies in both overestimating the power of the parent to shape the unique fate of each child and underestimating the myriad influences on the child which are outside − or at least originate outside – the home. In view of this, it is a little paradoxical that twentieth-century theorists, who have contributed so much to elevating the importance of parents, and especially the mother, such as D. W. Winnicott, Melanie Klein, René Spitz, John Bowlby and Anna Freud, were working out their ideas under the shadow of the Second World War. This leaves one wondering about how theories get developed and whether theories shape the world or the world shapes theories.

These observations are designed to raise awareness about the assumptions that are often implicit in discussions about the role of fathers and mothers. Moreover, these assumptions are often built into research on this subject, and failure to draw attention to them can further inflate the power of the underlying myths. In addressing questions about the role of fathers in the home, therefore, it is important to understand that these questions are being asked in the context of a set of beliefs which themselves need to be subjected to constant scrutiny and critique.

What Fathers do in the Home

'Nothing has a more powerful influence upon children than the life their parents have not lived.'

Jung

'A man without an abiding interest in his children and their future is a straw blowing in the wind.'

Colm O'Connor

It is easy to underestimate how much fathers in Ireland have changed in the past twenty-five years or so. The main picture of the father's role in the traditional Irish home, particularly in rural Ireland, comes from a study carried out in County Clare in the 1930s (Arensberg and Kimball, 1942). In that study, the authors describe family relationships as comprising:

1. complete separation between father and mother in terms of housekeeping, child rearing and farmyard and farm tasks;
2. concentration of authority in the hands of the father although the mother enjoyed areas of autonomy in her household and farmyard roles;
3. mothers playing a key role in managing tensions and being emotionally supportive while fathers often presented as severe and distant authority figures (*Ibid*).

It appears that these relationship patterns, not unique to Ireland, were so deep-rooted and pervasive as to be, in the words of Hannan, 'largely unquestioned and so "sacred" as to be unquestionable' (see also Hannan, 1973, p. 559). However, it was the work of Hannan in the 1970s which suggested that significant changes in gender relations were taking place in rural Ireland.

In a study involving over four hundred interviews with husband and wife couples in the western counties of Ireland, Hannan found considerable evidence of change in traditional sex roles. He found that over a quarter of all families departed from the traditional model in terms of household and child rearing tasks and had joint consultative patterns of decision-making. In these families, the husband was 'expressive and emotionally supportive in relation to his wife and children and emotions generally were openly expressed and supportive' (Hannan, 1973, p. 561; see also Hannan and Katsiaouni, 1997).

Notwithstanding the significant shifts which seem to have occurred in gender roles, there is also considerable evidence to suggest that the division of labour in the home still bears marks of the traditional pattern. Indeed, a number of studies have suggested that 'there is almost no evidence' (Lewis, 1993, p. 95) for the claim that 'today's fathers are caring for their children in radically different ways to their older counterparts' (*Ibid*; Lewis and O'Brien, 1978; Brannen and Moss, 1991; Kiernan, 1992; Kempeneers and Lelievre, 1992). The same finding has also emerged from a number of longitudinal studies (Coverman and Sheley, 1986; Lewis, 1986; Sanik, 1981). Even the social engineering efforts in Sweden at changing the division of labour between mothers and fathers in the home have had relatively little impact (Sandqvist, 1987; 1992). In English-speaking countries, especially the United States of America, attempts at social engineering by teaching fathers the skills of childcare (where these have been evaluated) have not demonstrated clear long-term increases in paternal involvement (Lewis, 1993; Hawkins and Roberts, 1992).

The main sources of change in the domestic division of labour seem to be occurring in dual-earner families. There is also some evidence that unemployed fathers tend to be more involved in housework and childcare than employed fathers, although the evidence for this is inconclusive (see Wheelock, 1991 and, for a contrary view, see McLoyd, 1989). As regards dual-earner families, one study found that fathers in these families do thirty hours of domestic work per week compared to fifteen hours by fathers in single-earner families (Ackerman-Ross and Khana, 1989). A number of other studies have shown a similar pattern (Crouter et al., 1987; Greenberger and O'Neill, 1990; Volling and Belsky, 1991). However, in dual-earner families, women still do considerably more domestic work and childcare than men.

This pattern seems to prevail throughout Europe according to the results of an EU-wide study of twelve member states, including Ireland, that was carried out in 1994 by the European Community Household Panel (Eurostat, 1997). The survey found that in families where both parents are in paid employment for a minimum of thirty hours a week, and where there are children under sixteen years of age, 77% of women and 50% of men claimed they looked after their children on a daily basis. However, the study also showed that working mothers looked after children more than working fathers in all countries. This is particularly true in Greece, Portugal, Luxembourg, Ireland, Italy and Spain where under 50% of men said they looked after their children as opposed to

80% of women; the differences were less marked in Denmark and the Netherlands. For those parents who claimed to spend time with their children, 32% of men and 6% of women said they spent fewer than two hours a day looking after them; by contrast, 69% of women and 27% of men claimed to spend four hours a day looking after their children (*Ibid*).

One group of researchers have suggested that the main reason why fathers in dual-earner families do less housework than mothers is that they spend much longer hours at work: 'for fathers, therefore, it appeared that heavy work commitments outside the home represented an obstacle to equal parenting and, as such, a source of conflicting pressures, particularly in families in which both parents were in full-time employment' (Ferri and Smith, 1996, p. 48). In these families, it appears that the domestic division of labour is driven more by the structural characteristics of the situation rather than by any ideological commitment for, or against, equalising the domestic division of labour between men and women. In other words, the fathers' involvement in housework and childcare may be negotiated with the mother, taking into account the work and other circumstances in which both parents find themselves. (This issue is discussed at greater length in chapter four.)

Impact of Fathers on Children

'Our lives may be determined less by our childhood than by the way we have learned to imagine our childhoods. We are ... less damaged by the traumas of childhood than by the traumatic way we remember childhood.'

James Hillman

'This poem came into being thirty-three years after my father died ...
when I was thirteen ...
I didn't have your love

to teach me how to love
and came to love my children through letting them love me.'

Niall Kelly

The impact of a father on children is mediated by his parenting relationship with the child. This may appear obvious, but for many years it had been thought that it was the father's characteristics as a man, rather than his characteristics as a parent, which mediated his impact on child development, particularly among boys. However, the research evidence suggests that it is the quality of the parent-child relationship rather than the gender of the parent that is most important in child development (see Lamb, 1997, p. 9). At an unconscious level, however, as the analysis in chapter two shows, the father's role is fundamentally different from the mother's because it symbolises and teaches the importance of a world outside the intimate relationship of the mother and child; at the unconscious level, therefore, broadly similar behaviours by mother and father have profoundly different meanings for the child's psyche.

At a conscious and practical level, the fact that good fathering and good mothering involve broadly similar behaviours has important implications for fathers, as Burgess has pointed out (1997, p. 188): 'The message emanating from this is that there is no free ride for fatherhood, no magical role for fathers just because they are fathers or just because they are men. It is what each man gives on a personal level that makes him a key player in his child's development. And, in the wider world, it is what men as a group will give to children in respect of intimate care and attention that will enable males to play a key role in their development. Otherwise a father's main value is limited to a pay-cheque and to a lesser extent a support system, and although these are valuable functions they in no way satisfy the aspirations of today's fathers, or their children.'

Some children grow up with little or no contact with their fathers. However, the research suggests that these children do not fare worse than children who have contact with their fathers, when all the other factors affecting the child's development are taken into account. The most significant of these other factors is the process by which a child loses its father. Children who lose a father through divorce, possibly after a period of sustained parental conflict, will tend to be more adversely affected than children who have never had a father living with them. As Lamb (1997, p. 11) has pointed out: 'since many single-parent families are produced by divorce and since divorce is often preceded and accompanied by periods of overt and covert spousal hostility, parental conflict may play a major role in explaining the problems of fatherless children'.

Fathers, or mothers, who have no contact with their children seem to have little impact on them – good, bad or indifferent. At the same time, almost without exception every child will want to know its biological parents and, in this sense, it is hard to imagine any child remaining entirely unaffected by its biological parents. Moreover, even children who have no contact with their biological fathers still need fathers and male role models. This implies that even 'fatherless' children can find in other men – and in their imaginations – the fathering that might otherwise be supplied by the biological father. There is no hard determinism, therefore, that turns a biological father into a psychologically real father, either for the child or the man. Being a father, therefore, involves choosing to become physically and psychologically connected with the child's life and development in whatever way seems appropriate, given the norms and circumstances of one's life.

There appears to be virtual unanimity among re-searchers that the more extensive a father's involvement with his children, the more beneficial it is for them in terms of cognitive competence and performance at school as well as for empathy, self-esteem, self-control, life skills and social competence; these children also have less sex-stereotyped beliefs and a more internal locus of control (see Pleck, 1997; Pruett, 1983; 1985; Radin, 1982; 1994). Conversely, children are less likely to become involved in delinquent behaviour or substance behaviour if their fathers are sensitive and attentive to them; even the children of fathers who have a criminal record are less likely to become delinquent if the father spends a lot of time with them.

Of particular importance here is the style of fathering: 'authoritative' fathering, which involves providing consistent values and boundaries and relating to the child with warmth and confidence, is beneficial to the child but 'authoritarian' fathering, which involves excessive discipline, control and an aloofness from the child, is not. One commentator has suggested that involved fathering promotes positive child development in the following way: 'the benefits obtained by children with highly involved fathers are largely attributable to the fact that high levels of paternal involvement created family contexts in which parents felt good about their marriages and the childcare arrangements they had been able to work out' (Lamb, 1997, p. 12).

In assessing the impact of a father's involvement with his children, some research distinguishes between two types of involvement:

- involvement through primary care taking such as preparing food, changing nappies, cleaning and clearing up;
- involvement through shared activities with the children.

The research evidence suggests that fathers tend to be more involved in the second sense and that this is the type of involvement that has the most positive impact on the development of the child (Drago Piechowski, 1992; Owen and Cox, 1988). Indeed it has been suggested that the first type of involvement may be inversely related to the second, particularly in very busy families where both parents work and time is scarce (Morgan, 1996, pp. 100–101).

Researchers have also tried to assess the impact of families on the likelihood of children becoming involved in crime; however, the independent effect of fathers is not always assessed in these studies. One of the key findings to emerge from three major longitudinal studies of delinquency in Britain suggests that the roots of crime lie within families, particularly inadequate or inappropriate parental supervision (Wadsworth, 1979; Kolvin et al., 1990; West and Farrington, 1973; West, 1982). It is true that most of those involved in crime and delinquency are boys or men from poor backgrounds (and this is why girls and women feature less frequently in this type of research), but the association between crime and poverty tends to diminish when poor parental supervision is taken into account. Poor parental supervision can, in turn, facilitate peer influences which may draw the young person into delinquency. As one team of researchers has pointed out, following a review of the research evidence: 'Those who have been least well-supervised by their parents when young and who have achieved least in primary school are more likely to mix with "the wrong crowd" of other anti-social children. In other words, the power of parents in a crime prevention context is at its greatest before their children reach the age of 10' (Utting, Bright and Henricson, 1993, pp. 14–15; see O'Mahony, 1997 for a recent review of the Irish evidence).

A further implication of this research is that involvement in crime and other anti-social behaviour is one of the ways in which boys who are poorly fathered express them-selves as men. Their involvement in crime is a way of participating in the outside world where they may enjoy the support of other boys and men who have had similar experiences of poor fathering. In this respect, girls seem to respond very differently, though not necessarily any more positively, to the experience of poor fathering.

Other studies have also highlighted the impact of family management practices on delinquency. In effect, delinquency is less likely in homes where the parents have a good relationship both with each other and with the children; it is more likely where these relationships are unhappy or neglectful. This is consistent with the findings noted above on the impact of divorce and lone parenthood: both British and American research demonstrates that where children are nurtured and loved, irrespective of whether the parents are divorced or whether the children are raised by a lone parent, they are much less likely to fall into delinquency (see Utting, Bright and Henricson, 1993).

Specific research on the impact of fathers on crime is much less extensive than research on families and crime, but the results nevertheless bear out the importance of the relationship between father and child. One study compared the families of five hundred delinquent boys with five hundred non-delinquent boys and found that fewer than half the former had sympathetic, affectionate fathers compared to eight out of ten of the latter (Gleuck and Gleuck, 1950). Moreover, this study found that the relationship with fathers was more significant than the relationship with mothers in predicting delinquency. Another American study found that children who grew into anti-social adults also had anti-social fathers in the sense that they drank excessively, were chronically unemployed and lost contact with their families after separation (Robins, 1966).

The reality is that most children – boys and girls – do not become delinquent or involved in crime. Many, however, suffer in less aggressive and destructive ways because of the absence of effective and affective fathering. It is difficult to know if poor fathering affects sons more than daughters, although the experiences of sons may be better documented, at least in Ireland (see for example, Hyde, 1996). The following poem, *My Father's Footsteps* by Colm O'Connor (1997), may speak to the experience of many sons and daughters:

> *My feelings toward my father were ones I never knew*
> *because I knew only his shadow*
> *Or the footprints of where he had been*
> *the after-images hanging after his departure –*
> *the smell of his after-shave*
> *his shoes on the landing after night-duty*
> *the sound of a car in the driveway*

Changing Fathers?

his 'Be Quiet' voice after lights went out
Or frozen moments held like rare coins:
Dad kicking a ball so high
A race on the beach at 10
His praise for a pencil sketch
The broad of his back swimming off the rocks
His reassuring voice over late-night algebra
His worry about the car on summer holidays
His unglamorous kindnesses
His letters
His unapplauded sacrifices
His absence.
Fathers linger
Like the echo of a long gone presence
in an empty room.

So in later years we men are left searching for
memories
for incidents around which we can make some purchase
in search of reassurances that we were fathered -
pictured moments that would allow us to feel that we
were blessed,
that we were substantial in our fathers' eyes.

And in your search a wave of anxiousness
surges through you
as you flick through your catalogue of childhood
memories
like some photo-album,
unable to find the Polaroids that would prove it all,
the evidence to yourself that your self-doubt
and fear and loneliness in this world
are all just temporary aberrations.

But can you find it?
Can you find the stained glass picture
that would look out at you
in clear blood,
that would mark your presence
that would allow you to say

'Yes that is me,
that is me and my dad.
Yes look,
that's my father's arm around my shoulder
and my father's smile
and my father's pride'
this picture that would show that you were chosen,
that your father blessed you,
and dipped you in the great river of his life
and baptised you into the world of men
and said
'You are my son, a man-to-be, in whom I am well
pleased.'

And you search for this memory among the scattered
photos at your feet and end up
like an unannounced Jesus at the water's edge
unannointed and unseen
searching out your father,
the look, the recognition,
but cannot find his eye
or hold his gaze.

And as men we go unseen and unblessed
as if unwelcomed into the intimacies of life
and we turn then –
we all turn then and walk into the desert
with a deep Hunger.

Researching the impact of fathers on children is clearly important. Of equal interest is the impact that children have on fathers. There is considerably less research on this aspect of the relationship, although some researchers have suggested that its impact on the development of fathers could be just as significant as the impact on the development of children (European Commission Network on Childcare, 1990; 1993). This is an area which would repay further investigation and we explore it further in chapters four and seven.

Conclusion

This chapter has reviewed the evidence on the impact of fathers on children. The results reveal that fathers who have warm, close and nurturing relationships with their children can have an enormously positive influence on their development. In this respect, the behaviours by which fathers impact on the development of their children are no different from those of the mother. The converse of this also applies, and children develop less well where their fathers are distant or uninvolved; these children may also become involved in crime where the parent-child relationship is weak. Thus, the quality of the parent-child relationship is what is crucial to the child's development. At the same time, in line with our psychoanalytic understanding of how mothers and fathers influence the unconscious development of the child, we wish to emphasise that similar behaviours by mother and father have profoundly different meanings for the child's psyche. In other words, at an unconscious level, the role of the father is not just to be a good mother, or vice versa.

Weak parent-child relationships can occur in a variety of settings and are influenced by a variety of factors. Where children become involved in crime, these settings tend to be characterised by poverty and other stresses such as unemployment or poor environment. The development of parent-child relationships in this context involves supporting families who lack the knowledge, skills and self-confidence to make them more effective parents, particularly when their children are young. This type of support would involve a range of measures to reduce poverty, increase childcare, establish family centres and neighbourhood projects, provide intensive support and education to vulnerable parents with pre-adolescent children, as well as specific measures to ensure that fathers are involved. The involvement of fathers in this type of work would probably require outreach work, particularly in disadvantaged areas, and a sensitive approach that addresses the obstacles constraining fathers – such as skills, attitudes, time, relationships with partner, relationship with child etc. – from being more involved with their children. Beyond the family and its immediate environment, it is also necessary to consider how the education of young people prepares them for their future role as parents by raising their awareness, understanding and skills for living in satisfying, intimate and respectful relationships.

Our analysis suggests that two broad changes are required to maximise the beneficial impact that fathers can have on their children. The first is to promote the ideal of good fathering among all fathers and potential fathers through the education system and through public education. This should be done in a variety of forums – family resource centres, parenting programmes, media awareness programmes etc – according to the needs of different categories of father and should elicit the active participation of fathers in discussing their own experiences of fathering and being fathered. We believe that being a father is not just a skill; it is a way of being a man and requires engagement with one's own life. Education about fathering needs to be sensitive to vulnerabilities, and strengths need to be supported and affirmed. We suggest that any initiatives in the area of education should be piloted beforehand.

The second change concerns the specific needs of fathers and potential fathers in disadvantaged areas. We suggest that measures to facilitate fathers in these areas need to be accompanied by a general improvement in the infrastructure of services in those areas; this could include employment and environmental improvements, increased childcare, family centres, neighbourhood projects and youth services for pre-adolescent and adolescent children. The involvement of fathers will require sensitive outreach work and a forum for participation, something that is highly skilled and urgently needed work and will require substantial resources and skills, if it is to be effective.

Chapter 4
Fathers and Home

Introduction

'Fathers should be neither seen nor heard. That is the only proper basis for family life.'

Oscar Wilde, *The Ideal Husband*

'My child arrived just the other day. He came into the world in the usual way.
But there were planes to catch and bills to pay. He learned to walk while I was away.
And he was walking, before I knew it, and as he grew he'd say, I'm gonna be like you dad.
You know I'm gonna be like you.'

Harry Chapin, *The Cat in the Cradle*

This chapter tries to answer the question: What do fathers actually do in families? The focus is on fathers 'at home', as opposed to fathers at work, however much the two are inextricably linked. What fathers actually do at home and in families is an empirical question. Researchers have examined the 'domestic' and 'caring' tasks that fathers and mothers carry out with children, the sexual division of domestic labour and responsibility for child caring and the amount of time each partner spends in such activity; all of this research is reviewed.

We shall show, however, that these are not just empirical questions which involve weighing who does what and when in the home. A number of philosophical and theoretical issues arise concerning not only *what* fathers do but *why* do fathers do what they do? And the related question of what they do *not do* and why? This takes us to the core of what is 'good enough' fathering and how such matters are determined, which has already been raised in chapter one. It brings us to consider the

95

nature of fairness; how to measure 'domestic democracy' and the fundamental question of where men and women differ in their orientations to care and nurturing their children, what determines this and how might it be changed?

We identify two key approaches to fatherhood which we set out and discuss in terms of the *fairness* perspective and the *developmental* perspective. We detect a key shift in debates on fatherhood that has arisen in the 1990s and attempt to elucidate the key features of the fatherhood paradigm that should govern public policy in the new millennium. This constitutes a perspective that integrates key aspects of the fairness and developmental perspectives and holds that, as well as promoting accountable fathering, the aim should be to support fathers in making the developmental transition to parenthood in ways that sustain paternal commitment to the benefit of children, women and men themselves.

Domestic Democracy: the Fairness Perspective

> 'He was, without question, the paterfamilias, governing and dispensing. As young children we often felt no more than mere appendages to the marriage, our mother his real concern, the one to be turned to and fondled. In the evenings, we had to respect his weariness, were schooled to become sensitive to his moods, gauging when to ask a favour of him. Secretly, he wished, I am certain, to be seen as a patriarch – that was his ideal – an unwavering provider ... This dedication to our upbringing becomes all the more poignantly abundant when set against the background of his childhood impoverishment and ensuing unease about money.'

> Derek Shiel, 1995

> 'A great many men have been falsely empowered by this culture's belief that discipline is not required in their domestic lives – relationships need not be actively worked on. 'A man is

*the king of his castle,' the old saying goes. And, while few
modern men would have the temerity to state such a belief
openly, a great many act on it..'*

Terrence Real, 1997

Traditionally, research into what fathers do in families has
examined three main areas:

- the amount of time fathers spend with their children;
- the kinds of activities undertaken;
- men's parenting styles (Burgess, 1997, p. 63).

More recent work has begun to deconstruct the nature of
domestic labour and childcare to render visible not only
the sexual division of the tasks that get done, but the
kinds of 'mental' labour and emotional work that men and
women do. Analysis of gendered ways of 'thinking about
the baby' reveals crucial issues about responsibility and
accountability for children and family life (Walzer, 1996).

Just as more and more men can be seen pushing
prams in public, research in the 1980s confirmed that,
from a very low starting-point, more men wanted to
become actively involved with children and some were
making efforts to do so. Nevertheless, the same studies
suggested that men in general had a very long way to go
before anything like equality of childcare and shared
responsibility with women could become a reality. Studies
in the 1970s and 1980s showed that while men had
begun to do more than they used to, women still tended
do the bulk of domestic work. Surveys showed that many
men supported more equal arrangements. However, a
gap was apparent between what men *said* and what they
actually *did* in relation to childcare – between attitudes
and behaviour. Longitudinal studies of fathering from the
1960s through to the early 1990s showed little or no
changes in fathers' participation in domestic tasks or
caring for their children (Lewis, 1993, p. 87).

There is a striking consistency in research findings of
paternal under-involvement in different countries. One
study of fatherhood in ten countries suggested that the

average daily time that fathers spent alone with their children ranged from 6 minutes in Hong Kong, 12 minutes in Thailand, 54 minutes in China, 48 minutes in Finland, 1 hour 36 minutes in the USA, to 3 hours 42 minutes in Belgium (Boyden, 1994). These findings are broadly in keeping with Hochschild's celebrated American study in the 1980s which found that, in families where both parents were working, men avoided most of the 'second-shift' labour, leaving the responsibility for childcare and housework to their wives (Hochschild, 1989).

Researchers have also attempted to break down what fathers and mothers do into types of activity. Thus American research on the nature of fathers' actual one-on-one interaction with the child – feeding, helping with homework, or playing catch – suggests that American fathers with pre-school children participate in, on average, about 26% of the total hours spent by mothers and fathers in direct childcare activities (Ishii-Kuntz and Coltrane, 1992). The same research found that men's participation in housework encouraged them to share child rearing activities with their wives. The level of paternal participation is substantially higher in two-parent families where the mothers are employed outside the home. Some American researchers have been at pains to point out, however, that this does not necessarily mean that fathers are doing proportionately more when mothers are employed, but that mothers are doing less. While proportionately more involved when mothers are employed outside the home, in absolute terms fathers' levels of involvement may not have changed significantly (Ishii-Kuntz, 1995).

Other researchers (Lamb et al., 1987) have distinguished three components of parental involvement with children:

- *engagement* which relates to the time spent in one-to-one interaction with the child;
- *accessibility* refers to activities with less direct interaction, such as a parent working in the kitchen while the child is in the next room;

- *taking responsibility* relates to the degree of accountability that is taken for the child's care and welfare, such as knowing when a child needs to go to the doctor, organising the visit and making sure the appointment is kept.

In two parent families where the mother is not employed outside the home, the study found that the father spent in the region of 20–25% of the time mothers do in direct interaction or engagement with the children. In such families where the mother is working outside the home, the levels of paternal engagement and accessibility stand at 33% and 65% respectively, which are higher than in families with a mother who is not employed outside the home. In terms of accountability, the study found no evidence that mother's employment outside the home has any effect on the level of responsibility taken by fathers (see, also Lamb, 1986).

So it appears that while there have probably been some increases over time in average degrees of paternal involvement, mothers spend more time than men in caring for children and continue to take day-to-day responsibility. The accumulated evidence suggests that 'increased participation of mothers in the labour force outside the home has not brought a corresponding participation of men in household tasks and childcare within the family' (Kiely, 1996, p. 147). When men have got involved, the apparent trend has been for them to do 'the more enjoyable bits', as researchers have tended to perceive them, like playing with the children and reading them bed-time stories. Segal (1990, p. 37), summarising the evidence, concluded that 'in the great majority of cases, men's participation is far removed from genuine sharing of responsibilities'.

Until the mid-1990s, much of this evidence was produced within a dominant paradigm on fatherhood, gender relations and childcare which was founded on feminist scholarship with the emphasis on issues of men's power, social justice and *fairness*. This perspective is based largely on a critique of patriarchy and power relations, and on empirical evidence supporting the hypothesis that men and male-dominated institutions in the public domain and the private world of the family systematically exploit women as carers. Men are seen as benefiting from being in a structurally powerful position where they can revert to traditional expectations and get out of housework and childcare. Women have no such option, being tied institutionally as well as personally to childcare responsibility by virtue of ideologies of motherhood, femininity and their ascribed identity as women.

In one way or another, domestic and caring/love labour is seen as ending up being carried out by women. In more affluent, middle-class households a further gender dynamic arises in that this can be the (female) paid help or au pair as well as the child's mother. Similar issues arise in the gendered nature of the public provision of childcare which is almost all done by women – in crèches, family centres, and so on – a theme we return to in chapters five and seven when discussing state services. Some have argued that the popular image of the so-called 'new father' has enabled many middle-class men to have it both ways. It gives them the license to choose to enjoy the emotional fruits of parenting while their position of class and gender privilege allows them the resources with which to buy or negotiate their way out of childcare (Segal, 1990). An *illusion* of equality was created where 'new fathers' could bask in the reflected glory of their heroic commitment when in reality it was their partners, supported by underpaid women house-workers, who were having to be 'superwomen' and carry the major responsibility, for which they got little acknowledgement. The juxtaposition of these apparent realities with all those carefully constructed marketing images of scantily clad men cradling babies and driving off in posh motor cars that arose in the 1980s has thrown into question whether, in reality, the 'new fatherhood' is more a matter of commercialism and post-modern style than of substance – of surface appearances rather than real changes in behaviour. The idea of the 'new father' is consequently thrown into doubt, having more to do with changing cultural expectations than behaviour. An important gap is revealed between *culture* and the *conduct* of fatherhood (Ishii-Kuntz, 1995). As we shall show later in our discussion of the developmental perspective, research in the 1990s has started to examine the constraints on fathers as well as on mothers which impact on men's ability to negotiate their fatherhood role and identity.

Thus in order to address the gap in gender equality, co-parenting has been framed within this fairness perspective as an issue of 'domestic democracy'. The development of anti-discriminatory policies and practices is viewed as essential to work against the traditional assumption that a woman is destined to do the childcare/domestic labour simply because of her gender. The key issue is *fairness*. When family work and responsibility are not shared equitably, unfair arrangements need to be changed. Public policy should actively seek to promote equal opportunities. It is notable that the focus of the fairness perspective has largely been on creating structures – childcare provision, reform of employment laws and practices – which can enable women to enter the workforce and compete with men on equal terms in the public domain. Men have been challenged to change by taking a more active nurturing role and being responsible co-parents. If (or, more to the point, *when*) men are found to be opting out, the fairness perspective holds that they must be made to feel their responsibility.

We should stress that we are not endorsing this position uncritically, but seeking to set out its key dimensions here as the basis for a critique which, by the end of the chapter, will help to clarify an integrated perspective on fatherhood that we believe could usefully inform public policy. As we go on to discuss, fatherhood scholarship in the 1990s, particularly from the developmental perspective, has challenged the fairness perspective by emphasising the complexity of judgements of fairness in domestic relations. Before proceeding to outline the developmental perspective, we first review some further empirical studies, including the only Irish study that has addressed this issue.

Lynn Segal's influential book *Slow Motion: Changing masculinities, changing men* (1990), captured a key aspect of the fairness perspective by arguing that anything that threatens to draw men out of the public world of work constituted a threat to their identity. She argues that men's apparent attitudinal changes towards fatherhood were not translating into widespread behavioural changes in terms of devoting more time to children and domestic work because of men's fears that increased parental involvement translates into a loss of power (Segal, 1990). Giddens has also argued that the 'basic question here is not so much whether men will be able to hold on indefinitely to their economic privileges, as whether they will be able to break with the ideals of masculinity pinned on performance in the public sphere, in the domain of work or in other activities' (Giddens, 1994). However, as we show below, some research in the 1990s has begun to paint a rather less exploitative picture of contemporary 'masculinity' to suggest that men, as well as women, can be caught in a structural trap which limits their choices to define their gender and parenting identities more equally and openly. For instance, the relatively simple fact that men are paid more than women, on average, influences decisions on the sexual division of labour that households make.

Recent research from within the fairness perspective has argued that the measuring of ultimate responsibility, or accountability, has a crucial bearing on such issues and needs to be taken fully into account. Again, our aim is simply to set out the findings which we shall then subject to a critique. Susan Walzer's qualitative study of fifty mothers and fathers (i.e. interviews with twenty-five couples) who were the first-time parents of babies, demonstrates in particular the importance of the invisible, mental labour that is involved in taking care of a baby and the gender imbalances that are apparent in such care. Her focus on 'mental labour' is intended to move on our understanding of parenting from the emphasis on simply evaluating physical tasks to take account of the 'thinking, feeling, and inter-personal work that accompanies the care of babies' (Walzer, 1996). Walzer identifies three particular areas of gender imbalance where the mental labour associated with childcare is predominantly women's work – worrying; processing information; and managing the division of labour.

The fathers in her study quite clearly loved their children and showed great devotion to them, but it was the mothers who did a disproportionate amount of worrying about them and about how to provide the best care. Walzer locates the reasons for this in the interactional dynamics between mothers and fathers, arguing that mothers worry about babies, in part, because fathers do not. The impact of the ideology of motherhood which held that mothers should worry was so strong that some mothers worried that they would be judged bad mothers because they did not worry! In many of the couples, the fathers saw it as their role to try and get the mothers to stop worrying, telling them to relax. Considerable marital tension was evident, many of the mothers expressing dissatisfaction that their husbands did not share more in the responsibility of caring. Walzer concludes that if the father offered to *share* the worrying, rather than tell the mother to stop worrying, the outcome might be quite different and happier.

The researcher also found that it is mothers who perform much of the mental labour around processing information about the child. It is they who consult childcare books, magazines and experts and, because they are better informed, both parents assume that the mother will orchestrate and implement the care. More-over, the ideologies of parenting presented in these magazines, books and expert discourses further reinforce expectations that it is the mother's role to be primary parent. Mothers who already felt that they had primary responsibility for their children did not find any disagreement about this in the advice literature. The role of fathers is invariably presented as a secondary – a 'helping' – one. Advice directs women to contain their responses to their husband's lack of participation – to keep a lid on their feelings, avoid conflict, try to entice the man into participation and not even to expect equitable arrangements. Such a suggestion reinforces the tendency for mothers to have the responsibility for getting the advice in the first place which, Walzer concludes, may also be a factor in the decreases in marital satisfaction that some couples experience.

The responsibility and practice of managing the division of labour between the couple was also carried disproportionately by the mothers. Even in situations where fathers reported that they split tasks equally, mothers often had the extra role of delegating the work. One such father who perceived that he split tasks equally with his partner said: 'Then at night either one of us will give him a bath. She'll always give him a bath, or if she can't, she'll tell me to do it because I won't do it unless she tells me, but if she asks me to do it I'll do it.'

Clearly some fathers who perceive themselves as sharing tasks with their wives do so when their wives tell them to. The division of labour is one where mothers are the ultimate managers. They also make decisions about what not to delegate (e.g., 'I do diapers. Joel can't handle it'). On one level, this appears to support the view that mothers are 'in charge' and may not want to relinquish control to their male partners because motherhood is a source of power for women. Walzer argues, however, that it is men who are in charge, because it is only with their permission and co-operation that mothers can relinquish their ties. The men had more freedom to come and go, some using it without even consulting their partners – who were left holding the baby – while the mothers had no such entitlement to do the same. Thus, while mothers may instruct their husbands, this data supports other studies in suggesting that husbands' responses to, and compliance with, orders are not compulsory (DeVault, 1991). In addition, Walzer concludes that while women may be the 'bosses' in the sense that they carry the organisational plan and delegate tasks to their partners, they have to manage without the privilege of being paid managers. Men, on the other hand, tend to have significant economic power, which is not affected or threatened in the same way by the onset of parenthood. Being a household manager involves expending huge amounts of physical and mental labour, not just in providing meals, for instance, but planning them, getting people to the table on time and managing relationships – doing 'emotional work'.

Walzer's research suggests that mental labour in child and family care is an important aspect in how women and men recreate motherhood and fatherhood as differentiated gender experiences. As a good provider and husband, a man, it is argued, can be perceived as a 'good' accountable father without thinking about his baby. Indeed, the baby may be perceived as a distraction to his doing what he is expected to do. Mothers, whether still employed or not, are expected to think about the baby simply in order to be seen as 'good' mothers. Marital dissatisfaction and struggles around fairness and equity in parenting will not be resolved simply by trading off who changes nappies. 'Only when the work of thinking about the baby is shared can new fathers claim to be truly equal participants' (Walzer, 1996).

While this perspective adds considerably to our knowledge of the visible and invisible 'work' that goes into caring for children, and how this tends to be unequally distributed between the sexes, we believe that – like the fairness perspective in general – it lacks a full appreciation of the complex nature of the *negotiated* nature of family care giving which appears to exist in some, and perhaps a growing number of, households. Crudely stated, can men and women be expected to do everything in families? Or is the reality that mothers and fathers are engaged in trade-offs in terms of who plays what role to maximise the social and economic well-being of the family? Thus in households where men continue to be the main breadwinners because, whether they like it or not, they can earn more than their wives, should fathers be expected to 'think about the baby' to the same extent as the mothers who have taken on the bulk of the caring role? As we show in chapter five, in Ireland younger fathers with children under the age of fifteen are more likely to be in full-time employment and work longer hours than any other category of men. How, in any case, are such men expected to know how to 'think' about children in the same way as women, and to have the skills of nurturing when their work role pulls them away from the domain of the intimate for most of their waking hours? What level and type of engagement by men in the lives of their children constitutes 'good enough' fathering? And who is to judge anyway when the good-enough standard has been reached?

Such questions bring us to a critique of the fairness perspective, and it is striking how little research has been carried out on the sexual division of domestic labour and parenting in Ireland. However, some important analysis and commentary on the broad social policy issues of balancing work and family life has begun to emerge (Drew et al., 1995; McCarthy, 1996). Just one study, carried out in the Family Studies Unit, University College Dublin (UCD) in the late 1980s, has partially explored what fathers do in Irish families. The study is partial in that it is based only on *mothers'* accounts of what fathers – their partners – do (Kiely, 1996). Fathers' own accounts of what they do, and the meaning they give to fatherhood and, indeed, to motherhood and childhood, is an essential aspect of a methodologically sound appraisal of who does what and why in family life. Research of this kind urgently needs to be done in Ireland. Nevertheless, while keeping its limitations fully in mind, the UCD study offers some interesting glimpses of fathers in families as seen from the perspective of women's perceptions and a feminist/ fairness perspective.

The study surveyed 'the attitudes and behaviour' of a sample of 513 urban mothers with regard to work and family roles. The research included an in-depth interview with mothers, all of whom had at least one child of school-going age. Almost 70% of the women said that their partners did participate in households as much as they (the mothers) would like. When this was explored in greater depth, however, by seeking information on specific behaviours, Kiely suggests that a very different picture emerged – although we are not convinced that the data he presents actually bears this out. According to Kiely, the evidence presented in Table 4.1 shows that, with the exception of household repairs, fathers took responsibility for very few household tasks.

Table 4.1 Who is responsible for household tasks?

Task	Father	Mother	Both	Children	Family
Breakfast	16.2	51.2	14.8	2.1	14.8
Dishes	4.7	48.1	17.3	13.6	15.0
Shopping	4.7	69.0	22.2	1.6	2.1
Ironing	1.2	78.1	4.9	4.1	8.6
Hoovering	5.7	51.6	18.9	6.4	12.5
Repairs	75.7	9.7	0.6	1.8	2.5

Source: Kiely, 1996, p. 149.

With regard to actual childcare tasks, Table 4.2 shows that fathers did quite a lot and, in some activities, such as playing and going on outings, took more responsibility than women. The latter, however, carried considerable responsibility for tasks such as discipline, putting children to bed and supervising homework. Mothers saw themselves as carrying most responsibility for childcare and household chores. Where men do get more involved than women, the researcher concludes that this usually involves tasks such as playing with the children, and taking them on outings. Mothers, Kiely concludes, are said to carry the weight of responsibility with respect to the less 'glamorous' tasks of disciplining children, helping with homework, getting them ready for bed, attending parents meetings at school.

Table 4.2 Who is mostly responsible for childcare tasks?

Task	Father only %	Mother only %	Both %	Other %
Putting to bed	11.7	42.7	41.7	4.0
Homework	23.0	43.3	30.4	3.4
Playing	18.9	13.1	66.1	2.0
Outings	15.5	10.7	72.1	1.6
Discipline	16.1	25.6	57.9	0.4
School meetings	3.4	52.7	43.1	1.0

Source: Kiely, 1996, p.149

Kiely suggests that employed fathers participated slightly more in preparing breakfast, washing the dishes and ironing than unemployed fathers, while significantly more unemployed fathers were involved in household repairs than employed fathers. In relation to childcare, there was no difference between the employed and unemployed groups, although slightly more unemployed fathers were involved in discipline and helping the children with homework (Kiely, 1996, p. 153). Of the 284 mothers who said that they were either presently working or had worked outside the home since marriage, some 68% considered that their involvement in domestic work had not been affected by their outside work. The mothers whose husbands did not participate in childcare or housework as much as the women would like were asked why this was so:

- 4.5% said he was 'too set in his ways';
- 11% said husbands believed it to be the 'wife's job';
- 6.5% of the women saw it as the wife's job and felt that their husbands were not good at it;
- 12.9% felt it was 'the way husband was reared';
- in 9 % the 'wife just does it, let's him away';
- 28.4% felt that their husband was 'lazy/not interested';

- 25.2% put it down to their husband having 'a demanding job';
- 2.6% gave 'other' reasons (Kiely, 1996, p. 150).

According to Kiely, the research demonstrates that 'the overall participation rates for fathers in household tasks and childcare are low ... The highest rates of participation, even though these are low, are found with young educated, employed middle-class fathers whose wives are also employed and who have fewer children and are in marriages of less than 16 years' (Kiely, 1996, p. 154). He suggests that the findings show that 'the mothers are clearly the managers. They manage the internal affairs of the family. They take care of the children, do the household tasks and make most of the decisions. The father, on the other hand, appears to do very little around the house except household repairs, play with the children, decide on what TV programme to watch, and are unlikely to change this low level of participation unless their wives become sick or go to hospital' (Kiely, 1996, p. 154).

On the basis of the findings presented, we find the certainty and judgement contained in this interpretation to be questionable. The data that Kiely presents (see Tables 4.1 and 4.2) could just as easily be read to suggest that fathers are doing more – or at least more than he is prepared to say. His account omits analysis of the crucial issue of the degree to which these parenting arrangements are *negotiated* by couples. The moral reasoning that appears to underlie his perspective – that fathers should be doing more and because they are not it is unfair – is not made explicit. This is despite the mothers' own moral reasoning which suggested a relatively high satisfaction level (70%) with the sexual division of labour that they themselves disclosed in the research. This figure is quite similar to the findings of (non-Irish) research carried out by Lamb (1986), where up to 80% of women surveyed did not want their husbands to be more involved than they were. Lamb identifies such 'support' as a factor in father's under-involvement, that is the degree to which mothers 'support' their partner in non-involvement. Other key factors he identifies as leading to low levels of paternal involvement are motivation – the extent to which the father wants to be involved and is prepared to act to achieve it – and skills and competence. Many men, he argues, feel that their role as father, or 'job description', is relatively less clear than women's and feel unskilled in childcare, thus regarding the children's mother as the 'real' expert.

Kiely goes on to link the findings to what he refers to as the cultural uncertainty currently surrounding fathers' roles and the considerable 'role strain' for men 'caught between attempts to respond to an old role that no longer fits new families, and attempts to respond to confusing societal expectations' (1996, p. 157). Whether the research actually reveals any evidence of such 'strain' is questionable. This is because Kiely makes little or nothing of the fact that the research is based solely on mothers' accounts. This is important, not least because it is characteristic for fathers and mothers to give different and, often quite literally, conflicting accounts of their involvement in family life. Where differences occur, men invariably report that they do more than their wives say they do, and men complain that what they do does not get enough notice (Marsiglio, 1995). The point here is not to cast doubt on the veracity of mothers' accounts. Nor is it a simplistic demand for men to be given an opportunity to present the 'case for the defence'. Interviewing fathers in no way guarantees that they emerge as 'innocent'. Men's own accounts of what they do at home invariably reveal important gendered assumptions about parenting. Men, like women – for better or for worse – reveal realities about how both genders 'do' gender (Coltrane, 1989).

A critical issue surrounds how the views of researchers, or the judgements of any 'outside' commentator, of what constitutes equity and fairness may be quite different from the actual judgements of mothers and fathers and the arrangements they adopt to care for the children. Thus, it may quite erroneously be the researcher's sense of fair-play and such ideological agendas that are dominating the assessment over and above the actual views of the mothers and fathers themselves. So, returning to the fairness perspective, we wish to make two points. Firstly, it is important to lay bare the moral reasoning that underpins different perspectives on fatherhood and gender relations so that the assumptions which determine debates and public policy can be made visible and their own fairness and legitimacy critically examined and debated. Secondly, it is important that men's voices are also heard if fatherhood is to be properly understood, as it should be, in terms of gender relations. Irish fathers' own accounts of their participation in childcare and domestic life remain to be documented. It bears emphasising, too, that children's voices are almost completely absent from research, whether it is in terms of their perceptions of their mother's and father's roles, or of their own role as children and house-workers in the family.

What can be said, drawing on other empirical research and conceptual work, is that questions of fairness in domestic life are complex. To some extent the UCD study already bears this out, since 70% of the mothers reported that their husbands did participate as much as they would like. Clearly, however, the impact of the social construction of motherhood and fatherhood is important as well as the actual choices which fathers and mothers have open to them.

Promoting 'Generativity': the Developmental Perspective

> *'I love him a lot. He will be with me one day. I'll see to that. I'm not gonna let him go through what I went through because I can see how much it does hurt. I want him to know that I am his father ... I'll do all I can for him.'*
>
> Lionnel (20), a non-resident new father (from Furstenberg, 1995)

In the 1990s, a new perspective is emerging which acknowledges the complexity of notions of fairness and accountability in child and family care from the perspective of *both* genders. It considers parenting not just as an issue of justice but of human growth and the management of developmental transitions. The implications of the *developmental perspective* are contradictory. On the one hand, it suggests that the social construction of gender, accountability and childcare norms are such that there has been relatively little change in actual behaviour, and there is a very long way to go before anything like equity in parenting becomes a reality. On the other hand, the assumption that men do not want to care and are exploiting their partners, and indeed children, at every opportunity has begun to be challenged. Some research is beginning to suggest that *some* men are caring much more actively than the paradigm of the 1980s and early 1990s suggested. and that in many respects men *want* to care, if only a re-organisation of work and social life could mean that they have the chance. Put another way, it is argued that men will not change until the institutional and social barriers to active fatherhood are removed and much more effort is focused on enabling men to make the developmental transition into fatherhood.

The evidence on which the developmental perspective is based appears to reflect changes in actual levels of paternal participation over the past decade, but it may also be a different way of reading and interpreting the available evidence. The developmental perspective looks behind the averages on which so much data on fatherhood are based to recognise variations in paternal behaviour. Thus, while one recent survey found that one in three fathers were 'minimally involved', it also found fathers who were spending 40–50 hours a week interacting with their children, and these were men who were in paid employment (Cohen, 1993; Burgess, 1997, p. 65).

As Burgess observes, studies based on father's self-reports about their involvement can be misleading because the men can even mislead themselves by greatly overestimating the amount of direct time they spend with children. One father she interviewed described himself as having a 'close and passionate' relationship with his three young children, yet he subsequently revealed that on weekdays he only saw them for a short time in the morning, never in the evenings, and also spent at least half of Saturday in the office. As she concludes, 'no one could doubt that this father had intense and passionate *feelings* for his children, but whether he had close and passionate *relationships* with them seemed unlikely, and it was clear that no one had challenged his perceptions. Because average levels of father involvement are so low, any father who does more than a very little can be rated "highly involved" by himself, his partner – and even by researchers' (Burgess, 1997, p. 66, original emphasis).

It has also been found that fathers' commitment to the non-provider aspects of their role may even be hidden in their public management of self so as to portray themselves as abiding by workplace norms that emphasise career commitment and honour the provider role (Pleck, 1993). These forms of 'impression management' by men around conventional corporate and masculine norms require careful consideration in any evaluation that seeks to excavate the reality of what fathers do in families.

It is, perhaps, understandable that minimally involved fathers get relatively large amounts of attention in public discourse, given that child welfare, gender justice and social order itself are reported to be so adversely affected by their lack of contribution. Yet it is crucial also to focus on those actively involved fathers who do exist, to acknowledge their presence and to attempt to learn from them and produce knowledge that can benefit other men and families, as well as childcare professionals and society at large. It appears that involved fathers are not inversely related to committed workers as has sometimes been thought. Marsiglio (1995, p. 17) points out that having a strong commitment to work identity does not preclude men from having a similar commitment to non-provider father roles too. Burgess (1997) found that the fathers who were most successful at work were those who were *most* involved and had quality relationships with their children. They were better time-managers and communicators at work. This speaks to another crucial theme of the developmental perspective: the positive effects that nurturing has on fathers' personal development, as well as on their children and the quality of marital relationships.

The developmental perspective on fatherhood is also being generated by a qualitatively different outlook and set of research questions. Closer attention is being paid to the fact that judgements on issues of fairness are complex, and researchers' judgements of equity may be quite different from the actual judgements of mothers and fathers (Hawkins et al., 1995). Moreover, if men are judged to be not caring or doing enough, the reasons for this are being explored in terms not simply of justice and fairness, but what men need, psychologically and socially, if they are to be *helped* to become good fathers. Caring has begun to be framed more positively as a personal development issue for men who have something to *gain* from active involvement with children and who need support in managing the developmental transition into fatherhood. The picture is being revised that fathers are resistant to taking on an active childcare role in the family and that they are exploiting mothers. Burgess' work exemplifies this shift in orientation; one strand of her analysis goes so far as to argue that men's under-involvement can arise from women's reluctance to 'give men room' and let go of the caring role, because it gives women whatever meaning or status they have (Burgess, 1997). Others argue that increased paternal involvement can create its own problems because 'women fear losing not only their traditional power and domination in the home if they allow men to assume even some of their former responsibilities, but their exclusive importance to children as well' (Pleck, cited in Segal, 1990, p. 48).

At the core of this perspective is recent theoretical work (see, especially, Hawkins et al., 1995; Marsiglio, 1995) which has begun to rethink the debate on fathering by attempting to move beyond a singular concern with justice and domestic democracy. A developmental perspective relates to the notion that development proceeds through the entire life-course, and is not just a matter for childhood and adolescence. Like childhood, adulthood contains key periods of qualitative change – critical times of *developmental transitions*. A developmental transition involves a 'qualitative shift in perceptions of oneself and the world' and behavioural shifts that can be observed by others (Hawkins et al., 1995, p. 43). Parenthood represents just such a developmental transition for men and women. Following Erikson's theory of psychosocial development, it is argued that the primary developmental task of adulthood is learning to care for others (Erikson, 1963). Erikson labelled this process *generativity*. Generativity, or care, is defined as an interest in establishing and guiding the next generation. For Erikson, nurturing one's offspring is the primary focus of this energy, although generativity can also be achieved by investing in other productive, creative or altruistic endeavours that make the world a better place for the next generation to live in (Hawkins et al., 1995, p. 44). The challenge of achieving generativity is the main developmental stage in the adult phase of the life-course identified by Erickson. The tension at the core of the developmental stage of early childhood is to emerge with a sense of basic trust and hope, while in adolescence the struggle surrounds developing a sense of faith in oneself and fidelity to an identity. How successfully generativity is developed is influenced by how the individual has negotiated the earlier developmental stages. For Erikson, problems in the developmental life-course which lead to difficulties in developing generativity result in 'self-indulgence and an obsessive need for pseudo intimacy ... often with a prevailing sense of stagnation and interpersonal impoverishment' (Hawkins et al., 1995, p. 45).

Like all developmental transitions, parenthood is characterised by periods of uncertainty, confusion and significant disequilibrium for individuals as their inner, psychological worlds are reorganised and their behaviour patterns altered accordingly. Thus transitions can be more or less successful, depending on how the chaos and dis/reorientation that characterises them is managed. Exponents of this perspective acknowledge that women have a certain 'biological advantage', so to speak, over men in that they have an opportunity to form some kind of emotional relationship with the baby as it develops inside them during pregnancy. Women are also better prepared psychologically and socially to make the transition because, for better or worse, girls are socialised for care-giving and boys for providing. Once the baby arrives, mothers tend to have numerous social supports to help them adjust to their roles, whereas society provides few supports for fathers (Hawkins et al., 1995, p. 51).

Thus concerted, conscious efforts have to be made if men are to make successful transitions into more active daily childcare/family work. The reason many men do not make a successful transition into being active fathers is not simply because they choose to exploit their wives, but because their generative energy gets focused outside their direct intimate relationships and they end up caring for the next generation through paid work and forms of (altruistic) endeavour. We are arguing that if these processes are properly understood, and developmental transitions carefully managed, men and women have a greatly increased chance of eventually having similar developmental pathways as carers and becoming true co-parents. For instance, men's capacity to nurture and their motivation to become involved with their children increases dramatically around the time of birth. This emotional energy needs to be capitalised on by health care professionals and other potential support networks for men. The more that secure bonding and attachment occurs between father and child at this formative time, the greater the likelihood that the man will focus his generativity within the family through active involvement with his children through the life-cycle.

Like all parenting, fatherhood involves a form of 'univocal reciprocity', a 'type of moral norm that encourages individuals to engage in social exchanges with others without expecting to receive direct or immediate reciprocation' (Marsiglio, 1995, p. 83). Yet such investment is recognised to have huge rewards in enhancing the self and intimate relationships. Within this paradigm, it is recognised, and indeed encouraged, that women – who know the struggles involved in making the developmental transition to parenthood well – can be mentors for men. Men can be helped to become more actively involved with children and develop generativity; the process of nurturing itself develops men's and women's nurturing capacities. Thus, not only does a father's involvement in childcare benefit his off-spring, but children can, in turn, be a potent developmental force in men's lives, helping to promote their ability to nurture and care. Above all, according to this perspective, men need to get the message that 'greater paternal participation need not be a personal sacrifice of patriarchal privilege for the sake of social justice; instead, it can be viewed as an important step in one's personal growth' (Hawkins et al., 1995, p.52).

Yet, as we discuss at length in chapter seven, virtually nothing is done in Ireland to enable fatherhood to be seen as an opportunity for personal growth, or to assist men in making the developmental transition into fatherhood or actively promote men's involvement in parenting. On the contrary, what we see are a series of barriers and dis-incentives to men getting involved, including the lack of paternity leave, generally better pay and working condit-ions for men, imbalanced socialisation and inadequate preparation of boys for intimacy, and an entire cultural context of negative imagery and lack of social supports for fathers that militates against men taking on an active fatherhood identity.

Once again, we need to acknowledge the plurality of men's responses to becoming fathers. Some men are still retreating from active fathering and no end of appeals to social justice and encouragement will alter that. Others are evidently struggling to (re)define themselves more directly in terms of their nurturing role and experiencing mixed results in terms of how they manage the tensions between their public role, self-definition and private worlds and commitments. Still others have successfully made the developmental transition to become 'new fathers' in the most active sense possible of caring for children. If a fairness perspective sensitises us to the scope for injustice and men's avoidance of responsibility, the developmental perspective takes us into considering the evidence concerning how men genuinely struggle to become 'good fathers' and, in some cases, actually achieve it. As one such father expressed it to a researcher: 'You feel like you're gifted by having a child, taking care of somebody and being responsible for their growth and development. It was just something I looked forward to ... someone being dependent on me, someone to share my life with, to take care of – that was my need, too' (Gerson, 1993, pp. 176–7).

So what can we learn from those men who *have* made the developmental transition into active fatherhood? Daly's study of a sample of 32 relatively new fathers with young children from 'intact families' is an exemplar of such qualitative research which aims 'to provide insight into the interactional and interpretative meanings of fatherhood identity as they emerge from the experiences of fathers themselves' (Daly, 1995, p. 23). The study confirms that an important reason why fathers and men in general have struggled with change is lack of exposure to appropriate paternal role models. In other words, whereas women have invariably grown up watching their mothers doing the childcare and identifying with that in terms of their role, men are disadvantaged by a lack of preparatory experiences. The absence of early identification experiences with their own fathers handicaps men in their efforts to become committed fathers. They have not seen men – their fathers in particular – engaged in emotionally involved parenting behaviour. Thus, 'men are attempting to meet heightened cultural expectations for fatherhood with a set of preparations that are rooted in the 1950s. The result of this lack of preparation appears to be an increased level of stress for fathers' (Daly, 1995, p. 22).

Traditional fathers were invariably presented by men in the study as *negative* role models and the new generation fathers generally reported feeling that they were making it up as they went along, without clear guidelines for good-enough fathering (Daly, 1995, p. 33). The men drew from diverse sources and role models in fashioning their identities and parenting styles. They culled desired skills or techniques from the quiet observance of other fathers, with a tendency to search for specific instances of good fathering behaviour among their peers (Daly, 1995, p. 35). Thus, 'the process of role modelling appears to be characterised by a quiet absorption rather than deliberate and interactive pursuit' (Daly, 1995, p. 36). The men's mothers and wives were viewed as a further source of practical and tangible guidance on how to parent well.

Thus, without a 'good father' mentor, and having to creatively forge new rules for themselves, new generation fathers tend to have disparate reference points. As Daly concludes: 'Without a readily available set of fatherhood models, these men have tended to focus on being a model to their own children to create for them a new set of standards for *who father is*. They seek to fill the space left by their own fathers with a fuller and more committed presence that they hope will be experienced and remembered by their own children. In the resonant silence of their own father's voices, they seek to proclaim a new expression of fatherhood' (Daly, 1995, p. 40).

Defining Good Fatherhood

'The point here is not that increased paternal participation in childcare leads directly and quickly to happier families. In some instances, greater involvement presents its own challenges to individual and family well-being. But whatever the consequences, fathers' intimate involvement in caring for children can facilitate generativity. Caring for children can become a symbol of togetherness, even when sometimes it is a source of conflict. And wives and husbands can relate to each other better not only because the division of childcare is 'fair' but

> *also because they are in similar developmental places, progressing along the adult path to generativity.'*
> Alan J. Hawkins et al., 1995

This chapter has reviewed the evidence concerning what fathers do in families and why they do – or do not do – what they do. The evidence we have reviewed suggests that there has broadly been an increase over time in fathers' level of active involvement in childcare and domestic tasks. There appears to be broad agreement, however, that paternal behaviour has not kept pace with changing attitudes and cultural expectations that fathers should become more involved. The reasons for why this is the case depend very much on how one reads the evidence and this, in turn, depends on the theoretical perspective and moral reasoning that is brought to bear on the evidence. We have, therefore, given considerable attention to deconstructing this moral reasoning and critically analysing the dominant perspectives on fatherhood.

We have identified two perspectives that have sought to account for fathers' roles in the home. The fairness perspective, which developed out of a feminist paradigm in the 1970s, suggests that fathers tend to be under-involved at home, leaving the bulk of responsibility with their partners. This perspective emphasises the promotion of equality and 'domestic democracy'. The developmental perspective, which emerged in the 1990s, emphasises that adulthood is a stage in the human life-cycle that is characterised by change, growth and development; generativity, or 'care' for the next generation, is viewed as central to the lives of adult men and women. As we have shown, the developmental perspective raises challenging questions about the complex nature of fairness in gender relations and domestic life. It does not deny the significance of issues of justice and democracy at home, but places the emphasis on what fathers – no less than mothers – need in order to make a successful developmental transition into parenthood and achieve generativity through an active commitment to care for their children. Unless adequate personal, institutional and cultural supports are in place for fathers as well as mothers, the chances are that men and women will continue to have differing ways of expressing care: women through active engagement in childcare and the domain of the intimate; men through investment in work, and forms of (altruistic) endeavour that extend beyond the home. The primary meaning that ends up being conferred on fatherhood is one that broadly defines it outside of the domain of the intimate and the direct nurturing of children.

The chapter has considered crucial questions which, in many ways, are at the heart of this book: Just what *is* a good father? What criteria should be used to make such judgements and determine public policy? The answers lie in an integration of the fairness and developmental perspectives. A good father, we suggest, is one who is open to developing his capacity for emotional communication and is active in nurturing, care work and being *fully* present for his partner and children within the parameters of what they have negotiated as constituting fairness and domestic democracy in this family. This must go beyond common-sense reasoning to take account of the impact of the social construction of motherhood and fatherhood, so that fairness is based on meaningful practices of accountability in parenting.

Despite all the difficulties that we have shown to exist around men becoming more active fathers, our analysis confirms the observations of other researchers who argue that 'fathers can establish as close and intimate bonds with their children as mothers can, and that they can be as competent as mothers are at providing nurturance, affection and stimulation' (Jump and Haas, 1987). A critical issue surrounds how more – and, at best *all* – men can be enabled to achieve such active fathering.

The overall implication of this analysis is that public policy should seek to create family-friendly measures, especially in the workplace, that maximise the choices men and women have in order to negotiate roles and responsibilities and which allow fathers, as well as mothers, the time and space for childcare. Increased involvement of men in childcare will not become a widespread reality until, and unless, there is real economic equality for women which makes it possible for couples to make affordable choices about which partner, if any, should stay at home. This will also require that greater value is placed on childcare. Quite simply, fathering must be institutionally rewarded in the public domain. Relatedly, care work needs to be valued and rewarded so that it will be seen as a positive choice for men as well as women, whether that work is done in the private domain of the family or in the public provision of childcare. Social intervention needs to understand the dynamics of generativity and to strategically focus on promoting men's caring capacities in making successful 'developmental transitions' into fatherhood. As ever, achieving this will rest heavily on individual men's motivation and their capacities for intimacy and open negotiation with women. It will also rest heavily on the provision of adequate supports for fathers, and on the willingness and ability of the State's family support services to include fathers in its work.

Chapter 5
Fathers and Work

Introduction

'Within the last decade someone upped the ante on the tokens required for manhood. A generation ago providing for one's family was the only economic requirement. Nowadays, supplying the necessities entitles a man only to marginal respect. If your work allows you only to survive you are judged to be not much of a man. To be poor in a consumerist society is to have failed the manhood test.'

Sam Keen

Working outside the home is a central part of the way in which men have been fathers and continue to be fathers. That, after all, is what patriarchy has traditionally meant. Paid work is how fathers traditionally played their breadwinning role within families while mothers did the unpaid work of caring for the children at home. In the traditional arrangement, men were the exclusive breadwinners and women were the exclusive carers. However, as the analysis in chapter one has shown, these arrangements are changing and, in 1996, fathers were the exclusive breadwinners in only half of all families in Ireland. As the proportion of women working outside the home has grown, fathers and mothers increasingly share the breadwinning role with the result that three out of ten families in Ireland in 1996 were dual-earners. Traditional arrangements have also been changed by the persistence of long-term unemployment among certain classes of men which has effectively erased their breadwinning role. In addition, the emergence of one parent families, the majority of which have no earners, has resulted in two out of ten Irish families having no earners. Thus, the relationship between work and family, and between work and fathers, is in the process of change. This, in turn, is impacting on relationships within the family and, as chapter four has suggested, this is likely to have longer-term impacts on the domestic division of labour between fathers and mothers.

Work outside the home is also one of the greatest determinants of a father's involvement with his children since it determines the amount of time he can spend with them. The traditional breadwinning role required little or no involvement by fathers in the physical or emotional care of children. This pattern, too, is changing, not just for economic reasons but also because expectations about what constitutes a good father are changing. The physical and emotional absences of fathers are less acceptable to both their children and their partners, and this is obliging some men to reflect on their respective commitments to work and family or, as Freud might put it, to work and to love.

It is against this background that a special analysis of the 1996 Labour Force Survey in Ireland was undertaken in order to find out about the characteristics of men and fathers at work, as well as women and mothers at work. The chapter examines this data in the context of policies designed to reconcile the competing demands of work and home and teases out the implications for parenting. Our analysis begins by looking at some of the characteristics of fathers, particularly those that have an impact on his relationship to work, namely housing status, employment status and hours worked, including unsocial hours. We compare fathers to other men and mothers to other women and also make cross-comparisons between fathers and mothers. We then discuss the policy implications of this analysis, particularly from the point of view of reconciling the competing demands of work and home. Specific attention is paid to childcare provision since this is one of the main ways of helping parents to meet their work and family obligations.

Socio-economic Characteristics of Fathers

'The differences between the sexes is being eroded as both sexes become defined by work. It is often said that the public world of work is a man's place and that as women enter it they will become increasingly 'masculine' and lose their 'femininity'. To think this way is to miss the most important factor of the economic world. Economic man, the creature who defines itself within the horizons of work and consumption, is not man in any full sense of the word, but a being who has been neutralised, degendered, rendered subservient to the laws of the market. The danger of economics is not that it turns women into men but that it destroys the fullness of both manhood and womanhood.'

Sam Keen

Our analysis distinguishes two types of father: younger fathers, at least one of whose children is under the age of fifteen, and older fathers, all of whose children are over the age of fifteen. Both categories of father, as the data in Table 5.1a reveal, are older than non-fathers; half of non-fathers are under the age of 35. The majority of younger fathers (62%) are aged 35-49 compared to the majority of older fathers (57%) who are in the age group 50-64. In general, as Table 5.1b reveals, fathers tend to be a little older than mothers and this suggests that women tend to enter motherhood at a slightly younger age than men enter fatherhood. This is influenced by the age at marriage, even if marriage and parenthood are not as closely tied as formerly: in 1990, the average age at marriage for men (28.6 years) was two years older than for women (26.6 years) (Department of Health, 1993).

Table 5.1a Ages of fathers compared to all men in Ireland, 1996

Age	Younger fathers (1) %	Older fathers (2) %	Non-fathers (3) %	All men (4) %
20-34	24	0	50	34
35-49	62	20	15	31
50-64	13	57	15	21
64+	1	23	20	14
Total	100	100	100	100

Source: 1996 Labour Force Survey, Special Tabulations by Anthony Murphy at University College Dublin.
(1) For the purpose of this analysis, a younger father is defined as a man over the age of 20 who has any child under the age of 15 years and lives with that child. Using this definition, there were approximately 373,000 younger fathers in Ireland in 1996 – 69% of all fathers.
(2) For the purpose of this analysis, an older father is defined as a man over the age of 20, all of whose children are over the age of 15 years and who lives with these children. Using this definition, there were approximately 166,000 older fathers in Ireland in 1996, equivalent to 31% of all fathers.
(3) Non-fathers are men over the age of 20 who do not have, or do not live with, their children.
(4) All men refer to men over the age of 20, both fathers and non-fathers, and amount to 1,156,000 men.

Table 5.1b Ages of mothers compared to all women in Ireland, 1996

Age	Younger mothers (1) %	Older mothers (2) %	Non-mothers (3) %	All women (4) %
20-34	35	0	43	33
35-49	58	26	11	30
50-64	7	53	17	19
64+	0	21	29	18
Total	100	100	100	100

Source: 1996 Labour Force Survey, Special Tabulations by Anthony Murphy at University College Dublin.
(1) For the purpose of this analysis, a younger mother is defined as a woman over the age of 20 who has any child under the age of 15 years and lives with that child. Using this definition, there were approximately

412,000 younger mothers in Ireland in 1996, equivalent to 67% of all mothers.

(2) For the purpose of this analysis, an older mother is defined as a woman over the age of 20, all of whose children are over the age of 15 years and who lives with these children. Using this definition, there were approximately 203,000 older mothers in Ireland in 1996, equivalent to 33% of all mothers.

(3) Non-mothers are women over the age of 20 who do not have, or do not live with, their children.

(4) All women refer to women over the age of 20, both mothers and non-mothers, and amount to 1,199,000 women.

Housing status

Around four-fifths of the dwellings in Ireland are owner-occupied. In view of this, it is not surprising that the majority of men and women – irrespective of whether they are parents or not – live in a house that they are buying or have bought. Nevertheless, it is worth noting that fathers and mothers are more likely to be in the owner-occupied sector than non-fathers and non-mothers (see Tables 5.2a and 5.2b). This reflects the fact that buying a house is usually part of the process of preparing for parenthood and, as will be seen, the ensuing financial responsibility seems to affect their overall participation in the world of work. As might be expected, younger fathers and mothers are more likely to be buying than to have bought their house. A minority of both younger fathers (8%) and older fathers (5%) live in local authority housing. Due to the higher incidence of lone parenting among women, a higher proportion of both younger mothers (11%) and older mothers (6%) also live in local authority housing.

Table 5.2a Housing tenure of fathers compared to all men in Ireland, 1996

Housing tenure	Younger fathers (1) %	Older fathers (2) %	Non-fathers (3) %	All men (4) %
Local authority rented	8	5	6	6
Private rented	5	2	16	10
Buying house	63	39	28	41
House bought	24	54	50	43
Total	**100**	**100**	**100**	**100**

Source: 1996 Labour Force Survey, Special Tabulations by Anthony Murphy at University College Dublin.

(1) For the purpose of this analysis, a younger father is defined as a man over the age of 20 who has any child under the age of 15 years and lives with that child. Using this definition, there were approximately 373,000 younger fathers in Ireland in 1996, 69% of all fathers.

(2) For the purpose of this analysis, an older father is defined as a man over the age of 20, all of whose children are over the age of 15 years and who lives with these children. Using this definition, there were approximately 166,000 older fathers in Ireland in 1996, equivalent to 31% of all fathers.

(3) Non-fathers are men over the age of 20 who do not have, or do not live with, their children.

(4) All men refer to men over the age of 20, both fathers and non-fathers, and amount to 1,156,000 men.

Table 5.2b Housing tenure of mothers and all women in Ireland, 1996

Housing tenure	Younger mothers (1) %	Older mothers (2) %	Non-mothers (3) %	All women (4) %
Local authority rented	11	6	5	7
Private rented	7	2	18	11
Buying house	59	36	27	40
House bought	23	56	50	42
Total	**100**	**100**	**100**	**100**

Source: 1996 Labour Force Survey, Special Tabulations by Anthony Murphy at University College Dublin.

(1) For the purpose of this analysis, a younger mother is defined as a woman over the age of 20 who has any child under the age of 15 years and lives with that child. Using this definition, there were approximately 412,000 younger mothers in Ireland in 1996, equivalent to 67% of all mothers.
(2) For the purpose of this analysis, an older mother is defined as a woman over the age of 20 all of whose children are over the age of 15 years and who lives with these children. Using this definition, there were approximately 203,000 older mothers in Ireland in 1996, equivalent to 33% of all mothers.
(3) Non-mothers are women over the age of 20 who do not have, or do not live with, their children.
(4) All women refer to women over the age of 20, both mothers and non-mothers, and amount to 1,199,000 women.

Employment status

Parenthood brings with it financial, as well as other responsibilities. In practice, this means that work outside the home is an extremely important aspect of being a responsible parent. This is particularly the case for fathers whose breadwinning role is important to the family finances as well as to their own self-image as a father. As indicated in chapter one, the father is the sole earner in about half of all households in Ireland (see Table 1.2). The data in Table 5.3a reveals that younger fathers are more likely to be in full-time employment than any other category of men: 81% of them are in full-time employment compared to 60% of older fathers and 55% of non-fathers. This clearly suggests a connection between the financial responsibilities of younger fathers and their participation in employment.

Table 5.3a Employment status of fathers compared to all men in Ireland, 1996

Employment status	Younger fathers (1) %	Older fathers (2) %	Non-fathers (3) %	All men (4) %
Full-time employed	81	60	55	64
Part-time employed	3	2	3	3
Unemployed	10	5	9	9
Not looking for work	6	33	33	24
Total	**100**	**100**	**100**	**100**

Source: 1996 Labour Force Survey, Special Tabulations by Anthony Murphy at University College Dublin.

(1) For the purpose of this analysis, a younger father is defined as a man over the age of 20 who has any child under the age of 15 years and lives with that child. Using this definition, there were approximately 373,000 younger fathers in Ireland in 1996, equivalent to 69% of all fathers.
(2) For the purpose of this analysis, an older father is defined as a man over the age of 20 all of whose children are over the age of 15 years and who lives with these children. Using this definition, there were approximately 166,000 older fathers in Ireland in 1996, equivalent to 31% of all fathers.
(3) Non-fathers are men over the age of 20 who do not have, or do not live with, their children.
(4) All men refer to men over the age of 20, both fathers and non-fathers, and amount to 1,156,000 men.

The employment status of mothers differs from fathers in two important respects. First, the proportion of mothers in full-time employment is much lower than for fathers, as Table 5.3b reveals. However, it is significant that the proportion of younger mothers in full-time employment (28%) is nearly twice as high as the corresponding proportion for older mothers (15%). Second, the proportion of mothers in part-time employment is much higher than for fathers. Younger mothers are more than four times as likely to be in part-time employment as younger fathers (14% compared to 3%) but are also nearly twice as likely to be in part-time employment as older mothers (14% compared to 9%). It is clear from this that the financial pressure on younger parents, both mothers and fathers, is making itself felt in their higher employment rates.

Table 5.3b Employment status of mothers and all women in Ireland, 1996

Employment status	Younger mothers (1) %	Older mothers (2) %	Non-mothers (3) %	All women (4) %
Full-time employed	28	15	40	31
Part-time employed	14	9	4	9
Unemployed	7	3	5	5
Not looking for work	51	73	51	55
Total	100	100	100	100

Source: 1996 Labour Force Survey, Special Tabulations by Anthony Murphy at University College Dublin.

(1) For the purpose of this analysis, a younger mother is defined as a woman over the age of 20 who has any child under the age of 15 years and lives with that child. Using this definition, there were approximately 412,000 younger mothers in Ireland in 1996, equivalent to 67% of all mothers.

(2) For the purpose of this analysis, an older mother is defined as a woman over the age of 20 all of whose children are over the age of 15 years and who lives with these children. Using this definition, there were approximately 203,000 older mothers in Ireland in 1996, equivalent to 33% of all mothers.

(3) Non-mothers are women over the age of 20 who do not have, or do not live with, their children.

(4) All women refer to women over the age of 20, both mothers and non-mothers, and amount to 1,199,000 women.

Hours worked

The level of contact between parents and children is affected less by employment rates per se and more by the number of hours which they spend at work outside the home each week. In general, there is a tendency for fathers to work slightly longer hours than non-fathers even if the overall average, as Table 5.4a reveals, is around 46 hours per week; one-third of fathers (33%) work 50 hours per week or more compared to only one-quarter of non-fathers (27%). This is significant in view of the fact that, under the Organisation of Working Time Act, 1997, the maximum working week is 48 hours.

Mothers, where they are employed, work an average of 31–32 hours per week outside the home, as Table 5.4b reveals. This is exactly 15 hours less than the number of hours worked outside the home by fathers. By contrast with men, non-mothers work longer hours than mothers.

It is particularly interesting to note that fathers whose partners are working outside the home spend fewer hours at work than fathers whose partners are not working (see Table 5.4a). This suggests that the hours worked by fathers are influenced by the employment status, and therefore the earnings, of their partners. The reverse, however, is the case with mothers: mothers whose partners are employed work longer hours than mothers whose partners are unemployed or inactive (see Table 5.4b). This suggests that mothers and fathers may have different ways of looking at work outside the home but this would require further investigation.

Table 5.4a Usual hours worked by fathers and men in Ireland, 1996

Usual hours	Younger fathers (1) %	Older fathers (2) %	Non-fathers (3) %	All men (4) %
Less than 35 hours	7	8	9	8
35-49 hours	61	58	64	62
50+ hours	32	34	27	30
Total	100	100	100	100
Average hours	46	47	45	46
Average hours (partner working)	46	46	-	-
Average hours (partner not working)	47	48	-	-

Source: 1996 Labour Force Survey, Special Tabulations by Anthony Murphy at University College Dublin.

(1) For the purpose of this analysis, a younger father is defined as a man over the age of 20 who has any child under the age of 15 years and lives with that child. Using this definition, there were approximately 373,000 younger fathers in Ireland in 1996, equivalent to 69% of all fathers.

(2) For the purpose of this analysis, an older father is defined as a man over the age of 20 all of whose children are over the age of 15 years and who lives with these children. Using this definition, there were approximately 166,000 older fathers in Ireland in 1996, equivalent to 31% of all fathers.

(3) Non-fathers are men over the age of 20 who do not have, or do not live with, their children.

(4) All men refer to men over the age of 20, both fathers and non-fathers, and amount to 1,156,000 men.

Table 5.4b Usual hours worked by mothers and women in Ireland, 1996

Usual hours	Younger mothers (1) %	Older mothers (2) %	Non-mothers (3) %	All women (4) %
Less than 35 hours	47	50	19	32
35-49 hours	48	40	74	61
50+ hours	5	10	7	7
Total	**100**	**100**	**100**	**100**
Average hours	31	32	38	35
Average hours (partner working)	32	32	-	-
Average hours (partner not working)	30	29	-	-

Source: 1996 Labour Force Survey, Special Tabulations by Anthony Murphy at University College Dublin.

(1) For the purpose of this analysis, a younger mother is defined as a woman over the age of 20 who has any child under the age of 15 years and lives with that child. Using this definition, there were approximately 412,000 younger mothers in Ireland in 1996, equivalent to 67% of all mothers.
(2) For the purpose of this analysis, an older mother is defined as a woman over the age of 20 all of whose children are over the age of 15 years and who lives with these children. Using this definition, there were approximately 203,000 older mothers in Ireland in 1996, equivalent to 33% of all mothers.
(3) Non-mothers are women over the age of 20 who do not have, or do not live with, their children.
(4) All women refer to women over the age of 20, both mothers and non-mothers, and amount to 1,199,000 women.

Irish men work the same average number of hours as British men − about 45 hours per week − but both categories work significantly longer than the average for the fifteen EU member states which was 42 hours in 1995 (Eurostat, 1996, p. 164). The usual working hours of Irish women, by contrast, is much closer to the EU norm (*Ibid*). Data on the hours worked by fathers and mothers is not available at EU level. However, selected studies indicate that Irish fathers work longer hours than some of their EU counterparts. In Denmark, where the maximum working week is 37 hours, fathers of young children work an average of 41 hours per week, five hours less than Irish fathers. However, Danish mothers worked longer hours than Irish mothers at 34 hours per week (Pruzan, 1993, pp. 168–170; Council of Europe, p. 104). Irish fathers also work longer hours than British fathers: 27% of fathers in Britain, but 33% of fathers in Ireland, work 50 hours a week or more (Ferri and Smith, 1996, p. 18). Irish mothers also work longer hours than British mothers: 23% of mothers in Britain, but 51% of mothers in Ireland work 35 hours a week or more (*Ibid*). The tendency for Irish fathers to work longer than non-fathers is also replicated in the Norwegian experience (Jensen, 1993, p. 160).

The hours that parents spend in work outside the home are a useful indicator of how they meet their financial responsibilities. However, they do not capture the distribution of those hours over the week, particularly where the parents may be involved in shift work, evening work, night work, Saturday work or Sunday work. The data in Table 5.5a reveals that a small proportion of fathers do shift work, nearly half do evening work, a quarter do night work, two-thirds do Saturday work and two-fifths do Sunday work. In this respect, there is almost no difference between younger and older fathers or between fathers and non-fathers. However, there are significant differences between fathers and mothers, as Table 5.5b reveals, with fathers being much more likely to work unsocial hours than mothers. British fathers do more evening and night work than Irish fathers, less Saturday

work and similar Sunday work (Ferri and Smith, 1996, p.
19). British working mothers are more similar to Irish
working mothers except that they do more evening work
than Irish mothers (*Ibid*).

**Table 5.5a Unsocial hours worked usually or
sometimes by fathers and men in Ireland, 1996**

Category of unsocial hours	Younger fathers (1) %	Older fathers (2) %	Non-fathers (3) %	All men (4) %
Shift work	16	13	15	15
Evening work	46	44	43	44
Night work	28	25	26	26
Saturday work	68	66	67	67
Sunday work	41	41	40	41
Work at home	15	19	14	15

Source: 1996 Labour Force Survey, Special Tabulations by Anthony
Murphy at University College Dublin.

(1) For the purpose of this analysis, a younger father is defined as a
man over the age of 20 who has any child under the age of 15 years
and lives with that child. Using this definition, there were approximately
373,000 younger fathers in Ireland in 1996, equivalent to 69% of all
fathers.
(2) For the purpose of this analysis, an older father is defined as a man
over the age of 20 all of whose children are over the age of 15 years
and who lives with these children. Using this definition, there were
approximately 166,000 older fathers in Ireland in 1996, equivalent to
31% of all fathers.
(3) Non-fathers are men over the age of 20 who do not have, or do not
live with, their children.
(4) All men refer to men over the age of 20, both fathers and non-
fathers, and amount to 1,156,000 men.

Table 5.6b Unsocial hours worked usually or sometimes by mothers and women in Ireland, 1996

Category of unsocial hours	Younger mothers (1) %	Older mothers (2) %	Non-mothers (3) %	All women (4) %
Shift work	13	11	16	14
Evening work	24	27	26	25
Night work	14	14	14	14
Saturday work	44	49	48	46
Sunday work	28	31	28	28
Work at home	9	14	7	8

Source: 1996 Labour Force Survey, Special Tabulations by Anthony Murphy at University College Dublin.

(1) For the purpose of this analysis, a younger mother is defined as a woman over the age of 20 who has any child under the age of 15 years and lives with that child. Using this definition, there were approximately 412,000 younger mothers in Ireland in 1996, equivalent to 67% of all mothers.
(2) For the purpose of this analysis, an older mother is defined as a woman over the age of 20 all of whose children are over the age of 15 years and who lives with these children. Using this definition, there were approximately 203,000 older mothers in Ireland in 1996, equivalent to 33% of all mothers.
(3) Non-mothers are women over the age of 20 who do not have, or do not live with, their children.
(4) All women refer to women over the age of 20, both mothers and non-mothers, and amount to 1,199,000 women.

One way of overcoming the enforced absences of work outside the home, and one that is increasingly feasible in sectors which utilise modern telecommunications, is to work from home. In view of this, it is worth noting that a significant minority (15%) of younger fathers usually or sometimes work at home; this rises to 19% for older fathers (see Table 5.6a). However, this trend does not seem to be influenced by fathering per se since the proportion of non-fathers who work at home is very similar to young fathers. However, it is noteworthy, as Table 5.5b reveals, that men are twice as likely as women to work from home, irrespective of whether they are parents or not. But this needs to be seen in the context that a much higher proportion of women 'work' in the home, albeit without pay.

The data analysed in this section was based on a distinction between fathers and non-fathers and between mothers and non-mothers. Beneath this distinction lies an assumption that parenting makes a difference to the way in which men and women participate in the world of work. Our analysis effectively confirms this, while also bringing out significant differences between fathers and mothers. Fathers are much more involved in the world of work outside the home than mothers and work much longer and more unsocial hours. This clearly reflects the gendered division of labour both inside and outside the home, even if that division is becoming less clear-cut. From the perspective of fathers, the analysis raises the question as to why some of them – particularly the 33% who work 50 hours a week or more – work such long hours. Are they constrained to do it by financial commitments, job insecurity and the pressures of the job? Do they want to do it because their employment role is central to their aspirations, ambitions, satisfactions and self-image? Do they experience any tension between their role as worker and their role as father? Is it even conceivable that some men prefer to stay at work in order to avoid the responsibilities of fathering and family life? The answers to these questions are unknown and require further research if we are to understand how men live out their role as fathers. The attitudes of mothers to the long hours worked by fathers, and their role in negotiating and deciding on those hours, would also have to be considered to understand how families share their parenting roles and responsibilities.

Reconciling Work and Home

'Merely breaking down the barriers faced by women on the labour market and in public life is not enough. The next breakthrough is a change in men.'
Ingvar Carlsson, Prime Minister of Sweden

'True reconciliation between work and family requires fathers' needs to be addressed alongside mothers.'
Adrienne Burgess and Sandy Ruxton

There is a growing recognition in policy circles that many parents have difficulty in reconciling the competing demands of work and family to the satisfaction of their employers, their children and their partners. At the same time, these difficulties are not insurmountable and some research evidence suggests how parents – both mothers and fathers – manage to reconcile the conflict. According to Burgess: 'When we began our interviews with fathers for this book, one surprising finding was how often our most involved fathers also turned out to be successful in career terms and conversely how often our least involved fathers seemed to be struggling' (1997, pp. 160–161). Among the reasons suggested for this are good time-management, communication and people skills; in addition, 'not one [father] had a consuming hobby or played much sport or was very involved in the community. These working fathers, like so many working mothers, seemed to focus on just two main areas; their work and their children' (*Ibid*, p. 163).

In recognition of the need to reconcile the competing demands of work and family, a number of EU countries have introduced, or are introducing, measures designed to make the workplace more family-friendly and flexible so that parents can become more involved in the care of their children. Family-friendly initiatives cover a wide range of measures, as Table 5.6 illustrates.

Table 5.6 Summary of family-friendly initiatives

Category of family-friendly initiative	Category of family-friendly initiative
Flexible working job-sharing flexitime flexiplace (working from home) part-time working term-time working	**Leave Arrangements** maternity leave paternity leave adoption leave parental leave compassionate / bereavement leave emergency leave eldercare care for people with disabilities
Breaks employment breaks sabbaticals secondments	**Other Initiatives** childcare support employee assistance programmes parenting workshops family days health care

Derived from Employment Equality Agency, 1996, p. 11.

The introduction of family-friendly measures in the workplace was, and to a large extent still is, seen as a way of helping women to reconcile the competing demands of home and work. This, however, is slowly changing as men are doing more domestic work (though still significantly less than women) and women are doing more paid work (though still significantly less than men). This finding, and its implications, were revealed in a multinational study of housework covering seven countries and three decades: 'Women (wives) with jobs do substantially less unpaid work now than equivalently placed women did one or two decades ago. And men (presumably their husbands) do significantly more domestic work ... And the consequence is, jobs can no longer be organised in ways that conflict with domestic responsibilities. Increasingly (if the trends we have described continue) the husbands of those women seeking the jobs will themselves need jobs which are organised in ways that allow them to fulfil their domestic responsibilities' (Gershuny and Robinson, 1991, p. 180).

In 1996, the Irish government and the social partners agreed – in Partnership 2000 for Inclusion, Employment and Competitiveness – to support the growth of 'family-friendly policies in employment, in line with the recommendations contained in the policy document issued by the Employment Equality Agency in 1996' (Government of Ireland, 1996, p. 30). One of these family-friendly measures is parental leave and the government committed itself to implementing the EU Directive on Parental Leave by June 1998 (*Ibid*); at the time of writing (June 1998), draft legislation had been prepared to bring this into effect. The main provision of this directive is to give 'men and women workers an individual right to parental leave on grounds of the birth or adoption of a child to enable them to take care of that child, for at least three months' (EU Directive on Parental Leave, 1996). The Directive also obliges member states to take the necessary measures to entitle workers time off from work for 'urgent family reasons' (*Ibid*).

The experience of parental leave in Sweden and Denmark is that the fathers who avail of it are typically men who are well-educated in well-paid, permanent jobs and married to women who are also well-educated and in well-paid jobs (Carlsen, 1993, p. 199). However, the uptake of parental leave by fathers in Denmark (3%) is much lower than in Sweden (50%). The reasons for this, according to one Danish commentator, are that 'the scheme is designed in such a way that not many fathers are likely to make use of it. It is available after 14 weeks of maternity leave, during which period mothers have learnt the caring role and – many at any rate – are still breast feeding ... At this point, established routines have to be changed and new ones established, which are changed once more at the end of the parental leave period after the first six months' (Pruzan, 1993, p. 174). One of the possibilities being considered in Denmark is that parental leave could be made part-time for fathers as a way of reducing their fears about losing contact with work while also facilitating the return of women to work (*Ibid*). The implications of this for Ireland should be carefully studied before the government implements the EU Directive on Parental Leave by June 1998.

Another factor contributing to the low uptake of parental leave by fathers is the culture of the workplace. Many workplaces do not expect men who are fathers to behave any differently from men who are not fathers. As a result, the provision of more flexible working arrangements for fathers may not lead to greater involvement by fathers in the care of their children unless it is seen as 'normal' for a father to wish to spend more time with his children (see Carlsen, 1993, pp. 204–5). Deeper still, perhaps, is the belief – possibly shared by both mothers and fathers – that the child needs the mother much more than the father and this can blunt the incentive to make adjustments at work that would allow fathers to spend more time with their children.

Experience in a number of countries suggests that the uptake of parental leave and other family-friendly measures by men is inhibited by considerations such as loss of earnings, increased workload resulting from taking time off and the overall impact on their career. One researcher has argued that 'the reasons for low take-up by fathers [of parental leave] are simple. Unless parental leave is paid at full salary, the family loses because the father is usually higher paid. Employers don't usually hire replacement labour for the short time the men are away, so a backlog develops at work, and in addition the men fear a negative impact on their careers. At home there are so few other stay-at-home dads that fathers often feel out of place, and spend most of the time on their own with their children' (Burgess, 1997, p. 166; see also Carlsen, 1993, p. 200). It should also be remembered that de-cisions about parental leave are rarely taken by the father alone but are negotiated by both parents in the light of their overall circumstances and priorities (Carlsen, 1993, p. 206). The key issue here is that fathers and mothers should be aware of the choices which they are making, insofar as their circumstances allow them to make choices, between their roles as workers and their roles as parents.

Paternity leave is different from parental leave which may be taken over a much longer period following the birth of the child by either or both parents. Paternity leave – at least as practised in Sweden and Denmark – usually involves two weeks leave by the father around the birth of his child; in Sweden, virtually all fathers take paternity leave and in Denmark, about half of all fathers take paternity leave (Carlsen, 1993). However, in both cases, it is rare for the full allowable period to be taken. Although there is no statutory provision for paternity leave in Ireland, a sample of fathers studied in one Irish maternity hospital reported that '51% of fathers took holiday leave, 3% had official paternity leave and a further 12% obtained compassionate leave. The average duration of time off was 1.4 weeks' (Council of Europe, 1995, p. 233). Provision of maternity leave is governed by the Maternity (Protection of Employees) Act, 1981 which provides for 14 weeks paid leave and a further 4 weeks unpaid leave.

The family-friendly measures proposed by the government in Partnership 2000 have the potential to facilitate greater involvement by fathers in the care of their children and families. However, the realisation of this potential will not be easy because fathers – and men generally – are less likely to avail of these measures than women and mothers. This was amply confirmed in a recent study of flexible working in Ireland which showed that 'job sharing, career breaks and extended parental leave encourage more women than men to trade full-time continuous jobs and careers for extra time off' (Fynes, Morrissey, Roche, Whelan and Williams, 1996, p. 227). As a result, flexible working arrangements can leave men's working lives almost untouched and can reinforce existing gender differences between men and women both at work and at home, as fathers work full-time and mothers work part-time.

The response of men and fathers to flexible working arrangements may itself be influenced by the way in which those measures are presented and promoted. As discussed in the introduction to this book, it is possible to advance four different reasons or perspectives for introducing family-friendly measures in the workplace, particularly from the perspective of employees:

1. benefits to women in the form of greater equality in the labour market and in the domestic division of labour;
2. benefits to men in the form of greater involvement as fathers with their children which can lead to their own personal development and growth;
3. benefits to children's development as a result of being emotionally close to both parents;
4. benefits to families in supporting the interdependent relationships – economic, social and emotional – which holds its members together, including members of the extended family.

In Ireland, most of the arguments in favour of family-friendly measures in the workplace are advanced from the perspective of women's equality in the labour market (see for example, Second Commission on the Status of Women, 1993, Chapter Three; Employment Equality Agency, 1996). The same also appears to be the case in other countries. There are inherent dangers in this, as the Danish experience has shown.

In Denmark, measures which are presented as 'equality measures' are seen as 'women's issues' and tend to elicit little involvement from men (Carlsen, 1993, p. 203). One researcher with the Danish Equal Status Council made the following observations about the equality perspective after reading 1,500 pages of transcribed interviews with Danish fathers on their low uptake of parental leave: 'the work towards equality is not accustomed to dealing with men, not accustomed to speaking men's language and perhaps does not even understand men's language ... It suddenly occurred to me that only one of the interviewees had used the word "equality" – and this was in spite of the fact that they knew that I was from the Equal Status

Council. It suddenly occurred to me that equality is not a word men normally use. Similarly, "care". Men do not *nurture* their children; they are *together* with their children. They *do things* with their children – whether it be sport, gardening or hoovering ... Men have many opinions about equality and not least about men's relationship with children but they use other words that we – the professional equality worker – are not accustomed to' (Carlsen, 1993, p. 203).

One of the lessons to emerge from this is that the agenda behind the introduction and implementation of family-friendly measures in the workplace needs to be broadened. This agenda needs to include men and children, as well as women, and the benefits that can accrue, over the course of a life, of sharing work and caring responsibilities more equitably. It should not be assumed that men and women will see the benefits of family-friendly measures in the workplace in exactly the same way.

We also wish to draw attention to the use of gender-neutral language in discussions of family-friendly measures. There is very little usage of the terms 'father' or 'mother' in this literature, even though it is precisely by virtue of being fathers and mothers that the need for family-friendly measures in the workplace arises. For example, a recent report on family-friendly initiatives in the workplace refers mainly to 'employees' and 'workers', occasionally to 'men' and 'women', but seldom to 'fathers' and 'mothers' (Employment Equality Agency, 1996). A similar gender-neutral language is used by the government and the social partners: for example, in *Partnership 2000 for Inclusion, Employment and Competitiveness*, their commitment to childcare and family-friendly policies in the workplace are cited without making any reference to 'fathers' and 'mothers' (Government of Ireland, 1996, p. 30). The issue here is not just pedantic; if it is an objective of government policy to promote greater involvement of fathers in the care of their children, while also promoting the involvement of mothers in the world of paid work, then the inherent value of those roles needs to be explicitly named. The absence of any references to fathers and mothers in matters designed specifically to support those roles is a little contradictory and may even undermine the potential of those measures to achieve their objectives. Both government and the social partners have a shared responsibility in ensuring that joint parenting is perceived as the ideal for both fathers and mothers and that the workplace must change to accommodate this ideal.

Finally, it needs to be emphasised that family-friendly measures, as the term is normally used, do not cover the issue of the number of hours worked by fathers, even though this is one of the most important factors determining employed fathers' involvement with children (see Ferri and Smith, 1996). In essence, family-friendly measures will only be effective in improving the balance between work and family life, and promoting joint parenting, if their net effect is to create real choices for couples, including reducing the excessive hours worked by some fathers.

Childcare Services and Fathers

'Fathers are exalted as breadwinners and scorned as intimate parents by a system which relentlessly promotes in-family care by mothers, not because it is the best option but because it is thought to the cheapest option.'

Adrienne Burgesse

Childcare is the bridge between work and family which helps to resolve the tensions that arise in meeting the competing obligations of both. In many countries, including Ireland, childcare tends to be seen as a women's issue, designed to help women enter or re-enter the labour force. For example, the Second Commission on the Status of Women states that childcare is an equality issue because women's responsibilities for childcare in the home means that, in the absence of childcare, they are not able to compete equally with men in the labour market: 'Childcare is an equality issue because the unequal distribution of responsibility presents barriers to participation by women with children in employment, education and training' (Second Commission on the Status of Women, 1993, p. 137). Reflecting this, the Pilot Childcare Initiative (introduced in 1994 and still ongoing) was introduced by the Minister for Equality and Law Reform with the following rationale: 'to enable women undertake education, training, re-training and employment opportunities which they would be unable to do, in the absence of a childcare facility' (see McKeown and Fitzgerald, 1997, p. 4). More recently, the government and the social partners in *Partnership 2000 for Inclusion, Employment and Competitiveness* affirmed their commitment to childcare in the following terms: 'childcare is clearly an important issue in promoting equality for women, and especially in promoting equal opportunities in employment' (Government of Ireland, 1996, p. 30; see also National Economic and Social Council, 1996, pp. 209–10; Government of Ireland, 1997, pp. 16–17).

It is true that childcare tends to be of most direct and immediate benefit to mothers in view of the private division of labour within many families between the father as breadwinner and the mother as carer of the children. Some fathers who are separated and have primary responsibility for the care of the children also benefit, but these are relatively few in number compared to the number of women. However, childcare can be of indirect benefit to fathers because it helps the mother share in the breadwinning role for the family and, other things being equal, creates the option for both parents to share the 'investment' and the 'involvement' roles of parenting with the possibilities for enrichment which that can bring. This applies as much to two-earner families as to families where the father is unemployed or families where the parents are divorced.

In Ireland, there is no overall coherent policy driving and shaping the development of childcare facilities for working parents. One recent report found that seven different departments of government have an involvement in childcare but no one department has overall responsibility for the childcare sector as a whole (McKeown and Fitzgerald, 1997, pp. 7–8). Moreover, most state expenditure on childcare facilities tends to have a predominantly 'child protection' function rather than a 'gender equality' function. From the beginning of 1997, the government and the social partners have committed themselves to 'develop a strategy which integrates the different strands of the current arrangements for the development and delivery of childcare and early educational services' (Government of Ireland, 1996, p. 30). This, in conjunction with the development of family-friendly policies and prac-tices in the workplace, could have a significant impact, depending on the scale of resources applied and the commitment to promoting childcare as a measure of benefit to both fathers as well as mothers.

One aspect of childcare that has not received adequate public attention is the virtual absence of men from this type of work. As growing numbers of women have en-tered the labour force, parents have handed the care of their children over to other women, since men are virtually absent from the childcare sector in the broadest sense, thereby retaining children in the sphere of women. One commentator has described this process as 'the femin-isation of childhood' (Jensen, 1993, p. 151). Viewed from this perspective, it is possible that the involvement of men with children may actually be diminishing as more children are being placed in childcare. This trend may also be compounded by the fact that the children of separated and unmarried parents may be brought up entirely by the mother in a process that is strongly reinforced by the law and the legal system (see chapter six).

The reasons for the absence of men from childcare and related work are many and inter-related. They involve pay since caring work is normally poorly paid. They involve attitudes since caring is often seen as inappropriate work for men; some men may see it as 'sissy' work rather than 'macho' work. In a mutually reinforcing cycle, the predominance of women in childcare and related work may itself be a disincentive to some men entering this work because it involves entering a 'woman's world' without the support of other men. It is also worth noting that men are often perceived as dangerous in the context of childcare and this has probably even further alienated them from involvement in this sector. There can be little doubt that the perception of men and fathers as 'dangerous' is attributable to the widespread – and wholly appropriate – reporting of child physical and sexual abuse cases and statistics, even if only a tiny minority of men are known to be involved (see chapters six and seven). Any strategy to involve more men in childcare would need to address the issue of low pay (which needs to be addressed irrespective of men) and the attitudes and values of men about care work.

The consequences of gender imbalances in the childcare sector seem likely to have long-term consequences in terms of perpetuating, in the minds of children, the image that women, but not men, are the 'natural' carers of children. As a result, the gender imbalance in the delivery of childcare may itself undermine the objective which it is trying to promote – namely, reducing the gendered division of labour between home and work. As a result, the potential of these services to promote radical cultural changes in attitudes about men's potential role in childcare are being missed. In addition, children are missing the benefit of having men within these services. In our view, any long-term strategy for childcare would need to address the issue of gender imbalance in the staffing of these services, possibly by setting targets and taking appropriate action to achieve them.

Conclusion

'When I was growing up to become a man in a society which was more patriarchal than today, the attitude which I acquired was that work was, to a great extent, a chance for me to be something. What I could become myself was actually more important than the results of my work. The most essential thing

about an occupation was that it was a means of acquiring power (mainly, but not solely, because it could lead to wealth). If I worked, I could acquire a position which would give me a value in other people's eyes. This attitude made work a strain. Life became a struggle, in which I had to fight in order to progress as far as possible on the career ladder.

Nowadays, I have another view of work and its meaning. This view affects me as a man, since working-life is such an important part of a man's life ... Work is not a means by which I must prove my worth or acquire ascendancy, but a means by which I can create. It is the results of my work which are of importance, not what it can make me. I exist to serve life ... I am to create together with other people. My work is not a context in which I struggle against others to win influence. It is a context in which I have the best chances of achieving something if I open myself up to a spirit of community with others. I do not need to compete with women or with other men. After all, we are all essentially equal. But we all have different abilities when it comes to handling problems. And we are best able to make progress when we combine our different abilities.'

Goran Bergstrand

This chapter has examined the different ways in which fathers have been involved in the world of work. Drawing upon the results of a special analysis of the 1996 Labour Force Survey, the chapter has shown that younger fathers, defined as fathers with any child under the age of fifteen, are more likely to be in full-time employment than any other category of men: 81% of them are in full-time employment compared to 60% of older fathers and 55% of non-fathers. The proportion of mothers in full-time employment is much lower than for fathers although the proportion in part-time employment is much higher. In general, there is a tendency for fathers to work slightly longer hours than non-fathers, even if the overall average for both is around 46 hours per week; a third of fathers (33%) work 50 hours per week or more. Mothers typically work outside the home an average of 15 hours per week less than fathers. Fathers are also more likely to work unsocial hours than mothers: two thirds of fathers do

Saturday work, nearly half do evening work, and two fifths do Sunday work, and a quarter do night work. In this respect, there is almost no difference between younger and older fathers, or between fathers and non-fathers. In general, Irish fathers and mothers seem to work longer hours outside the home than some of their EU counterparts.

Many countries are introducing family-friendly measures in order to help parents cope with the competing demands of work and family. These measures include flexible working, breaks, leave arrangements and other initiatives, notably childcare. In Ireland, the government and the social partners committed themselves in 1996 to introducing more family-friendly measures in the workplace, including the EU Directive on Parental Leave by June 1998. Our review of the literature suggested that the introduction of family-friendly measures in the workplace does not automatically imply that those measures will be taken up by fathers. The reasons for this are many but include loss of earnings which can have a negative effect on the entire family, increased workload resulting from taking time off and the fear that taking leave for family reasons may have a negative impact on one's career. In addition, the culture of the workplace can discourage men from availing of family-friendly measures because it does not expect men who are fathers to behave any differently from men who are not fathers.

In Ireland, as elsewhere, there is a danger that family-friendly measures in the workplace may be perceived *solely* as measures to promote the equality of women. This is a danger because the net effect of these measures, however unintended, could be to reinforce rather than reduce the existing gendered division of labour, both at home and in work. In other words, the manner in which family-friendly measures are implemented and promoted could be just as important as the measures themselves. Accordingly, we recommend that the government and the social partners give serious consideration to ensuring that family-friendly measures in the workplace are promoted as measures designed to facilitate both fathers and mothers in meeting their parenting responsibilities. It should not be assumed that men and women will see the benefits of family-friendly measures in the workplace in exactly the same way. To date, almost all of the arguments in favour of family-friendly measures in the workplace are presented as having benefits for mothers; unless the corresponding benefits for fathers are also highlighted, these measures are likely to be taken up disproportionately by mothers. In this regard, we would also recommend that the language used to promote family-friendly measures is less gender-neutral and neutered and uses terms like 'father' and 'mother' to indicate that it is precisely for them and their children that the measures are being introduced.

It also needs to be emphasised that family-friendly measures, as the term is normally used, do not cover the number of hours worked by fathers, even though this is one of the most important factors determining employed fathers' involvement with children. In essence, family-friendly measures will only be effective in improving the balance between work and family life – and promoting joint parenting – if their net effect is to create real choices for couples, including reducing the excessive hours worked by some fathers.

Childcare is an extremely important initiative within the overall context of family-friendly measures in the workplace. From the beginning of 1997, the Irish government and the social partners have committed themselves to 'develop a strategy which integrates the different strands of the current arrangements for the development and delivery of childcare and early educational services' (Government of Ireland, 1996, p. 30). As with other family-friendly measures in the workplace, our analysis revealed that childcare tends to be seen as a women's issue, and this can reduce its overall effectiveness from the point of view of breaking down the gendered division of labour in the home and at work. We acknowledge that change in this area appears to be slow and complex, but it would be helped if the arguments in favour of childcare addressed themselves specifically to the needs and benefits of fathers rather than assuming that what is of benefit to mothers is automatically of benefit to fathers. In other words, we recommend that more attention is given to the way in which childcare is presented and delivered with a view to ensuring that it is seen as relevant and of benefit not only to children and mothers, but to fathers as well.

Our analysis drew attention to the virtual absence of men from childcare work. The reasons for this are many and inter-related. They involve low pay, the attitude that sees it as inappropriate work for men and the fears of some men about entering a world that is presently the almost exclusive domain of women. However, we also suspect that many men have become alienated from childcare because the wholly justified reporting of child abuse cases involving men has created a more generalised perception that all men are dangerous in the context of childcare. Whatever the reasons, we believe that the consequences of gender imbalance in the childcare sector are likely to have long-term consequences in terms of perpetuating in the minds of children the image that women, but not men, are the 'natural' carers of children. As a result, the gender imbalance in the delivery of childcare may itself undermine the objective that it is trying to promote, namely reducing the gendered division of labour between home and work. In our opinion, this gender imbalance is also a loss for the children who miss the benefit of having caring men in these services. Accordingly, we see the need for a discussion document on gender imbalances in the childcare sector that would include a strategy for addressing the barriers inhibiting men's involvement in this sector and the measures required to overcome them, consistent with maintaining the highest level of service for children.

Chapter 6
Fathers and the Law

Introduction

'Honour your father and your mother so that you may live long.'
The Bible, Book of Exodus

This chapter critically examines the salient features of the law as it relates to fatherhood in Ireland. We begin by considering the Constitution and comment on the absence of any constitutional recognition for the rights of unmarried fathers. We also examine the law of guardianship and the rights of married and unmarried fathers in this regard. The throughput of family law cases in Ireland in 1993–1994 is analysed in order to throw some light on the uses that men and women, fathers and mothers, make of the family law system in Ireland. The way in which the law is implemented through the courts is as important as the law itself and this seems to be particularly true in the case of fathers. This observation provides a context for highlighting the legal and other difficulties facing separated and unmarried fathers and the impact that this can have on contact with their children. As with other themes addressed in this book, issues affecting fathers cannot be considered in isolation from children's rights, motherhood and gender relations generally. We review joint custody in the context of the emergence of fathers' rights groups and argue in favour of joint custody where this is shown to be in the best interests of the child. Some fathers also come in contact with the law – both civil and criminal – as a result of the abuse of children and their wives/partners and we discuss some of the social and legal implications of this.

Fathers and the Constitution

'In truth, we owe our courts an enormous debt of gratitude for the clarity with which they have cut through the "humbug" of modern Ireland. For what they have done is outline in public the unadorned fact that the State, through its Constitution and laws, continues to hold the woman's place is in the home, and the man's is in the workplace.'

John Waters, 1998
(on the judgement of the Supreme Court that a deserted husband does not have the same entitlements as a deserted wife)

The family which is recognised and protected in Articles 41 and 42 of the Irish Constitution is the family based on marriage. By implication, the rights and responsibilities of fathers are those which come through marriage. Unmarried or 'natural' fathers do not exist in the Constitution.

The Constitution makes no explicit reference to fathers, married or otherwise. Mothers are explicitly mentioned – if not to the delight of all women – in the context of their contribution to the common good by working at home (Article 41.2.1) and the need to ensure that they do not neglect their home duties by having to engage in outside work (Article 41.2.2). Married fathers, unlike married mothers, do not have a constitutionally-protected right to their children. All of this is symptomatic of giving a greater social value to the ideology of motherhood than fatherhood and of symbolically strengthening motherhood while weakening fatherhood. We are emphasising the ideological context of parenting here because, as many feminist critics have pointed out, actual supports for mothers, such as childcare services, fall far short of the ideal suggested in the valuation of mothers. Mothers are too often expected to get on with parenting and are left, quite literally, holding the baby. Yet both men and women are diminished by a system that over-identifies women with motherhood and under-identifies men with fatherhood.

In 1966, the Supreme Court decided in the case of The State (Nicolaou) v an Bord Uchtála that, under the Irish Constitution:

1. a natural or biological father is not a member of a family within Article 41;
2. a natural or biological father is not a parent within Article 42; and
3. a natural or biological father has no personal right in relation to his child which the State is bound to protect under Article 40.3.

The Constitution Review Group pointed out that 'there has been much criticism of the continued constitutional ostracism of natural fathers' (Constitution Review Group, 1996, pp. 325). To redress this, it proposed the following: 'The Review Group considers that the solution [to giving constitutional rights to natural fathers] appears to lie in following the approach of Article 8 of the ECHR [European Convention on Human Rights] in guaranteeing to every person respect for "family life" which has been interpreted to include non-marital family life but yet requiring the existence of family ties between the mother and the father. This may be a way of granting consti- tutional rights to those fathers who have, or had, a stable relationship with the mother prior to birth, or subsequent to birth with the child, while excluding persons from having such rights who are only biological fathers without any such relationship. In the context of the Irish constitution it would have to be made clear that the reference to family life included family life not based on marriage' (Constitution Review Group, 1996, p. 326).

The reference to Article 8 of the European Convention on Human Rights, which involves the right to respect for family life, is particularly significant in the Irish context since this was the basis of a successful legal action taken by an Irish unmarried father to the European Commission of Human Rights in 1991. The case was taken by Joseph Keegan who complained that his right to respect for family life had been violated because his child had been placed for adoption by its mother without his knowledge or consent; in addition, he complained that Irish law did not afford him even a defensible right to be appointed guardian.

The facts of the case are that Joseph Keegan had a stable relationship with the mother of his child over a period of two years, during one of which they co-habited. The conception of their child was a deliberate decision by both of them and they had also planned to get married. In order to establish that Keegan's 'right to respect for his family life' had been violated – which the European Court of Human Rights established – the Court first established that he had a family life in the following way: 'The Court recalled that the notion of the 'family' in this provision is not confined solely to marriage-based relationships and may encompass other *de facto* 'family' ties where the parties are living together outside marriage. A child born out of such a relationship is *ipso iure* part of that 'family' unit from the moment of his birth and by the very fact of it. There thus exists between the child and his parents a bond amounting to family life even if at the time of his or her birth the parents are no longer co-habiting or if their relationship has then ended' (European Court of Human Rights, 1994, p. 3).

This judgement is significant in showing that one of the rocks upon which family and fatherhood rests is the social relations between the parents rather than their physical or biological relationship alone; or indeed their legal relationship based on marriage. A stable relationship between the parents – either before or since the birth of the child, or both – is thus seen as a minimal prerequisite to becoming a father. By the same token, the definition excludes those exceptional cases, such as rape or incest, where a normal relationship between the parents does not exist and any claims to fatherhood based on such a relationship would not be regarded as socially acceptable. However, the definition fails to clarify those more nebulous cases where the parents did not have a steady relationship before or since the birth of the child, but each may wish to develop a bond with their child.

The Commission on the Family, in its submission to the All-Party Oireachtas Committee on the Constitution in March 1997, indicated guarded support for the view of the Constitution Review Group: 'The Commission agrees with the Review Group that providing in the constitution for a guarantee of respect for family life, to include non-marital family life, may be a way, *inter alia*, of granting natural parents rights in relation to access and/or custody of their children or consent to their adoption. Such rights would be subject to what is in the best interests of the child' (Commission on the Family, 1997, p. 18).

An alternative approach, and one which we would favour, would involve drafting a constitutional provision which guarantees that a mother and father have equal rights to a child where the child is conceived through their mutual consent. The right of each child to know and be cared for by both its parents, whether living together or not, should also be enshrined in the Constitution. The exercise of these rights would be regulated by law and always in the best interests of the child.

The reasoning behind our views is that every child needs to have the opportunity to know its mother and its father. Children who are brought up without knowing their biological parent(s) usually retain an undying need to know where they came from – to know their lineage and kinship – as the adult reminiscences and experiences of adopted children testify (Milotte, 1997). The Irish writer, Hugh Leonard, described his experience of not knowing his biological father as follows: 'On my birth certificate, in the space designated "Name of Father", there is a single pen-stroke. Blaise Pascal said that if Cleopatra's nose had been shorter, the whole face of the earth would have changed; well, if my mother had thought to invent a name for my father, my own life would certainly have been different ... I have a deep-rooted belief that what I would describe as my maverick qualities must come from my father, who is forever lost to me in time and space. I have always been a cuckoo in any and every Irish nest ... I am by nature a loner who has never found his natural home ... I say this as a simple reality, not to boast or strike an attitude, and my father, whoever or of what race he was, simply must be the culprit' (Leonard, 1995, p. 36).

A biological father is more likely to play the symbolic role which is entrusted to him (see chapter two) if he is appointed to that role by having his name on the child's birth certificate; and there is a greater likelihood that he will actually *perform* that role in an active sense if he is included from the outset through having rights of guardianship, (joint) custody and access to the child. The failure of the Irish Constitution to recognise the existence of unmarried fathers undermines the fathering role by failing to state the universal symbolic importance of the father to each child. In turn, the father's role, as seen from the perspective of the child, does not depend on the relationship between the parents and some abstract ideal of 'family life', as seems to be suggested in Article 8 of the European Convention on Human Rights. As we see it, a positive statement of a mother's and father's constitutional rights would also be a positive statement of the rights of children vis à vis their parents.

Guardianship

Guardianship is a common law concept and essentially defines a relationship between an adult and a child such that the adult who is designated a guardian has the right to make all decisions affecting the welfare of the child; for example, where the child may live, who may have access to the child, how the child is brought up, what type of education it receives, the type of health care which the child may receive (such as an operation) etc. Guardianship also means that a child cannot be placed for adoption without the consent of the guardian, unless a court makes an order dispensing with that consent.

Married parents typically share guardianship rights to their children. However, when married parents separate, their guardianship rights can become the subject of dispute, particularly their guardianship rights of access or custody to a child. In these instances, a District Court is empowered to decide under section 11 of the Guardianship of Infants Act, 1964 as to how the guardianship rights should be divided between the parents.

All married parents are automatically guardians of their children. However, unmarried fathers do not have automatic guardianship rights to their children. Under the Status of Children Act 1987, non-marital fathers have the right to apply to the District Court for guardianship. The Children Act, 1997 provides that application to the court for guardianship is only necessary when the unmarried father fails to reach agreement with the child's mother. This is virtually identical to the law on granting 'parental responsibility' to unmarried fathers in England and Wales under Section 4 of The Children Act 1989 (see Lord Chancellor's Department, 1998).

Some of the key differences between married and unmarried fathers, as seen from the perspective of guardianship and related rights, are summarised in Table 6.1. Three features are particularly worthy of note. First, a man's paternity is usually presumed rather than proven. In the case of a married father, it is automatically presumed that he is the biological father if he is married to the child's mother; the mother's maternity, in turn, is presumed by the fact that she gave birth to the child. In the case of unmarried fathers, the presumption that a man is the biological father of his child depends on the mother's consent through, for example, agreeing to have his name placed on the birth certificate. There is anecdotal evidence to suggest that some mothers refuse this consent for fear that the father may claim guardianship rights to the child, something they do not wish to happen.

An important implication of this is that a child's paternity may not be established if the parents are unmarried and the man's paternity is denied by either the father or the mother. In effect this means that, under Irish law, a child born outside marriage does not have a right to have paternity legally established. This, in turn, would appear to be contrary to the UN Declaration on the Rights of the Child, Article 7, Paragraph 1 of which states: 'The child shall be registered immediately after birth and shall have the right from birth to a name, the right to acquire a nationality and, as far as possible, the right to know and be cared for by his or her parents'.

Table 6.1 Differences in guardianship rights of unmarried and married fathers in Ireland, 1997

Unmarried fathers	Married fathers
Paternity is presumed if: Both father and mother sign their names on the birth certificate. There is a Maintenance Order citing the man's name as father of the child.	Paternity is presumed if: the father is married to the mother of the child.
Paternity is not presumed if: The father refuses to put his name on the birth certificate. The mother refuses to allow his name on the birth certificate.	Paternity is not presumed if: both parents agree that the man is not the father of the child.
Paternity is proven if: a DNA test proves that the man is father of the child.	Paternity is proven if: a DNA test proves that the man is father of the child.
The unmarried father has the right to apply to the courts for joint guardianship of his child where paternity is presumed.	The married father has automatic joint guardianship rights to his child.
The unmarried father with joint guardianship rights can apply to the courts for custody of, and access to, his child.	The married father has automatic rights to joint custody and access to his children.
The rights of an unmarried father to custody of, and access to, his child may be restricted by the courts if it is deemed to be in the best interests of the child.	The rights of a married father – as well as fathers who are separated or divorced – to custody of, and access to, his child may be restricted by the courts if it is deemed to be in the best interests of the child.

Second, the establishment of paternity does not confer any guardianship rights on unmarried fathers. Married parents have automatic guardianship rights as do unmarried mothers. Following the Status of Children Act 1987, unmarried fathers were given the right to apply to the District Court for guardianship rights. However, in the light of the Keegan case, it is doubtful if the father's right to his child – and the mutual enjoyment of each other's company – are adequately protected under the Status of Children Act, 1987. This is clear from the court's inter-pretation of Article 8 of the European Convention on Human Rights: 'According to the principles developed by the court in its case-law, where the existence of a family tie with a child has been established, the State must act in a manner calculated to enable that tie to be developed and legal safeguards must be established that render it possible as from the moment of birth the child's integ-ration in his family. The mutual enjoyment by parent and child of each other's company constitutes a fundamental element of family life even when the relationship between the parents has broken down' (European Court of Human Rights, 1994, p. 4).

In our view, the right to apply for guardianship falls short of a father's right to respect for his identity as a parent in the meaningful sense of an opportunity for him to have a relationship with his child and for his child to know and relate to him as a father. The Children Act 1997 provides, inter alia, that an unmarried father does not have to apply to court for his guardianship rights if the child's mother acceded to his claim. This, however, also falls short of redressing the unequal status of unmarried fathers vis à vis every other category of parent. In England and Wales, where the situation is almost identical, there is now official recognition that this situation is no longer acceptable: 'Discrimination between married and unmarried fathers in respect of parental responsibility is increasingly seen as unacceptable, in view of the large number of children who are now born to unmarried parents, many of whom are likely to be in stable relationships. It is clearly impossible to assume that most unmarried fathers are irresponsible or uninterested in their children, and do not deserve a legal role as parents' (Lord Chancellor's Department, 1998, p. 15). Our view is that unmarried fathers should have automatic guardianship rights, as proposed by the Law Reform Commission (Law Reform Commission, 1982); the grounds on which these rights should be challenged or restricted – such as a child conceived through rape or a father with a history of violence and abuse against the mother or other children – should be clearly defined.

Third, the rights of all fathers – married, separated, divorced, unmarried – to custody and access of the children can be restricted by the courts under the Guardianship of Infants Act, 1964. These proceedings are held in camera and accordingly, it is impossible to know how judges apportion these rights between parents. Some anecdotal evidence suggests that the Irish courts tend to weigh custody and access decisions in favour of mothers. In 1995, the Department of Social, Community and Family Affairs, replying to a Council of Europe questionnaire on the rights of fathers stated that: 'In cases where parents separate, custody can be awarded to either parent. In practice, it is far more common to be awarded to the mother than the father' (Council of Europe, 1995, p. 230). The same practice applies in the English courts (Richards, 1982).

The law as it stands allows District Courts to award joint custody but, while there is no systematic research evidence available in Ireland, it seems that the joint custody provision is not widely used in practice. Nor is it known just how many fathers actually apply for such custody arrangements and what outcomes result when they do apply; this information is not collected by the courts or the Department of Justice, Equality and Law Reform. In Canada, for instance, while mothers get sole custody of children in 86% of cases, this represents the mutual decision of both parents to award sole custody to the mother; when fathers apply for custody it is either almost equally distributed to mothers and fathers, or the majority of decisions are made in favour of fathers (Bertoia and

Drakich, 1995, p. 237). Thus any assessment of out-comes in custody and access cases needs to take account of factors such as who applies to the courts, whether the case is contested or not, and the possibly differential impact of fathers and mothers as petitioners. We return to the issues of joint custody and fathers' rights below.

Fathers and the Family Law System

'Separated men have few rights, but unmarried fathers have absolutely none.'

David Hanley

The practical application of the family law system in Ireland has been analysed by Fahey and Lyons (1995) and provides some useful insights into the relationship between fathers and the law, particularly in the area of family breakdown. Before examining this data, it is worth pointing out that a large proportion of family breakdowns in Ireland, possibly as high as two thirds depending on how one interprets the data in the 1991 Census of Population, occur without being processed through the courts. As such, the image of family breakdown as presented through the court system represents only a subset of this reality and probably the more conflictual and acrimonious subset. Moreover, since family cases are heard in camera, it is impossible to know precisely how decisions are made – on what basis and in whose favour.

Table 6.2 gives the breakdown of married and separated persons in Ireland in 1996. This reveals that in 1996, around 6% of the ever-married population described themselves as separated or divorced. However, only two fifths (41%) of these appear to be legally separated or divorced, thus indicating that the majority of ever-married men and women involved in family break-up do not have recourse to the court system in Ireland.

The family law system is implemented through the District Courts and the Circuit Courts. The analysis by

Changing Fathers?

Fahey and Lyons covered family law cases in 1993–1994 and found that the District Court handled about two-thirds of all family law cases in that year; by comparison with the Circuit Court, the District Court is 'the more important locus of family law proceedings in Ireland' (Fahey and Lyons, 1995, p. 20).

Table 6.2 Marital status of ever-married men and women in Ireland in 1996

Marital status	Men	Women	Total
Total ever-married (1)	710,616	733,789	1,444,405
Total of separated/ divorced	35,661	52,131	87,792
Deserted	*6,363*	*16,785*	*23,148*
Marriage annulled	*920*	*1,287*	*2,207*
Legally separated	*11,863*	*14,616*	*26,479*
Other separated	*11,741*	*14,430*	*26,171*
Divorced	*4,774*	*5,013*	*9,787*
Separated/ divorced as % of ever-married	5	7	6
Legally separated/ divorced as separated	47	38	41

Source: Census of Population, 1996.

(1) Total ever-married includes all married, re-married and separated persons and excludes widows.

Table 6.3 is based on an extrapolation of data presented by Fahey and Lyons (1995, chapter two) and is presented with a view to highlighting the uses made by fathers and mothers, both married and unmarried, of the District Courts in the resolution of family disputes.

Table 6.3 Size and composition of family law cases in the District Courts in Ireland in 1993–1994

Category	Numbers		Characteristics of applicant		
Type of Application	N	%	Gender status	Parental status	Marital Status
Barring/ protection order	4,500	56	Women	Mothers (75%)* Not mothers (25%)*	All married
Maintenance order	1,750	22	Women	Mothers (100%)	Married (75%) Unmar-ried (25%)
Guardian-ship	1,750	22	Men (66%) Women (33%)	Fathers (66%) Mothers (33%)	Married (60%) Unmar-ried (40%)
Total	8,000	100	Women (85%) Men (15%)	Mothers (71%) Not Mothers (14%) Fathers (15%)	Married (86%) Unmar-ried (14%)

*Estimated according to the proportion of married women who have children (75%) and who have not children (25%), using the 1994 Labour Force Survey (Table 43). Main Source: Derived from Fahey and Lyons, 1995, chapter two.

A number of features are particularly worth noting. First, the family law system in Ireland, as Fahey and Lyons (1995, pp. 39–41) observe, performs two main functions: a protection function and a separation function. The protection function, involving barring and protection orders, accounts for more than half (56%) of the family law cases coming before the District Court. It should be noted that since the sampling period covered in Fahey and Lyons' work, the 1996 Domestic Violence Act has extended the right to apply for barring and protection orders to non-married spouses and other relatives of abusers, and the early indicators are that use of the protection function of the court has correspondingly increased (for 1996 figures, see Task Force on Violence Against Women, 1997, p. 51). The marital separation function involving maintenance and guardianship – as well as judicial separations in the Circuit Courts – is more diffuse and involves two court levels. Commenting on these two functions, Fahey and Lyons point out that 'the protection of women and children against violence at the hands of husbands/fathers is as important a function of the family law system as the regulation of separation in the more usual sense' (*Ibid*, p. 22).

Some recent research has shed light on the prevalence of domestic violence in Ireland and on women's accounts of the dynamics of abuse and the role of the law in protecting abused women and children (Kelleher and Associates and O'Connor, 1995; Task Force on Violence Against Women, 1997, pp. 49–61). However, virtually nothing is known about the precise content of the protection function as implemented through barring and protection orders. As Fahey and Lyons point out, the statistics on barring and protection orders 'tell us nothing about the nature of the violence (how often it is psychological rather than physical, how repetitive it is, how severe it is), about the victims and the perpetrators (we do not know, for example, how often children as well as women are victims), about the kind of responses the courts give (we do not know, for example, why more than half the barring applications made in 1993–94 were not granted), about the pattern of enforcement of orders issues, about rates of recidivism, or about any other practical outcome as far as families are concerned' (*Ibid*, p. 2). Thus, a more systematic understanding of the precise role and functions of the courts in promoting the protection function remains to be established.

Second, most of the family law cases are initiated by women (85%). In turn, most of these are mothers. Men and fathers (15%) are a distinct minority in terms of using the District Court to resolve family disputes. In effect, this means that the family law system, as applied in practice in

Ireland, is 'a woman's resource rather than a man's resource' (*Ibid*, p. 136).

Third, guardianship is effectively the only area where fathers use the family law system to redress family 'disputes'. Moreover, this is the only area of the family law system where the applicant is more likely to be a man than a woman. In 1993, for example, there were 3,665 applications to the District Court for guardianship of which 531 (14%) were from unmarried fathers; on the basis of the data presented in Table 6.3, this clearly implies that most of the applications for guardianship by men came from married fathers. In their study, Fahey and Lyons found that the most common issue in guardianship cases coming before the Dublin Metropolitan District Court was access followed by custody (*Ibid*, p. 29).

The traditional stereotype of the unmarried father – and to a lesser extent, the separated father – is that he is not interested in having custody of, or access to, his children. Stereotypes sometimes have a grain of truth. However, the apparent growth in numbers of separated and unmarried fathers who apply for joint custody of their children seems to reflect, at least in part, a desire by these fathers to remain involved with their children. It may also reflect a fear that this involvement could be cut off unless protected by law. Commenting on the significance of joint custody cases in England, where the mother is reputedly awarded sole custody in the vast majority of cases, Richards (1982, p. 137) writes: 'In legal terms, it might not seem that a joint custody order makes very much difference ... However, psychologically, a joint custody order affirms the continuing role of both parents in the lives of their children. I will suggest that this is something that may have great significance for the children. A further advantage of such [joint custody] orders is that they can avoid the implication that the disposal of custody is a winner-take-all situation'.

In Ireland, there has been a steady increase in the number of unmarried fathers applying for guardianship over the past few years, as Table 6.4 illustrates. The table reveals that the number of applications has risen by over

800% in the period 1989–1996; this is a much faster rate of growth than applications for barring or maintenance (see Fahey and Lyons, chapter two).

Table 6.4 Applications for guardianship by unmarried fathers in Ireland, 1989–1996

Year	Applications for guardianship N	Applications for guardianship granted N	Applications for guardianship granted %
1989	76	25	33
1990	215	190	88
1991	276	251	91
1992	347	312	90
1993	531	477	90
1994	562	436	76
1995	727	556	76
1996	700	400	57
% Change 1989–96	821	1,500	-

Source: Department of Justice, Equality and Law Reform.

In part, this reflects the introduction of the Status of Children Act 1987 but, at a deeper level, it may reflect a greater interest in active fathering by unmarried fathers through having their rights to guardianship, custody and access acknowledged by the court. It is true that the number of applications for guardianship by unmarried fathers in 1996 (700) amounted to little more than one-twentieth (6%) of all registered births outside marriage (12,484) in that year; equally, however, it is known from one Irish study that up to half of fathers remain in a relationship with the unmarried mother of their child (Richardson, 1991, p. 177), thus suggesting that legal remedies are only resorted to in a minority of cases.

In some instances, applications for guardianship by unmarried fathers may trigger applications for mainten-ance by mothers, and vice versa. However, it is not necessary for the two to be connected in each particular case to draw the inference that both guardianship and maintenance are part of the legal ground on which the rights and responsibilities of unmarried fathers and mothers are worked out. To some extent, it reflects the traditional division of labour between fathers and mothers, where fathers are seen to control the money and mothers are seen to control the children and each can be used as resources in granting or denying the rights of the other.

Fathers and the Legal System

In assessing the impact of the law on fathers, it is important to remember that 'the way the law is implemented is as important as the content of the law in shaping its practical effect' (Fahey and Lyons, 1995, p. 137). This is probably as true of family law as other types of law, but is more than ordinarily difficult to prove in the case of family law because cases are heard in camera and complete records of proceedings are not kept, much less published. As a result, there is almost no public information on how the system actually works. In their study of the family law system, Fahey and Lyons were extremely critical of the official monitoring statistics that are available: 'These statistics provide little information on the elementary facts of the system – how many family law cases arise each year, how many go to court and how many are resolved by agreement outside the court, how many have a history of repeated recourse to the law, how many involve children, what the social and family circumstances of the litigants are, what kinds of decisions the courts offer, how far these decisions are put into effect, and so on' (*Ibid*, p. 2).

It is known that quite a large number of fathers who have come into contact with the family law courts are extremely dissatisfied with the operation of the system. These fathers form the core membership of Parental Equality: the Joint Custody and Shared Parenting Support Group, which was set up in 1993 to promote equality

171

between mothers and fathers in the custody and parenting of their children, particularly in the wake of marital breakdown. Table 6.5 summarises some of the common experiences of its members.

Table 6.5 Summary of experiences of members of Parental Equality: the Joint Custody and Shared Parenting Support Group Ireland, 1993–1997

A total lack of appreciation of the value of fathers and fatherhood among the judiciary.
A failure by the courts to justify the removal of a father's custody rights and obligations.
A failure to even ask a sole custody applicant to give reasons or justification for seeking to remove custody rights and obligations from the respondent.
A prevailing view among solicitors that mothers always get custody and resultant lack of willingness on their part to vigorously defend a father's custodial rights and obligations.
A failure by the courts to impose any conditions on sole custody awards other than granting very limited access to non-custodial parents.
A failure and unwillingness by the courts to deal effectively with breaches of access orders.
A general perception that non-custodial parents have no rights other than access which the courts may not/will not enforce.
Little understanding among the judiciary of the concept of joint custody and a general unwillingness to even consider it.
An amazing tolerance by the courts of perjury which, even when proven, incurs no sanctions.

Source: Parental Equality, 1997.

Studies in England and Wales also report similar representations of experiences of the court system to that reported by Irish fathers (see for example, Richards, 1982; Lowe, 1982; Eekelaar and Clive, 1977). Moreover, the gendered nature of court outcomes seems to apply as much to criminal as to civil cases. For example, a study of 228 larceny cases appearing before the Dublin District Court in 1979 found that 'females were treated more leniently than males' (Lyons and Hunt, 1988, p. 129). This is in line with a similar study in Britain that also found more lenient sentences for women because 'marital status, family background and parenthood were more important factors in the sentencing of females than males' (Farrington and Morris, 1983). More recently, a study of 2,000 cases coming before the Dublin District Court in 1988 and 1994 found, when account is taken of the fact that the number of men appearing before the court is much greater than the number of women, that there is a 'sentencing bias' against male offenders as well as those who are younger and come from disadvantaged areas (Bacik, Kelly, O'Connell and Sinclair, 1997, p. 129).

In this study, disadvantage was measured in terms of five indicators – unemployment, low social class, lack of a car, living in rented accommodation, and overcrowding – and seems to suggest that, in passing sentence, judges take into account the economic role of men. Men who do not conform to the patriarchal ideal of male provider are treated more harshly than other men, while women, particularly mothers, seem to be assessed on traditional maternal roles. Moreover, the profile of men in Mountjoy Prison confirms a picture of young men who have never found an economic role within their families or society generally; even though three-quarters (72%) of all prisoners in Mountjoy are fathers, more than half (59%) considered themselves 'permanently separated' from their children (O'Mahony, 1997, p. 38). For these men, it appears, the wages of patriarchy are unemployment, long prison sentences and separation from children.

In drawing attention to such gender bias in the application of the law, it needs to be emphasised that the impact of the law cannot be measured simply in terms of court appearances. While the weight of the criminal justice system falls heavily on already marginalised men, we also know that women – particularly marginalised women – are regulated by the State in terms of motherhood to a greater extent than are men and fatherhood. As we discuss at length in chapter seven, in the range of social interventions that seek to ensure the promotion of children's welfare, 'parenting' tends to be synonymous with 'mothering' and fathers are systematically ignored by statutory social workers and other health and social service professionals. Thus, in implementing the prov-isions of legislation such as the Childcare Act 1991, it is mothers whose childcare is judged, monitored, and placed under surveillance. Moreover, the majority of these women come from socially disadvantaged backgrounds and are struggling to cope with the demands of childcare in very poor circumstances (Ferguson, 1995; Thorpe, 1994). Thus, for these women, it appears that the effects of patriarchy are having to parent in chronic poverty and poor housing with minimal social supports, sometimes in a context of experiencing violence from their partners – all the while running the risk, if not the reality, of losing their children to State agencies.

Our view is that a radical alternative to the court system should be considered for dealing with family disputes in Ireland. It is not possible to form an entirely rounded view regarding the impact of the court system on fathers – or mothers and children – given the lack of systematic evidence. We do, however, see considerable merit in an idea, contained in one of the submissions to the Commission on the Family (1996, p. 104), that a family commission should be set up covering five core functions:

- a national counselling service;
- a national mediation service;
- family tribunals;
- a commissioner for children;
- a research and information office.

Contact Between Non-Resident Fathers and their Children

The term 'non-resident father' is used here to denote fathers who do not live full-time with their children. The State is obliged to promote and facilitate contact between non-resident fathers and their children. This is part of the concept of 'family life' enshrined in the European Convention on Human Rights, discussed earlier. It is also enshrined in the UN Convention on the Rights of the Child, which was ratified by Ireland in 1992. This convention legally obliges the State to uphold the right of every child 'to know and be cared for by his or her parents ... as far as possible' (Article 7, paragraph 1, in Council for Social Welfare, 1991, p. 97). The convention also obliges the State to 'respect the right of the child who is separated from one or both parents to maintain personal relations and direct contact with both parents on a regular basis, except if it is contrary to the best interests of the child' (Article 9, paragraph 3 in Council for Social Welfare, 1991, p. 98). This clearly implies a reciprocal right and obligation on the part of non-resident fathers.

No studies have been carried out across a representative sample of non-resident fathers in Ireland to determine the level of contact with their children or the factors affecting it. As such, it is difficult to form a view of their experiences. However, it is known that many non-resident fathers in Ireland want to be involved in the care and upbringing of their children but have difficulty in affirming their rights as an equal parent of their child. This has been articulated in the work of Treoir: Federation of Services for Unmarried Parents and their Children (Dromey and Doherty, 1992) and more recently in the work of Parental Equality: the Shared Parenting and Joint Custody Support Group.

The work of Treoir has revealed three areas where the non-resident father's rights to a relationship with his child can be undermined or denied. First, the child may be given no information about the father, and his name may not even be registered on his child's birth certificate. This practice was, and to some extent still is, informed by the stereotype – often shared by mothers and professionals alike – that unmarried fathers would not be interested in their children. The practice is further cemented by the attitudes of some mothers that the child 'belongs' to them and not to both the parents. As a result, mothers have been known to block the registration of the father's name on the birth certificate for fear that it may give him any guardianship rights to the child (which it does not).

Second, the child may be given only negative information about the father. All children have an image of their father, even those who have never seen their father. In the case of non-resident fathers who are not in contact with their children, this effectively means that the image of the father will be formed from the mother. Treoir presents evidence that suggests that 'too often the messages about absent fathers to their offspring are negative. Comments such as "your dad was a rotter"; "you're turning out just like your dad"; and "I wish I'd never had you" can be all too common' (Dromey and Doherty, 1992, p. 6).

Third, fathers can be excluded from the opportunity to share with the mother in the parenting of their children. In recent years, Treoir has become aware of an increase in the number of calls to its information centre from fathers who have problems in having access to their children – either any access at all or an amount of access that they regard as fair – mostly because the mothers refuse to grant access. Typically a mother refuses access because:

- her relationship with the father breaks down;
- she enters a new relationship with another man;
- she wishes to place the child for adoption against the father's wishes.

In some instances, fathers are refused access after being involved with their child for a number of years.

Parental Equality was set up in 1993 and, in the four years to 1997, has received calls from over 5,000 people, many of them unmarried or separated fathers who are experiencing difficulties in obtaining shared custody and access to their children. One such father made a submission to the Commission on the Family and painted the following scenario facing working-class and lower middle-class parents as a result of their legal separation (see Table 6.6).

Table 6.6 Scenario facing working-class and lower middle-class parents as a result of their legal separation in Ireland

Mother gets custody of children.
Mother gets home.
Father removed from home.
Father cannot afford a second home.
Father lives in a bedsitter/small flat.
Father continues to work and pay maintenance and mortgage to enable wife and children to continue living in comparative comfort in family home.
Father has access to children but cannot have them overnight and must meet them in public places due to unsuitable accommodation.
Father becomes a 'MacDonald's Dad'.
Father loses all self-esteem.
Father effectively destroyed.
Father eventually becomes dysfunctional (may opt for suicide).
Children effectively lose their father.
Children see father's life disintegrating.
Children psychologically damaged for life.

Source: Based on a submission to the Commission on the Family, March 1997.

Outside Ireland, there has been extensive research on the factors that facilitate or hinder contact between non-resident fathers and their children. These include:

- the judgements of the courts, which have tended to see the mother as the primary care taker and have awarded her custody of the children;
- the closeness of father-child relations before the separation;
- the physical distance between the father and child after separation;
- the strained relations between father and mother which makes contact with the children difficult and unpleasant;
- the entry of a new man into the mother's life;

- mother's hostility towards the father, particularly where she controls access to the children and uses it to reap revenge on the father;
- the views of fathers themselves who sometimes see their role vis à vis the children as secondary, even insignificant and replaceable.

No doubt, there are always two sides to such invariably acrimonious stories and the perspectives of mothers, and indeed children, need to be heard as well as the fathers'. However, some research evidence and the experience of professionals in this area suggests that the traditional stereotype of the non-resident father who loses contact with his children simply because he does not care is too simplistic. As one commentator has sought to emphasise: 'Contact with fathers is broken not because they don't care, but because they cannot deal with the pain, or they have nowhere to take the children, there is hostility from the mother, or the child is angry and doesn't want to see them, or through lack of money' (Robinson, 1995).

A number of studies show that, when parents separate, contact between non-resident fathers and their children tends to diminish with time and distance (Wallerstein and Kelly, 1980; Seltzer, 1991; Furstenberg and Nord, 1987). In Britain, for example, a 1991 study showed that up to 40% of non-resident fathers lose contact with their children after five years (Bradshaw and Miller, 1991). However, preliminary results from a more recent British study involving a more representative national sample suggest that 'even 5 to 10 years after the break-up, three out of four fathers are still in contact with their children and one out of three sees them at least fortnightly' (Burgess, 1997, p. 192). Research evidence from Australia indicates that two-thirds of non-resident fathers see their children at least fortnightly (Gibson, 1992), while in California nine-tenths of children had contact with their children four years after divorce (Maccoby and Mnookin, 1992).

A key factor affecting the level of contact between non-resident fathers and their children is the level of contact established in the years immediately following separation; if a pattern of regular contact is established and reinforced by shared physical custody and children staying overnight, then the level of contact is likely to be much higher (Wallerstein and Kelly, 1980; Leupnitz, 1986; Maccoby, Depner and Mnookin, 1990; Albiston, Maccoby, and Mnookin, 1990; Ottosen, 1996). One implication of this is that contact between non-resident fathers and their children may not be a matter simply of the father's interest or disinterest in his children; it may also be affected by the access which he is afforded to his children. In this regard, a mediated process of separation, particularly in situations of intense conflict, could help to ensure that the children's need for regular contact with their father is maintained and could be much less damaging for the children (see Law Reform Commission, 1996). Where possible and appropriate, father-children contact needs to be promoted separately as a relationship in its own right which is distinct from the dynamics of the post-separation spousal relationship.

A further implication, though not one that has been fully tested in the research, is the relationship between the father and his children prior to separation: it would seem likely that fathers who have a close and positive relationship with their children prior to separation – notwithstanding their marital difficulties – are likely, other things being equal, to maintain this after the separation. This is an area that would merit further investigation. The introduction of step-fathers, who may physically but not psychologically replace the father, has also been shown to reduce contact between non-resident fathers and their children (Furstenberg and Cherlin, 1991; Kock-Nielsen, 1987).

One aspect of contact between non-resident fathers and their children is the payment by fathers of 'maintenance' or 'child support' as it is variously called. One study found that contact and maintenance are linked in that those fathers who have most contact with their children pay the most maintenance (Maccoby and Mnookin, 1992). Also, richer fathers are, understandably, better payers

(Bradshaw and Miller, 1991). In Britain, the Child Support Agency was set up in April 1993 to determine and collect maintenance from all non-resident parents, irrespective of their previous marital status. There is no such agency in Ireland. The relevant social welfare legislation refers to non-resident fathers as the 'liable relative' and contributions from the non-resident father are sought by the department on a case-by-case basis. The experience of Treoir is that the enforcement of maintenance by the Department of Social, Community and Family Affairs can hinder rather than help the objective of joint parenting, particularly in the case of poorer people, as both parents effectively become worse off if they are 'officially' joint parents. As things stand, therefore, the social welfare system may act as a disincentive to some joint parents where the parents do not live together; moreover, it is precisely in these situations where the objective of joint parenting should receive all the support it can get in the interests of both children and parents.

Other measures that have an impact on families, such as income support payments from the Department of Social, Community and Family Affairs, would need to be re-adjusted to make joint parenting/custody a viable option. For example, Child Benefit (Children's Allowance) and the One Parent Family Payment can be paid to one parent only, typically the mother, even in those cases – which are admittedly small in number – where both parents have joint and equal custody and access. In these cases there are both practical and symbolic grounds for making separate payments to each parent to reflect and support the parenting role which each plays. The level of these payments would also need to be considered in the context of the costs of running two separate households.

Fathers' Rights and Joint Custody

In this section we focus in more detail on the issue of joint custody and fathers' rights. The Children Act, 1997 gives the court power to grant joint custody – a power that it already has – as set out in Section 9: 'For the avoidance of doubt, it is hereby declared that the court, in making an order under section 11, may, if it thinks it appropriate, grant custody of a child to the child's father and mother jointly'. The wording stops short of giving full weight to joint custody as the preferred option. In light of what we have argued above, there is a strong case for joint custody being established as the norm for all parents who are legally separating – with the presumption that both parents have *equal* rights of custody and access – and that the onus should be on the courts to prove why joint custody would not be in the best interests of the child.

In discussing joint custody, it is useful to distinguish between 'joint *legal* custody' and 'joint *physical* custody' since this distinction helps to throw light on the factors that promote or hinder contact between fathers and children. The experience in California, for example, suggests that joint legal custody may not be enough to ensure contact between the father and his children, nor give fathers a say in their upbringing; joint physical custody is much more effective in this regard (Maccoby and Mnookin, 1992).

In many countries, the issue of joint custody is almost inseparable from the emergence of fathers' rights groups (see Coltrane and Hickman, 1992). Over the past decade, fathers' rights groups across the Western world have actively promoted the ideal of joint custody and equality in parenting. We have already referred to the work of Parental Equality in Ireland whose emergence and agenda appears very similar to those of groups formed in other countries. These organisations began to emerge in the USA in the 1970s and expanded rapidly until, by the 1980s, there were over two hundred such groups, with some in almost every state. Some examples include: Husbands Against Dirty Divorce (Seattle, WA), Fathers for Equal Rights (Jackson, MI), the Coalition of Paternal Rights Attorneys (Phoenix, AZ), and the Joint Custody Association (Los Angeles, CA).

The 1990s have seen the rise of new and larger American fathers' advocacy groups. Fathers United, for

Changing Fathers?

instance, seeks to restructure divorce and custody laws, including calling for mandatory joint custody, unless one parent is unable or unwilling to parent. According to one commentator, joint custody seems to be a guiding principle for all fathers' rights organisations (Clatterbaugh, 1997, p. 70).

Notwithstanding the emergence of fathers' rights groups and their advocacy of joint parenting, the North American research suggests that many separated fathers do not actually apply for custody – joint or otherwise – whereas mothers invariably do and, not surprisingly, when it is uncontested, they get it (Bertoia and Drakich, 1995). In Canada, for instance, mothers get sole custody of the children in 86% of cases although this represents the mutual decision of both parents (*Ibid*, p. 237). When fathers petition for custody, however, it is either almost equally distributed to mothers and fathers, or the majority of decisions are made in favour of fathers. Some research suggests that applications for sole custody by fathers tend to be extremely rare. In the USA, some researchers argue that an almost equal distribution of custody awards occurs in contested cases (Polikoff, 1983; Weitzman, 1985). This is disputed, however, by the work of Maccoby and Mnookin (1992) which claims that mothers are favoured in contested cases. As already indicated, we have almost no information on these matters in Ireland.

A study of two fathers' rights groups in Ontario, Canada examined the men's reasons for joining the group, their conceptualisation of fatherhood, and their opinions on topics such as joint custody, child access, divorce, mediation and support payment enforcement programmes (Bertoia and Drakich, 1995). The authors of this study were particularly struck by the fact that many of the fathers wanted liberal access to, but not necessarily custody of, their children. As one father told the researchers: 'All I want is good access so that I am not a visitor. I want to have the freedom to phone them, and I want the freedom for them to phone me. I want to be able to see them when they want to without asking permission all the time' (Bertoia and Drakich, 1995, p. 239).

Many of the fathers interviewed seemed to have a notion of fathering which involved 'helping' rather than being a fully accountable co-parent. According to the authors, 'not one of them realised that to speak of "helping" was to delegate the task of childcare to mothers' (*Ibid*, p. 239). The researchers concluded that this reflects how fathers take for granted mothers' primary responsibility for childcare. While some fathers referred to the joys of being with their children, 'not one father talked about wanting to have the responsibility of the everyday care of his children' (*Ibid*, p. 241). The researchers suggest that the fathers in these organisations were seeking a traditional father role that did not involve full equality in physical custody and everyday care but a right to exercise the level of parenting that existed prior to the divorce (*Ibid*, p. 241). In other words, 'the post-divorce fatherhood role for many fathers means a continuation of their pre-divorce role and not a reconceptualised role of the equal parenting dad typified in the fathers' rights public rhetoric' (*Ibid*, p. 242).

This research is significant in drawing attention to deep-seated assumptions about the roles of father and mother and how the physical and emotional care of children is often seen as the main responsibility of the mother, even in organisations which advocate joint custody. It bears emphasising that the Irish situation may be different although the assumption that the mother is the primary parent is probably quite widespread among many fathers, irrespective of whether they are married, single or separated. This research evidence is also useful in terms of showing how concepts of parental justice and parental equality are grounded in assumptions and lived realities about motherhood and fatherhood. As a result, the decisions of the courts in granting sole custody to mothers is often no more than the application of everyday assumptions about the roles of mothers and fathers in families. It is precisely these assumptions which we have endeavoured to challenge in this book.

Another aspect of joint custody is whether it works in practice and under what circumstances it is in the best interests of the children. One review of the evidence in a number of American states cautions that joint custody arrangements may not always be in the best interests of the children: 'Laws favouring joint custody arrangements effectively abolish the best interests of the child standard for making custody determinations. The best interests standard requires the judge to carefully analyse the facts to determine which of the parents is better able to parent the child given the child's particular needs. Laws favouring joint custody presume that joint custody is in the best interests of all children. The fact that joint custody is not the best arrangement for a particular child is often not enough to overcome a joint custody presumption. Usually the parent opposing it must show that joint custody is actually harmful to the child or meet a higher burden of proof than preponderance of the evidence' (Zorza, 1992, p. 922). In some American states, it appears that the parent opposing joint custody has an almost impossible burden to meet to convince the court that it is not in the best interests of the child. Many US statutes make it clear that courts may impose joint custody awards even if only one parent requests it. Judges have been found to generally prefer joint custody provisions because they make their jobs much easier. They 'hardly need to look at what the particular child needs or how capable each parent is relative to the other in parenting' (*Ibid*, p. 923).

In cases of domestic violence, joint custody is dangerous for women and children, as some Irish commentators have pointed out (Ferguson, 1997c; Task Force on Violence Against Women, 1997). This, however, is an argument against the improper use of joint custody; it is not an argument against the underlying principle of joint custody.

It is not always the woman who is the victim and the man the perpetrator. In what appears to be a minority of cases, it is women who are the abusers. The organisation AMEN (Abused Men) was started in Ireland in 1998 to provide a helpline service for, and advocate on behalf of, the 'battered husband'. In its first few months alone it received hundreds of calls from men in need of help (AMEN, 1998).

Taking all the evidence we have reviewed here into account, we believe that the courts should have a *discretionary* – as opposed to a mandatory – power to award joint custody. In our view, joint custody is the appropriate option for the court to consider, unless the evidence and the circumstances suggest otherwise; where the evidence and the circumstances do suggest otherwise, the best interests of the child should be the organising principle on which court decisions are based.

It is clearly wrong for fathers to be adversely judged purely on the basis of being fathers, just as it is unjust for women to be punished by the courts simply because of unquestioned assumptions about mothers. Meeting the best interests of children on a case-by-case basis can be established by eliciting children's views, as well as each parent's, and by taking full account of the distribution of responsibility and the nature and quality of relationships in the family prior to the marital breakdown. There is a compelling case for separating couples, and indeed children, to have routine access to mediation and counselling services to promote communication, conflict resolution and healing.

Abusive Fathers and the Law

'... and no one knew
my father was eating his children ...
and yet as he lay
on his back, snoring, our lives slowly
disappeared down the hole of his life.'

Sharon Olds: from the poem *Saturn*

A further point of contact between fathers and the law – both the civil and the criminal law – involves the abuse of children and women by fathers/husbands. There can be little doubt that, while most men do not abuse, one of the factors that has contributed to the negative perception of men and fathers is the new public visibility of domestic violence and the widespread reporting of child physical and sexual abuse cases and statistics.

In the area of sexual abuse towards children, the number of cases confirmed by the health board suggests that, in Ireland, at least one in every 1,000 children is sexually abused (McKeown and Gilligan, 1991). However, a national survey of adults in Ireland revealed that up to 6% of the population claim to have been sexually abused as children (Market Research Bureau of Ireland, 1987). Of particular interest in this context is the fact that about 90% of child sexual abusers are men (McKeown, Gilligan et al., 1993, p. 107). Fathers are the abusers in 35% of confirmed cases compared to 3% of mothers; in other words, fathers are over ten times more likely to sexually abuse their children than mothers – the remaining categories of abusers are outside the immediate family, e.g., baby-sitters, relatives, neighbours, although they are still men in the vast majority of cases (*Ibid*, pp. 110–111). While child sexual abuse by women is gaining greater recognition, studies in other countries also confirm that fathers are much more likely to sexually abuse their children than mothers. It is worth emphasising, however, that the vast majority of fathers do not sexually abuse their children.

A number of problems are known to exist in fully implementing the criminal law in child sexual abuse cases. The prosecution rate of confirmed child sexual abuse cases is less than 10% (McKeown and Gilligan, 1991). This arises, in part, from the decision of the Director of Public Prosecutions not to proceed in a large number of cases. The precise reasons for these decisions are rarely publicly disclosed as, in maintaining its independence, the DPP's office is not obliged to be publicly accountable. It is known, however, that most of the cases that are prosecuted rely on guilty pleas from the accused. In defending his office from criticism for its failure to prosecute more cases where the offence is denied by the accused, the DPP has argued that the conditions of his role preclude him from prosecuting any case unless a conviction is a likely outcome (McGrath, 1996, p. 66). He has also argued that the adversarial nature of the criminal justice system is 'singularly unsuited' to dealing with child sexual abuse cases: 'Child sexual abuse is a crime, and one of the worst. It needs to be addressed vigorously by the criminal justice system. I do not believe the criminal justice system is up to the job. It is a very blunt instrument for ascertaining truth. In the case of child sexual abuse, it is at its worst' (Barnes, 1995, cited in McGrath, 1996, p. 66).

As McGrath (1996) points out, perhaps the major issue here is that the legal system is anti-child, or pro-adult. This includes the presumption of unreliability on the part of children in giving evidence, particularly in cases involving alleged sexual offences. In reality, however, children are no less reliable witnesses than adults and, as McGrath (1996, p. 67) argues, are in many respects more reliable informants because of their less developed ability to lie or deceive. The net result is that many sex offenders go unpunished. Not only is justice not done, but the implications of so many sex offenders remaining free and untouchable in the community are very worrying indeed for child protection, as this is known to be a compulsive form of behaviour which offenders do not give up voluntarily (Finkelhor, 1986). Sanctions and 'treatment' programmes are the only way to ensure that offenders will have any chance of stopping abusing and future victims will be protected – initiatives that are discussed in more detail in chapter seven.

The situation with regard to the physical abuse of children is quite different in terms of the roles of mothers and fathers. Child physical abuse, and especially neglect, are more commonly recognised than sexual abuse; they comprised two-thirds of all confirmed child abuse cases coming to the attention of health boards in Ireland in 1995 (Ferguson, 1996b). Some research suggests that mothers are just as likely to physically abuse their children as fathers and to seriously abuse them (Sternberg, 1997). Research that points to similar trends in child neglect suggests that these patterns have to be seen, in part, in the context of women spending proportionately more time with, and carrying greater responsibility for, children. A striking feature of such cases is the absence of resident fathers. Lone-parent mothers are over-represented in child protection cases, and high proportions of these women have been shown to experience addiction problems and other indicators of vulnerability, such as social isolation and exclusion through being from ethnic minority groups (Thorpe, 1994). Routinised concerns about the competencies of mothers and fathers from the Travelling community in Ireland to provide good enough parenting is a case in point. Relationships between violence against women and other forms of child abuse, including maternal neglect where the woman's capacity to parent well is weakened by the male violence, are also emerging as significant in Irish and international research (Ferguson, 1997b). Again, it is worth emphasising that the vast majority of fathers or mothers do not physically abuse or neglect their children.

The use of the criminal law in cases of child physical abuse and neglect is extremely rare. Most cases are not serious enough to warrant consideration of criminality as such. In any event, conceptualising such cases in criminal/punitive terms goes against the kind of therapeutic/welfare approach which has come to characterise models of good practice in responding to the needs of these children and parents. Legal intervention in such cases is usually restricted to civil actions to protect abused and neglected children, the loss of the children constituting a major sanction in its own right. It is much more rare for sexually abused children to go into care given that there is usually at least one non-abusing parent available to care for the child. It is the sex offender who requires removal from the child, rather than the other way round. That said, procedures surrounding the 'criminalisation' of child physical abuse and neglect have been tightened up in recent years through the introduction in 1995 of new Health Board and Gardaí guidelines on the investigation and management of child abuse (Department of Health, 1995). Largely as a result of how failures in communication between Gardaí and health board officials are known to have contributed to tragic failures to protect victims, such as in the Kilkenny incest case (McGuinness, 1993), health board personnel are now required to routinely notify *all* cases of suspected child abuse to the Gardaí, and vice versa. While this has undoubtedly led to significant increases in social worker-Gardaí collaboration, initial evaluations of the practical application of the procedures suggest that considerable discretion is operating in the system which means that it remains exceptional for criminal investigations to be instigated in cases of physical abuse or neglect (Ferguson, 1997b).

The research evidence indicates that men are much more likely to be violent to their partners than the reverse. Children who are witnesses to 'domestic' violence in its many forms – physical, psychological, emotional, isolating or other forms of 'coercive control' of the women – are experiencing abuse in its own right, often in addition to other forms of child abuse directly perpetrated against them (Kelleher and Associates and O'Connor, 1995; Ferguson, 1997b).

As indicated above, aside from the key child protection provisions of the Childcare Act 1991, the main legal protections for women and children who are the victims of domestic violence and abuse are barring and protection orders, applications for which constitute more than half the entire family law system in the courts. The study by Fahey and Lyons (1995, p. 32) revealed that 4,500 Barring or Protection Orders were processed through the District Court in 1993–1994. In the case of unmarried spouses, there is now provision for protection in the Domestic Violence Act 1996. It must be stressed that huge problems have been shown to exist in regulating abusive fathers. These include:

- uneven implementation of pro-arrest policies by the Gardaí which results in missed opportunities to arrest and charge violent perpetrators;

189

- relatively small numbers of cases getting to the courts;
- the downgrading of offences by the courts, such that inadequate penalties are given;
- the need for a court accompaniment and advocacy service for abused women to support victims and increase their confidence in the system, empowering them to follow through on civil and criminal proceedings (Task Force on Violence Against Women, 1997).

It must also be emphasised that the Report of the Task Force on Violence Against Women, as well as helping to point out these difficulties, has set out a comprehensive, coordinated strategy for effecting change in promoting the protection of abused women and children and rendering abusers accountable. In chapter seven, we go on to review in greater detail the development and orientation of services for working with abusive fathers.

Conclusion

This chapter has reviewed some of the main ways in which the role of fathers is defined and regulated by law. The Irish Constitution makes no reference to fathers; unlike mothers, they do not have a constitutionally-protected right to their children. However, the position of unmarried fathers is particularly weak since, under the Irish Constitution, they are not recognised as either a parent or as part of a family and have no constitutional rights to their child. Both the Constitution Review Group and the Commission on the Family have considered this issue and have suggested that the adoption of Article 8 of European Convention on Human Rights (which guar-antees every person respect for 'family life,' this being interpreted to include non-marital family life) would be one way of granting constitutional rights to unmarried or 'natural' fathers. An alternative approach, and one which we favour, would involve drafting a constitutional provision to guarantee that a mother and a father have equal rights to a child where the child is conceived through their mutual consent. The right of each child to know and be cared for by both its parents, whether living together or not, should also be enshrined in the Constitution. The exercise of these rights would be regulated by law and would always be applied in the best interests of the child.

Moving from the Constitution to statute law, our analysis revealed that unmarried fathers do not have automatic guardianship rights to their children. Our view is that this legal situation is not conducive to joint parenting and is not sufficiently supportive of the child's right – as enshrined in both Article 8 of European Convention on Human Rights and Articles 7 and 9 of the UN Convention on the Rights of the Child – to be brought up by both its parents. Nor is it sufficiently supportive of the child's right to have paternity legally established. We have also considered the evidence, albeit much of it anecdotal in Ireland, concerning separated fathers and the apparently low rates of joint custody of children. This effectively undermines joint parenting since it gives the mother total responsibility for bringing up the child and leaves the father's access to his child almost entirely at the discretion of the child's mother.

The law relating to guardianship, custody and access has an important impact on the level of contact between children and their non-resident fathers. Our analysis suggests that many non-resident fathers in Ireland want to be involved in the care and upbringing of their children but have difficulty in affirming their right as an equal parent of their child. This has been articulated in the work of Treoir: Federation of Services for Unmarried Parents and their Children and, more recently, in the work of Parental Equality: the Shared Parenting and Joint Custody Support Group.

This chapter drew upon existing analyses of family law cases through the courts in 1993–1994 in order to look at the uses which fathers make of the family law system. The analysis, based on Fahey and Lyons (1995), revealed that only a small proportion of family disputes and separations are resolved in the courts. Most family law cases are initiated by women, and many of them are against men in the sense that they involve barring and protection orders. Guardianship is effectively the only area where fathers use, or can use, the family law system to redress family disputes. Applications for guardianship have increased significantly in recent years, possibly reflecting an increased interest by unmarried fathers in their children, although they still amount to only 6% of all registered births outside marriage. The court system has an independent effect, over and above the content of the law, on the resolution of family disputes. In general, our analysis suggests that the court system needs to do more to be supportive of fathers who are separating or un-married. Our view is that a Family Commission, which would effectively remove family cases from the remit of the courts, could be the best way to proceed.

Evidence from elsewhere suggests that the concept of 'joint legal custody' may not be sufficient to promote contact between non-resident fathers and their children unless it actually means 'joint physical custody'. More-over, other measures which impact on families, such as income support payments from the Department of Social, Community and Family Affairs, particularly Child Benefit (Children's Allowance) and the One Parent Family Payment, may need to be re-adjusted to make joint custody a viable option.

We agree with the argument that joint custody should be established as the norm for all parents who are legally separating – with the presumption that parents have equal rights of custody and access – and that the onus should be on the courts to prove why joint custody would not be in the best interests of the child and its parents. We believe that, on balance, the discretionary power given to the courts to award joint custody is appropriate. It leaves in place the best interests of the child as the organising principle on which decisions must be based, while at the same time establishing joint custody as the appropriate option for the court to consider, unless the evidence and the circumstances suggest otherwise. In forming this view, we have at-tempted to acknowledge the complex interactions between notions of parental justice on the one hand and assumptions about parental roles on the other.

Fathers also come in contact with the law because a minority are known to abuse their children and, in some cases, their partners as well. Some of the key statistics in this area were reviewed. It is our view that the widespread and wholly appropriate reporting of child abuse cases has contributed to the sometimes widespread and negative perception of men and fathers; it is worth emphasising, however, that the vast majority of fathers do not abuse their children.

In summary then, our analysis reveals a number of areas within the law where the rights of fathers – particularly the rights of unmarried fathers – require attention. It is our impression that the rights of separated fathers to joint custody of their children do not receive the enthusiastic support from the courts that it deserves and this needs to be addressed. Within the Constitution, we favour a declaration which enshrines the equal rights of father and mother to the guardianship of their child where the child is conceived through consent, irrespective of whether both parents live together. As elsewhere in the book, our analysis is informed by the primacy of the best interests of the child and our belief that this is usually best served when the child knows and is cared for by both its parents, irrespective of the legal or personal relationship between those parents.

Chapter 7
State Services and Supports for Fathers

Introduction

'Suddenly, I heard the first boy cry out, 'Ndiyindola!' (I am a man!), which we were trained to say in the moment of circumcision. Seconds later, I heard Justice's strangled voice pronounce the same phrase ... Before I knew it, the old man was kneeling in front of me. I looked directly into his eyes. He was pale, and though the day was cold, his face was shining with perspiration. ... Without a word, he took my foreskin, pulled it forward, and then in a single motion, brought down his assegi. I felt as if fire was shooting through my veins; the pain was so intense that I buried my chin into my chest. Many seconds seemed to pass before I remembered the cry, and then I recovered and called out, 'Ndiyindola!'

... I felt ashamed because the other boys seemed much stronger and braver than I had been: they had called out more promptly than I had. I was distressed that I had been disabled ... and I did my best to hide my agony. A boy may cry; a man conceals his pain.'

Nelson Mandela, *Long Walk to Freedom*, 1994

Fathers, as it has been stressed throughout the book, do not form a homogenous group. They differ greatly in social and legal status, as well as in orientation and style. One thing that seems common to all fathers, however, is the need for support and guidance. Precisely the same must be said of mothers. Yet, as the analysis presented in this chapter shows, fathers tend to be largely avoided by State and social services, which still tend to assume that childcare is about 'mothering'. The result is an almost total absence of supports for men from all social backgrounds, and an astonishing lack of services which seek to engage fathers. This betrays the pervasive assumption that males are meant to become fathers simply by 'being' men. Little or no concept of men's development, or of fatherhood involving a developmental transition (as discussed in chapter four), seems to exist or inform how fathering is understood or approached. This also tells us a great deal about the kinds of absent or, at best, 'helping-out' fathers it is assumed men are meant to become. We show that this situation arises from the fact that little or no concept of men as carers or of men's vulnerability exists at a public level, either in society in general or, more specifically, within the professional caring community.

This has much to do with how dominant forms of 'masculinity' are constructed and perceived in Irish society, not least by men and male-dominated institutions themselves. Thus, in this chapter we seek to provide at least a start in deconstructing the myth of the invulnerable man and father. In deconstructing dominant constructions of manhood – what Connell (1995) calls 'hegemonic masculinity' – we give particular attention to identifying the needs of those men who have to father in marginalised communities and circumstances, such as the long-term unemployed and disadvantaged young men, and consider strategies for social intervention. These strategies include engagement with men in a 'clinical' context on a one-to-one basis, the development of men's groups, and also education and youth work programmes for young men that place the fatherhood role and responsibility at the core of their masculine identity.

Universal State services and Fathers

'Some men live with a limp they don't hide,
stagger, or drag
a leg.

Their sons often are angry.
Only recently I thought:
Doing what you want ...
Is that like limping? Tracks of it show in sand.'
Robert Bly, My Father's Wedding

In countries such as Ireland, parenting and family life are deeply influenced and constituted by expert knowledge. Expertise has taken over from tradition and the passing on of wisdom and knowledge through families and communities (Giddens, 1991). This does not mean that extended families and significant others such as mothers and fathers no longer have influence on parenting practices. However, it does mean that a structural shift has occurred during the twentieth century where the balance of influence is firmly with the State and, more broadly, with the expert. Childbirth has been medicalised, and child rearing mediated and thoroughly colonised by expertise, from public health nurses to GPs, to schools, social services and so on. Parents – and especially mothers – also increasingly regulate their own behaviour by using expert knowledge through consulting advice books, magazines and other media. The power of expertise is such that social intervention and knowledge no longer merely reflect and act on a pre-existing reality of child rearing. Expertise inherently shapes and actually *constitutes* parenting norms. Thus, an interrogation of the gendered norms and perspectives on parenting that characterise expertise and social intervention in Ireland today has much to contribute to our understanding of how fathering is constituted, and ways in which it can be changed through public policy.

Social intervention into parenting and family life can be conceptualised as occurring on a continuum. At one end, there are universal State services such as hospitals, maternity care, general practice and public health nursing to which all citizens have a right in order to promote their children's and their own well-being and competence as parents. At the other end, there are specific, selective services which intervene pro-actively in the interests of child welfare to regulate deviant parenting. The most significant of these that we examine here are those governed by the duties of the health board community care teams under the Childcare Act 1991 and the Child Abuse Guidelines (1987; 1995) to investigate and manage suspected child abuse (Ferguson and Kenny, 1995). A new Domestic Violence Act (1996) also places increased obligations on health boards, the Gardaí and the justice system to protect adult members of households and regulate gender relations in the private domain. In the majority of cases, this involves protecting women from men's domestic violence (Kelleher and Associates and O'Connor, 1995). Our review of the evidence suggests that not only are women still the primary focus of social intervention in their capacities as mothers, but that women are the main childcare workers and providers of public childcare services. Men are largely absent from involvement with children in public provision, yet are over-represented in management positions – a gendered division of power and childcare work that, we suggest, public policy will have to seek to proactively change if fatherhood, masculinity and gender relations more generally are to be genuinely recast in ways that advantage children, women and men themselves.

It would be too much to say that fathers are completely ignored, or that men never seek help from the caring professions. Research and clinical experience show, for instance, that some fathers do use therapy services (Carr, 1998) and that at least a proportion of men who go for marriage guidance counselling are so motivated to get help with their situation that they are prepared to attend alone (Ferguson, 1998). However, research and practice suggest that, at every point on the continuum of State services and supports, fathers tend to be avoided by professionals, and there is a great deal of uncertainty among professionals about how to approach men and work with them. Traditionally, in the mainstream of social intervention, 'parenting' has implicitly been synonymous with 'mothering'. Intervention has focused on women as the primary carers, while the place of men and engagement around fathering has at best been ambiguous; at worst, men are ignored entirely.

An illuminating example is a recent qualitative study of 35 lone-parent fathers in the north-east of England. This showed that a number of the men interviewed were surprised and disappointed by the lack of attention they received as lone parents (Barker, 1994). Apart from some initial contact with court welfare officers, when custody issues were being clarified, social work intervention was minimal. Some of the lone fathers were critical of this hands-off approach, feeling that 'social welfare agencies were failing in their duties by not ensuring that everything was satisfactory in new lone father households'. The study also disclosed 'a surprising lack of involvement by health visitors in the lives of lone fathers and their children'. It concluded that 'a sizeable minority of lone fathers felt they would have benefited from some professional being available to give them advice and validation in their parenting roles, [and] health visitors would have been ideally placed to have adopted such roles, and some lone fathers were surprised that they had not' (Barker, 1994). The author makes no substantive claims as to what caused this tentative approach, but speculates that it could arise from mis-management, a respect for patriarchal rights to authority and privacy, difficulties in (female) health visitors relating to (male) parents, or some other cause. But the result was clear: what the author calls 'fit fatherhood' was neither being nurtured nor monitored.

While no equivalent research has been carried out on intervention with lone fathers in Ireland, there is much anecdotal evidence to suggest that similar patterns exist here and, moreover, that fathers in general – whatever their status – tend to be avoided by welfare professionals. In conducting teaching sessions with public health nurses, for instance, many will admit to not being pro-active in engaging fathers and, at worst, regarding them as a nuisance if they do stay around during the visit, getting in the way of the 'real' business that must be done with mother and child. There is also much anecdotal evidence that the general pattern is for general practitioners to spend relatively little time in consultations with men as compared to women. The very language we use – 'maternity services' – betrays how we have institutionalised the absent father in the health and social services. While we accept that men are now much more included in ante-natal classes and at childbirth, it is no exaggeration to say that there simply are no 'paternity services', and the sooner this changes the better it will be for all.

This avoidance of men occurs despite the fact that socio-economic changes have resulted in there being many more 'vulnerable' fathers, such as long-term unemployed men who are at home with children. In chapter one, we estimated that there were 5,000 lone parent fathers with children under the age of 15 in Ireland in 1996, of whom about 40% were unemployed (see Table 1.2, chapter one). At the very least, such men, like all fathers, are in need of engagement around how they see their role, and what their needs as fathers are in terms of advice and support services. There is also evidence that the absence of fathers from welfare intervention and support programmes is a two-way process. Just as professionals avoid men, many fathers tend to resist engaging with welfare practitioners, regarding such encounters as 'women's business' (Milner, 1996). Typically, mothers and professionals such as public health nurses are left to get on with it.

The attitudes and general orientation of the welfare professionals undoubtedly have a significant bearing in shaping such bias in social intervention. But so too do men's attitudes to becoming involved with the services, and the degree to which they define themselves as active fathers and co-parents. In practice, many men are not available due to work and other commitments during the hours when services are being delivered.

Selective Intervention with Abusive Fathers

'Think of an infant boy warmly wrapped up in his baby blanket, expecting the best from life and having no reason to believe that anything other than good things would come to him. What's the word that comes to mind when you think of this baby? Violent? Potential Rapist? Cold? Distant? Unable to express his feelings? Boorish? Hardly; for he is innocent and gorgeous. So what happens?'

Peter Kieran (1997)

At the other end of the continuum, even in those situations where there is reason to be deeply concerned about fathers who are known or suspected of putting their children and/or partners at risk of abuse, the bulk of the work has gone into mothers. Recent research into child protection work in Ireland demonstrates how social workers and other professionals place women at the centre of intervention in ways that can empower and support them and their children; equally, however, it disempowers them because it is a form of discriminatory practice that simply expects too much of women and little or nothing of men (Buckley, 1997). One Irish study that examined the response to cases where there was concern about both domestic violence and child abuse, found that while the man was the suspected abuser in the vast majority of cases, most of the work went into the mothers as generally the (violent) men were ignored, avoided or themselves managed to avoid the prof-essionals (Ferguson, 1997b).

These findings are supported by official reports concerned with child abuse, such as the *Report of the Kilkenny Incest Investigation* (McGuinness, 1993), which notes the absence of work with men and the importance of trying to get more fathers involved in family support services as a way of preventing abuse and parenting difficulties. Similar trends have been disclosed in research into UK policy and practice (Milner, 1993; DHSS, 1995).

Professional avoidance of men who are abusive in intimate relationships arises from a number of factors. Such men generate fear for personal safety and a sense of hopelessness that they cannot or will not change, no matter what is done. It is a symptom of a lack of confidence that has arisen from the general neglect of work with men and the skills deficit that needs to be corrected in the health, social and criminal justice services (Ferguson and Synott, 1995). The upshot is that 'social workers unwittingly collude with ... the effective minimisation of father's roles and behaviour by concentrating on women who provide a softer target for their efforts' (Milner, 1996, p. 119).

As one social work academic and former practitioner has wisely observed, it is one thing to recognise deficits in skills and confidence around work with men, and quite another to change it (O'Hagan, 1997). As well as changing attitudes and awareness of gender issues, the institutional development of actual programmes that work with abusive men has a crucial role to play. Intervention programmes based on group work with violent men have been developing in Ireland since the late 1980s, and there are now two distinct programmes in existence: the MOVE (Ireland) – Men Overcoming ViolencE – programme, and the Cork Domestic Violence Project (Ferguson and Synott, 1995; O'Connor, 1996; Cork and Ross Family Centre, 1995). A failure to engage violent men is at least in part a product of the limited intervention options available to practitioners. Once such 'treatment' options become available, then the more professionals in the community become aware of and use them, practice can be re-orientated to focus more strategically on abusive fathers.

It is crucial that the specific development of work with abusive men takes place through the adoption of core principles for best practice which have now been set out as the basis for government policy in this area (Task Force on Violence Against Women, 1997, chapter 10). These include the importance of an approach that is based on accountability, which can best be achieved through an inter-agency approach that ties the 'treatment' of male batterers into sanctions and the criminal justice system. Intervention programmes are known to be most effective if they operate through a groupwork approach. They need to be accountable also to the abused woman, whose safety must be the guiding concern of all work with batterers. Programmes need to have ways of verifying the woman's safety and well-being at all times, ideally through developing support groups for survivors of abuse (O'Connor, 1996). These can also play a vital role in boosting victim confidence to carry through legal actions and, more generally, to promoting healing. The aim of intervention programmes is not 'treatment' in the conventional medical sense which implies illness. Men who batter are not sick; their behaviour is learned and the decisions they make to be violent are motivated by a desire to exercise power and control over their partners. What is required, therefore, are intervention programmes that seek to re-educate abusive men into forming non-violent intimate relationships. While there is always a need for caution in measuring the outcomes of such programmes, research evidence suggests that out of all the options available – including voluntary attendance at batterers' programmes, fines, a caution, arrest with no subsequent prosecution, probation – men who have been mandated by the courts, and have completed groupwork programmes that operate through an inter-agency ap-proach around the principle of accountability, are the most likely to become self-regulating and non-violent. Crucially, becoming non-abusive is defined here in the broad sense of ceasing all forms of violence: physical, sexual, emotional, economic, and isolation and control of victim's movements (Dobash and Dobash, 1996).

Perhaps the most disturbing feature of the failure to work with abusive men is the fact that so few attempts are being made to work with *known* offenders, especially those who have been imprisoned for such offences. It is now broadly accepted within the professional community that sanctions and 'treatment' programmes are the only way to ensure that offenders will have any chance of stopping abusing and to protect future victims. Yet, treatment programmes for sexually abusive fathers and offenders of all types are scandalously undeveloped in this State. This is despite the best efforts of front-line professionals, such as probation officers and psychologists, who are working with offenders and who advocate the extension of treatment facilities (Geiran, 1996). Existing treatment programmes include the Northside Inter-Agency Project in Dublin, a community based groupwork intervention focused on adolescent male sex offenders (McGrath, 1992). The National Forensic Psychiatric Service at the Central Mental Hospital, Dublin works primarily, though not exclusively, with intra-familial offenders. The Grenada Institute in Dublin works primarily, though not exclusively, with sex-offending priests. The best known programme is that at Arbour Hill Prison, Dublin which is jointly run by the Probation and Welfare and the Psychological Service of the Department of Justice, Equality and Law Reform. This caters for a mixed group of imprisoned sex offenders and is the one Irish programme with official backing at a central policy level. As Geiran (1996, p. 140) observes, while there are some 300 sex offenders in Irish prisons at any one time, just 10 of these at a time participate in the Arbour Hill programme, which commenced in June 1994. Low rates of take up arise, in part, because participation on the programme is voluntary and it is left up to offenders themselves as to whether they wish to seek rehabilitation. We believe strongly that participation of sex offenders in treatment programmes should be mandatory. Unless it is made compulsory, large numbers of known sex offenders will continue to be released into the community without any real attempt having been made to directly address their offending behaviour. But in demonstrating such administrative ir-rationality and failure to even attempt to reform (rather than simply contain) most offenders, responses to sex offenders merely exemplify how the Irish criminal justice system fails to work in general (McCullagh, 1996).

Similar issues of accountability arise once convicted sex offenders are released into the community. While far from being a panacea, we welcome the announcement in August 1998 by the Department of Justice, Equality and Law Reform of its intention to create a Register of sex offenders to monitor offenders after release.

Men are not always the abusers nor, more generally, the person in the family who is the cause of the problem. At its most extreme, some argue that violence against men by wives – 'battered husbands' – is a major, if hidden, social problem in Ireland which is on the increase (Stitt and Macklin, 1997). Such concerns led in 1998 to the founding of the organisation AMEN, a helpline for male victims of domestic violence. This organisation already claims to have received huge numbers of calls from abused men (AMEN, 1998).

The whole point of intervention into the lives of abusive fathers should be to enable them to do the kind of work on themselves that leads them to form non-violent, respectful, intimate relationships. When this process does work, the man has the opportunity to become a co-parent – a true resource for his partner who, very often in such cases, is herself struggling to parent well. Thus, in less serious cases of child welfare involving borderline parenting, the resourcefulness of fathers to protect and promote the welfare of children in vulnerable family situations is rarely considered, let alone promoted by State intervention.

While child sexual abuse tends to gain more media attention, child 'neglect' is still the most commonly reported problem investigated by health boards (Ferguson, 1996b). It is a complex phenomenon which is characterised by the inter-relationship of poverty, disad-vantage, deficits in parenting skills and personal coping resources, all of which require that, where present, fathers as well as mothers are mobilised as active carers. In practice, the majority of abuse cases involve children who are 'in need' and who are being parented in circum-stances of material and emotional adversity. A strategic focus on fathers needs to be part of an overall approach which is not only concerned with intervention after the fact of 'abuse', but which also identifies and integrates vulnerable households into supportive childcare services in a manner that seeks to prevent either abuse or the need for children to be received into care (Ferguson and Kenny, 1995).

Thus, it is clear that in 'high risk' parenting, public policy faces a major challenge in re-focusing practice from its primary concern with the ability of mothers 'to protect' their children. There are undoubtedly situations where, for reasons of safety to women, children and the professionals themselves, it is quite legitimate not to be man-centred or father-centred in intervention. However, the general absence of work with men means that many are being illegitimately 'missed' by the services, with a high cost to women, children and men themselves.

Fathers, Men and Public Childcare Provision

> 'The less sleep I need,
> The more pain I can take,
> The more alcohol I can hold,
> The less I concern myself with what I eat,
> The less I ask anybody for help, or depend on them,
> The more I control and repress my emotions,
> The less attention I pay to myself physically,
> The more masculine I am.'
> Herb Goldberg, *The New Male*

It has already been noted in chapter five that men are virtually absent from childcare and related services. As Murphy's comprehensive analysis of Irish child welfare and family support services shows, the involvement of men in the public provision of childcare, in crèches, family and day care services is virtually non-existent (Murphy, 1996). While women have engaged enthusiastically in the vast array of community and personal development initiatives that have developed in recent years, mainly in the voluntary sector, men are virtual strangers to such services. Ryland's study of parenting programmes in Ireland confirms that the take-up by fathers is minimal (Ryland, 1995). It would be too much to claim that all childcare services have been established for women to the conscious exclusion of men. This can happen, but in general the process is more subtle than that. Family centres, crèches and such like, are theoretically open to men, but the impact of deeply gendered assumptions and practices concerning who the primary parent is results in their uptake by women, avoidance by men and the pervasive identification of such services with mothers.

Moreover, it is women who do the bulk of professional childcare work. In the Irish Pre-School Playgroups Association, about 20 of their 1,700 members are men (fact derived from personal communication). In primary schools it is rare for male teachers to take infants classes; only one man in the Cork area, for instance, is currently known to do so. The prevailing ideology is that teachers get 'promoted' out of junior infants, the implication being that the 'real' work of teaching goes on with older children and adults (personal communication with Dr Francis Douglas, University College Cork). At second level, the subject of Home Economics is taken by a third of all pupils, mostly girls, and all who teach it, with one or two exceptions, are women.

The under-involvement of fathers in parenting and support services is underpinned by perceptions of the 'feminised' nature of child rearing, which aptly reflects the gendered reality that childcare work – both in public and private domains – is predominantly women's work. Similar patterns are evident in social work and other helping services. As Doherty's analysis of service providers in the Midland and Mid-Western Health Boards has shown, 85% of the front-line social workers employed in those two Health Boards are women (Doherty, 1996). Management structures, however, are male-dominated as senior positions are overwhelmingly held by men.

Changing Fathers?

A picture emerges of a dominant form of State inter-vention into family life that is deeply gendered. While the day-to-day work of public and private childcare is essentially feminised, being predominantly done by women, men's roles are largely restricted to childcare 'managers'. They are the administrators of family life; bureaucratic men whose (paternal) authority lies in organisational rationality and accountability, but not in the emotional depth and commitment that true intimacy and mentoring of the next generation demands. At best, then, men are the *imaginary* heads of public and private 'households', as it were. For while men have very real administrative power, they have limited involvement in terms of day-to-day childcare practice, and their direct impact on the domain of the intimate appears limited. That said, the ways in which men perform these administrative tasks in terms of promoting openness and emotional communication for staff are crucial.

This suggests to us that it is not only vital for fathers to take an active paternal role with children, and to be acknowledged for doing so, but for welfare agencies and practitioners to adopt perspectives on intervention which are open to acknowledging and fostering men's active role with children and in family life. Thus, in saying that social intervention essentially ignores fathers, we are not arguing that this reflects a simple reality where women are the primary parents and men do nothing at home. That may be the case in some households. We are arguing, rather, that there is a palpable gender bias in how expertise and intervention actually shape the sit-uation that encourages mothers, but not fathers, to be the primary carers. It is a bias that effectively ignores the work done by fathers and prevents the fatherhood role from developing to its full potential by keeping men stuck in traditional roles and, at worst, discouraging them from getting involved with children at all.

The professional community must become fully aware of guiding assumptions and practices around gender roles. It needs to reconceptualise and reshape its re-lationship to fathers and mothers if it is to genuinely allow

208

for the empowerment of men as well as women as active parents. This argument links directly to that made in chapter four concerning the developmental perspective and the urgent need for professionals to understand, and capitalise on, father's generative energy as a way of helping them to engage in childcare and acquire similar developmental pathways around responsibility and caring as their partners. As Murphy concludes: 'The real challenge for public policy will be to convince fathers and men in general that there are real gains to be made for them and their children from acknowledging and developing emotional literacy. Authoritarian child-rearing approaches will need to be replaced by the skills of nurturance and negotiation in the more democratised personal relationships of a post-modern society' (Murphy, 1996, p. 95).

In our view, this represents just as great a challenge for 'public' fathers who hold administrative power and the reins of public policy in the State, as it does for the parenting practices of fathers in private.

Intervention with Vulnerable Fathers

'I didn't confront life, or myself, until my father died ... But then my dad's death was totally unexpected. He was 64, fairly young, in good shape but had a massive coronary. Fortunately our relationship was really good at the time. We definitely were very comfortable with each other. Whereas, for years, we'd had a fierce relationship.
Drink played a part, in a kind of subtle, middle-class way. Dad's drinking was disguised. He never lost his grip on things, but he allowed our relationship to deteriorate. And it was the band that finally gave me the strength to leave home. And the money I needed. But, even during all that time the love was never completely blotted out. It's just that the way he expressed love was so hard. And even in the end, we never really did talk, in depth, about the love we really felt for each other.'
Liam O Maonlai (of Hothouse Flowers, quoted in *The Irish Times*, 29 May 1998)

Although we tend not to view men as vulnerable, there is increasing evidence to suggest that vulnerability is at the heart of the male condition, no less than it is for women. What differs between the sexes is how vulnerability is experienced and responded to. The most tragic and alarming indicator of this is the apparent increase in suicide among men. While the female rate has remained relatively stable over time, suicides by men have risen in recent years to the extent that the male-female ratio is now about 4:1. The largest increases are among young men, aged between 15 and 25 years, for whom suicide is now the most common cause of death, greater even than road accidents (National Task Force on Suicide, 1998). While the reasons why people take their lives are clearly complex, the gender differences are such that commentators now broadly accept that the impact of social changes, such as increased unemployment, on men's identities, and the greater difficulties males have in admitting to personal distress and accessing help, are contributory factors (Kelleher, 1996). Moreover, research is showing that suicide is a predominantly rural phenomenon in Ireland, making its links with social factors such as isolation all the more pronounced (Kelleher et al., 1997). Clearly, finding ways of linking vulnerable men and fathers into social networks, and changing how men cope with their distress, are crucial to helping prevent such tragedies and promoting men's health in general.

Fathers from different social backgrounds have different needs in terms of State services and supports. The specific issues pertaining to non-resident fathers, and working fathers, for instance, are dealt with elsewhere in the book. Particular concern needs to be focussed on the situation of what can be called 'vulnerable' fathers and especially men who are socially excluded. Before elaborating further on their particular needs, it should be stressed that 'mainstream' men, even those who are middle-class and relatively affluent, can be extremely vulnerable fathers in the general sense of experiencing major problems with intimacy and forming worthwhile relationships with their children and partners – and indeed other men.

Terrence Real, an American family therapist and academic, in his book *I Don't Want to Talk About It: Overcoming The Secret Legacy of Male Depression,* names and gives shape to the huge problem of depression among men which is so often ignored and misunderstood. This is not least by men themselves. *Overt depression* is characterised by feelings of worth-lessness, worry, poor concentration, helplessness, poor sleep and so on. Clinical work with men who are depressed shows that their poor experiences of being fathered are central motifs in their problems with intimacy and depression and their difficulties in forging meaningful emotional connections with their own children and partners. What Real calls *covert depression* settles below the level of consciousness as the man desperately defends against the onslaught of acknowledging such pain. Whereas overt depression involves surrendering to and enduring the toxic relationship to the self, covert depression involves warding off all toxic shame, at any price. The covertly depressed man relies on external stimulants to rectify an inner baseline of shame. His life is governed by ways of relating and activities (work, 'achievements', addiction to alcohol, drugs, sex, dieting) which, rather than enhancing an already adequate sense of self-esteem, desperately try to prop up an inadequate one. It is an experience of depression that 'is not about feeling bad so much as losing the capacity to feel at all' (*Ibid*, p. 55).

Real argues that such problems have to be understood in the context of how men acquire a gender identity. The traditional process of becoming masculine, he argues, 'teaches boys to replace inherent self-worth with performance-based esteem. It insists that boys disown vulnerable feelings (which could help them connect) while reinforcing their entitlement to express anger' (Real, 1997, p. 276). Gaining an identity from performance-based es-teem – over-valuing work, sport and countless other public achievements – to the neglect of inherent self-worth means that how boys become men is a negative achievement; not so much an acquisition as a disavowal, a rejection. The achievement of masculine identity, Real (1997, p. 130) argues, is not so much a process of development as one of elimination of the nurturing self – a successive unfolding of loss. Feminine socialisation also brings costs, of course, although women have been pressurised to give up different things, in particular the development of a self-concept and skills that belong to performance and success in the public world.

The implications of this analysis has relevance to men from all social backgrounds. It reveals the hidden pain apparently experienced by many (but obviously not all) 'driven', affluent and outwardly successful men. At worst, especially if such men have had other painful experiences, such as abuse and humiliation by their own fathers (O'Connor, 1997), the need to stay disconnected from feelings and stay 'in control' can lead them to become violent and batter their spouses and children, demonstrating that such violence is prevalent in all social classes (Task Force on Violence Against Women, 1997). Alternatively, they may even end up trying to kill themselves, too often succeeding.

Real distinguishes between *active* trauma and *passive* trauma in men's lives. The latter refers to the routine repudiation of the nurturing self that males tend to experience in the process of becoming men. Their capacity for intimacy is chipped away in small bits, through passive trauma from the most ordinary interactions and the demand that they relinquish the relational side of themselves. This leads to an acceptance by males of psychological neglect, a discounting of nurture and the turning of the vice of such abandonment into a manly virtue (Real, 1997, p. 134). This means that male conditioning not only leads to the experience of such trauma, but also a requirement that men carry their pain 'silently' as disclosure of it is culturally restricted within the dominant norms of acceptable masculinity.

Some men brought up in flagrantly abusive environments experience active trauma from sexual abuse, beatings and so on, and they are at high risk of losing their capacity for intimacy in great chunks. The same is true of female victims of abuse, but in the context of the primary concerns of this book, a clear focus also needs to be maintained on the needs of male survivors. While not all sexually abused boys grow up to be offenders, without adequate treatment there is a greatly increased possibility that they will. A high incidence of childhood sexual victimisation has been found among sex offenders. Boys can have particular problems disclosing abuse and accepting the victim role and treatment because of the corrosive impact of an ideology of masculinity that says males should be invulnerable and able to defend themselves. Treatment needs to engage both with boys' victimisation and their sense of spoiled gender identity. In a homophobic culture, a fear of 'becoming gay' can lead men to develop a hypermasculinity which leads to sex crimes, such as rape, to prove they are men. It is a cruel paradox that this can lead to men to revisit on boys, as well as girls, the very crimes they are seeking to compensate for.

In his book *The Male Survivor*, Mendel (1995) shows that a critical distinction between victimised men who go on to perpetrate abuse and those who do not is the ability of the latter to integrate their experience of victimisation and access their feelings of pain, loss and vulnerability. Sex offenders, by contrast, may emerge from their childhood victimisation primarily experiencing anger, which is expressed via sexually abusive acts. The crucial variable shown up in all studies is the provision of treatment in adolescence to overcome the trauma of the abuse. It is crucial that adequate resources are provided so that treatment services for victims can be offered to promote the kind of healing that can equip male survivors to form healthy intimate relations.

Real draws out the contradictory experiences and expectations that now surround masculinity which compound the difficulties vulnerable men have in coming forward for help. Society on the one hand now wants men to be more in touch with their inner-selves and feelings and, on the other, colludes in not allowing men to be vulnerable by often punishing those men who do take the risk of intimate exposure. He cites American studies of college room-mates where female students reached out to their room-mates for support about being depressed and were met with caring and nurturing reactions. By contrast, when male students disclosed depression to their room-mates, they were met with social isolation and often outright hostility. Real concludes: 'It is true that men do not easily disclose their depression. But it also seems true that many may have good reason to hide' (*Ibid*, p. 38). He also shows that GPs, for instance, tend to know little or nothing about men's inner-lives and how to approach and assess them on an effective level in non-traditional ways. This kind of research and clinical experience exposes the shadow side to Western manhood, and the price of power that many men experience, and the need for men to re-define masculinity and gender relations in more self-regarding, mutually supportive and caring ways (Kimmel, 1994).

Such studies are also significant because they recognise the urgent need to develop *methodologies* of working with men. It is one thing to recognise that some vulnerable men/fathers, and those they live with, are in trouble. It is quite another to get them to come forward, engage directly about their problems and use help. The challenge is to get them to identify problems like depression and move beyond 'our love of invulnerability' (Real, p. 38) and defences to achieve intimacy and learn the 'hard discipline of learning to love from within' (*Ibid*, p. 57). This has to involve the man 'stopping running' and dealing with the pain that has driven his behaviour. 'First, the covertly depressed man must walk through the fire from which he has run. He must allow the pain to surface. Then, he may resolve his hidden depression by learning about self-care and healthy esteem' (Real, 1997, p. 63).

For Terrence Real, in the midst of adversity, there is considerable hope for men and signs that increasing numbers are prepared to do the personal development work necessary to lead fuller lives. 'In the men I treat', he writes, 'there is often an initial resistance, a kind of shudder, at having to give up the traditional notion that a man need not work much, either emotionally or physically, in his own home, but most of the depressed men I work with are grateful to find new courses of action that actually improve their family's lives. They are pleased to be with a happier partner in a more loving household. I have also found that a great many men want more for themselves as well. They want to experience themselves more fully, even if it means encountering pain. Just as many depressed women are tired of their oppression and willing to risk security to begin asserting their needs, many depressed men are tired of their disconnection and ready to tolerate the humility, the fall from hubris, implicit in listening to the needs of others' (Real, 1997, p. 311).

Working with Men, Masculinities and Socially Excluded Fathers

Men from different social class and ethnic backgrounds appear to have different needs in terms of vulnerability and support. This is not to say for one moment that all men from socially disadvantaged communities are worse fathers than men from better off circumstances. That is palpably untrue. What can be said, however, is that we do need to pay particular attention to those men whose (traditional) identities have been thrown into turmoil through being excluded from the labour market through long-term unemployment, and, in the case of traveller men, marginalised from the settled community. The traditional ways in which Traveller men made a living, such as through scrap metal and making various household goods for sale, have been eroded in recent times, thereby weakening their economic base. Some within the Travelling community, such as Ellen Mangan, argue that their sense of themselves as men has similarly been weakened. This process of increased marginalisation is exacerbated by the men's apparent reluctance to get involved in employment training schemes established for the settled community (Ellen Mangan, cited in the *Sunday Independent*, 17 May 1998).

In situations involving vulnerable long-term unemployed men, redefining their role can be literally a matter of survival. The pain and struggles involved in such processes are vividly illustrated by the experience of 37 year-old Pat, a father of three, who has been unemployed on and off for the past ten years. Pat's story is related in an article by Ray Smith (1995, pp. 36–7), a community worker in Dublin who has been active in working with long-term unemployed men and in the development of men's groups:

'I became unemployed when the company I worked for closed down. I had a very good relationship with my employer and felt secure in my work. I was very happy there. I remember feeling shattered when the job went. I felt insecure and wondered if I could get a job anywhere else.

I particularly remember one day at rush hour outside a factory. People were coming out of there looking tired, I saw them achieving something and saw myself as having nothing. I decided at that point never to go out again at that particular time.

Shortly after losing my job I began walking from place to place looking for work with little success. I really felt angry and betrayed by the company owner, but as I looked for other jobs, I really did not want to go into another place of work, I wanted my old job back.

I felt that I was a failure, I owed rent on my accommodation, I had lost contact with friends and I had lost contact with the people I worked with. I was not looking after myself well and had let my appearance go.

I managed to pick up casual work but found myself moving from job to job. I was constantly late for work and at that time I returned to bed-wetting habits. When I was young I used to wet the bed. My mother would always change the sheets the next day, she never made an issue of it. Sometimes when it happened she would just change the bed without mentioning it.

The time that followed was a horrible time. There was real poverty in my life and I could not include myself in any social activity. I also could not bear to say to people I was unemployed as I saw myself as a complete failure and worthless.

I used to wake several times at night, get up and make coffee and smoke. I'd then sleep late. I felt my children had little respect for me and saw me as doing nothing. When I did get work over the past few years I would blame myself when the job closed down, thinking I brought that on.

During that time I developed stomach ulcers and I also suffered from excessive tiredness. I'd go to bed in the middle of the day, sometimes just to escape the boredom. More recently I've developed rheumatoid arthritis but I drink a lot of tea and smoke which does not help.

Through my involvement in groups I have reflected on my life experience. I have learned of my fear of loss of control of events. I have also moved from achievements based on influences outside of myself to internal ach-ievements. I work with youth in my community, I learned to play the guitar and sing and play at sessions for which I am paid for my performance.'

Pat's story painfully illustrates the trauma involved for men in the loss of identity and meaning that can arise from long-term unemployment. As Smith (1995) observes, such men can get stuck in grief, mourning for the loss of the 'productive' self, and have huge problems finding meaning in domestic roles and intimacy. It should be emphasised that no amount of personal development work can ever be allowed to take the place of political action to provide meaningful roles for men, both at work and without work, or excuse the sheer poverty that socially excluded fathers and their families are forced to suffer. Yet, as Pat's story shows, personal development work alongside other men in a men's group played a key role in his survival and redefinition of himself. In essence, applied to the argument of this book (see chapter four), what Pat was able to do in turning his life around was to (re)discover his generative energy, gaining meaning in caring for youth – the next generation. Taking on an active fatherhood role can also be a way for socially excluded men to find a meaningful place and value in society. At the core of this is helping men to replace what Terrence Real (1997) calls performance-based esteem with inherent self-worth. In Pat's insightful words, moving 'from achievements based on influences outside of myself to internal achievements'.

The perspective adopted in working with socially excluded men/fathers is crucial in determining successful outcomes. Adopting a conventional pro-feminist approach which emphasises to these men that they should become more involved in childcare for reasons of social justice, because they have power, is problematic. This is because they usually feel powerless, and this aptly reflects the subordinate structural position they find themselves in. An approach that just emphasises fairness and equality issues, as discussed in chapter four, is unlikely to work with men who themselves feel that they have been treated unfairly. Indeed, it is likely to make things worse for these men and their families as they eventually refuse to engage at all with the services and become even more isolated.

We are not arguing that such men should be approached as victims and not be challenged as well as supported in how they manage change. The key point is both methodological and substantive. Men who are suffering in such circumstances need primarily to have their pain, loss and struggles affirmed. They need help to (re)negotiate a new masculine identity and (re)discover their essential worth as human beings, inherent self-worth, their capacity for generativity and to have an opportunity to give value to, communicate and to *receive* such care in social relationships. Through this process, which is as much a spiritual journey as a psychological or sociological one, men may be helped to (re)claim new meaning in fatherhood and intimate relations more generally (Arthurs, Ferguson and Grace, 1995).

Vulnerable men, in particular, need to be linked into wider social networks and need to engage in development work around fathering and masculinity in general in the presence of other men. The further development of structures such as men's groups can actively reach out to such men and break into their isolation and sense of failure and create structures for mutual support. Through this process, which can be a genuinely healing one, a space is created in which issues of justice and responsibility can be addressed, and men can reach an operational definition of themselves as 'good fathers' that is in tune with their own needs and perspectives and those of their partner and children (see also chapters one and four). It should be stressed that such personal development work is relevant to vulnerable men who *have* problems, such as depression and social isolation, but not to those men, such as abusive fathers, who *are* problems. As we argued earlier, it is crucial that the latter are approached through models of work that are based on accountability and sanctions where men are compelled to take responsibility for the problems they cause (Ferguson, 1998).

Fergus Hogan (1998) has argued that, rather than being 'challenged' to get involved, the spirit of work with men who have problems requires that such vulnerable men, and indeed boys, are *invited* into intimacy. Hogan brings his rich experience of working with families in a child guidance setting to bear on theorising about ways of working with males. Many young men are brought to him as either having or being problems, and a key therapeutic task is to try and get through their often solid defences to access their emotions and their view of their lives. Creative use of language and story, he argues, holds a key. Drawing, for instance, on his own experience of the confusion of adolescence which manifested itself in pains in his bones, he invites young men to speak of their 'growing pains'. While equipped with the traditional skills of storytelling that tend to characterise the Irish, Hogan argues that the impact of the social construction of (a non-expressive) masculinity means that what men tend to lack is skill in telling *intimate* stories about their inner-lives. What he calls 'soulful storytelling' is based on the use of poetry and story by both the therapist and the client, and is a way to crack open the armour and access the male imagination and emotions, thereby promoting healing and personal development. His work has important reson-ances with the 'mytho-poetic' tradition of working with men pioneered in the United States by Michael Meade (1993) and Robert Bly (1990).

The men's spouse and children also need support. Families of distressed men may worry about the stigma that surrounds depression and, because of an impulse to 'protect the male ego', may collude in the man's denial of his problem and reluctance to receive help. But as Terrence Real remarks, 'when we minimise a man's depression, for fear of shaming him, we collude with the cultural expectations of masculinity in a terrible way. We send a message that the man who is struggling should not expect help. He must be 'self-reliant'. He must resolve his distress on his own' (Real, 1997, pp. 38–9).

Based both on our reading of the literature and, perhaps more importantly still, our experience of working with men's groups, men coming together in men's groups to discuss their lives as men have much to offer in how they can resolve their distress. More generally, leaving aside problems such as depression, other men are a major but still largely untapped resource for men to gain support and develop personally. Undoubtedly, men's needs for support can be met by their partners and perhaps other close relatives and friends. In arguing for the further development of men's groups as productive ways to in-tervene in men's lives, we are not seeking to invalidate the mutual support that can be found in modern marriages, but are recognising the limits to intimacy that can often be achieved within the couple or other privatised relationships. Nor are we prescribing that all men should be in men's groups. Clearly, some men do not feel the need for them while others would actively wish to avoid them, irrespective of their needs. As Alan O'Neill, a full-time men's development worker and co-ordinator of the South-East Men's Network suggests, men enter men's groups 'because life is hard. Our relationships with women, children, men and our colleagues prove to be more difficult than we imagined. A growing number of Irish men have realised that it's time for men to take responsibility for ourselves and that the best way of doing that is getting together with like minded men' (personal communication with Alan O'Neill).

All men's groups are not the same in terms of their approach and ideology. The so-called men's movement is replete with what Connell (1995) calls 'masculinity politics': differing views on what it means to be a man and what the project of men working together should essentially be about (see, Clatterbaugh, 1997). The key polarities of the debate surround whether men and men's groups see themselves as trying to transcend traditional power relations between the sexes – essentially seeking to promote men's development into new forms of social relations between men and children, men and women and men and other men based on equality and open, emotional communication – or as operating from a 'men's rights' perspective to challenge what they perceive as the post-feminist dominance of women in society, trying to 'win back' men's entitlements (to work, for instance), reassert traditional masculinity and reinvent patriarchy (for an extended discussion, see Kimmel, 1995).

The kinds of men's groups that seem most suited to promoting good fatherhood are those which focus on the domain of relationships and self-concepts. This does not mean avoiding issues such as father's rights, but that men's groups that are orientated around personal development can provide an important reference point for the collective (re)negotiation of men's roles and identities – a challenge that all men face today, whether we like it or not. All men should at the very least have the opportunity to engage in such personal development with other men should they wish and this needs to be regarded as a legitimate thing for men to do.

221

While, by definition, working with men and masculinities means focusing in particular on the male gender, this should not be seen as a simplistic argument for a separatist agenda for men. Traditional patterns of gender socialisation have meant that men tend to lose touch with the emotional basis of society and themselves, while women became the 'specialists in love and the emotions' (Giddens, 1992). Thus, a real value of men working together, separately from women, is that it leaves men without the traditional support of women to do the 'emotional work', challenging men to provide mutual care and develop relational responsibility for ourselves and other men. In addition, Alan O'Neill, co-ordinator of the South-East Men's Network argues that 'it's good for men to address men's issues on their own because some of the misinformation that men carry about themselves is very nasty and it's safer that men admit to and acknowledge this nastiness in men only gatherings' (personal communication with Alan O'Neill). Yet in a crucial sense the aim of such work is to promote men's capacities to develop satisfying relationships with women and children, as well as other men (Kieran, 1997).

Despite the growing awareness and popularity of men's groups, significant barriers remain to men meeting with men for the primary purpose of critical reflection, support and personal development. This has much to do with how we have constructed dominant forms of masculinity and the impact of homophobia which appears to underlie many people's fears of men engaging with other men in this self-conscious way. The leap in imagination, understanding and conceptualisation of masculinities that it takes to view men as vulnerable and in need of such support should not be underestimated. We are simply not accustomed to seeing men as vulnerable. The dominant construction of masculinity in Ireland constitutes an ideology – a series of images and cultural rules against which manhood tends to be assessed – which adds up to the view that men are essentially invulnerable. While men (and women) never buy into these ideologies in any simple sense, they still impact hugely on what men internalise and how men feel about themselves and others, and their capacity for intimacy (for an extended discussion of these issues, see Ferguson, 1997a; Bannon, 1976).

A critical issue here is the social relations of power that exist, not only between men and women, but also between men where value is given to some forms of masculinities more than others (Connell, 1995). There is, then, a hierarchy of masculinities which means that, while men in general hold social power, some have far more power than others, and some are actively subordinated and have lost the 'patriarchial dividend' (Connell, 1995). At a public level, the hegemonic definition of masculinity still values power which is exercised – mostly by men – in such a way that alternative ways of being and viewing men are closed off. Within this exemplary form of masculinity, qualities and practices of care and nurture are subordinated and associated not merely with femininity but, at worst, with gayness – a form of masculinity which is constructed as the worst thing a man can be, containing all that is eliminated from hegemonic masculinity: from 'real manhood'. Homophobia refers here to the fear not just of sexual contact with other men, but of any forms of intimate contact between men. Men come to fear revealing a self which we have constructed culturally in terms of 'feminine' or gay characteristics, accentuating the neglect of the nurturing self. Even though many men and fathers can transcend the worst effects of such an ideology and go on to form nurturing relationships, its toxic effects can be seen in the difficulties many men have in acknowledging their personal problems and in experiencing emotions and communicating them. Thus, all men have to bargain with the dominant ideology that constitutes hegemonic masculinity. Challenging gay oppression and homophobia is crucial, therefore, to reconstructing masculinity to include more 'acceptable' caring qualities and to opening up opportunities for men to access the necessary social supports and, where necessary, to recognise their vulnerability in order to promote their well-being as men and fathers (Ferguson, 1998).

Recent research has begun to challenge the prevailing image of male invulnerability by showing, for instance, that men are often extremely frightened by being the victims of violent crime. One study looked at 33 men who were the victims of violent assault by men and how they were affected by it. The study found that the men's experiences of being victims were traumatic and similar to women's. The men reported feelings of fear, phobias, disruption of sleep, hyper-vigilance, aggressiveness, personality change and a considerably heightened sense of vulnerability as a result of the attack (cited in Newburn and Stanko, 1994).

None of this is particularly surprising. It is the *idea* that men are invulnerable, and are not affected by such things, that stops us from seeing how many do, in reality, suffer. Thus, 'Services which assume that men do not need help or will not accept help merely collude in the reproduction of an ideology which places the traits of "strength", "resilience" and "emotional independence" at the centre of the dominant conception of masculinity' (Newburn and Stanko, 1994, p. 163).

At least some men feel vulnerable some of the time, though some are unlikely to admit to feeling so. Men 'are, as such, emotional beings capable of asking for support' (Newburn and Stanko, 1994, p. 161) and we need to maximise the opportunities for men to make such requests and come forward with their distress and worries and express their need for support. We believe that recognising men's vulnerability, and enabling them to surrender to it, constitutes an urgent agenda for professionals in the health and social services.

Interventions that focus on fatherhood in the wider context of promoting reflection and learning about masculinity and gender issues should extend into schools as well as youth and community work. Such intervention needs to address young men's definitions of themselves and their active participation as future fathers (Furstenberg, 1995). A clear concept of responsible fatherhood in the definition of masculinity needs to be clarified and adopted in intervention with young men. The beginnings of just such an initiative are being developed in Ireland by the Department of Education and Science. The project, which explores the social construction of masculinity, is aimed at all second level students in single sex boys schools and encourages boys and young men to critically reflect, in a supportive environment, on their masucline identities (Department of Education and Science, 1998).

In terms of social exclusion, strategic efforts need to be made to engage those young men who are vulnerable, and for whom the whole notion of employment has become meaningless; who do badly out of the education system and who cannot get work. The loss of a traditional masculine identity has left some such vulnerable young men impoverished in terms of a place in society. Many who become fathers are not only excluded from work, but are also excluded from parenting, either by themselves or by their partners.

The dynamics of these processes, and the possibilities for more pro-active intervention strategies, have begun to be vividly shown up in research into vulnerable young men and fathering in the inner-city. Furstenburg (1995) and Marsiglio (1995) consider how intervention pro-grammes can attempt to encourage young fathers' long-term paternal involvement and alter vulnerable young men's views about fatherhood and masculinity. Furstenburg's study is an analysis of the accounts of inner-city young men about their lives, masculine identity and struggles to become actively involved fathers. He also interviewed the young women who were mothers of the children. The meaning of fatherhood for these young mothers involved more than just helping to support children financially. 'Concern that fathers remain emo-tionally involved in their children's lives ran high' (Furstenburg, 1995, p. 125). The young men themselves mostly had similar aspirations of fatherhood – 'doing for your children' – as involving more than material assis-tance. Fatherhood meant something important to the young men as a chance to redeem themselves in the context of their unemployment with no other real opportunities for them to be a man (*Ibid*, p. 133). In practice, however, a number of the men, by their own admission, found it difficult to live up to their standards. The theme of broken promises loomed large. The fathers who disappeared from their children's lives felt real shame and loss. The rare men who managed to stay involved with children were esteemed by everyone the researcher spoke to.

The young men had no preparation at all for parenthood; most pregnancies were unplanned, and the community was suspicious of their ability to honour their pledges. In short, they were expected to fail. Nearly all of the men spoke of being emotionally undernourished by their biological fathers, leaving some feeling inadequately trained in how to be a caring father (*Ibid*, p. 134). They were faced with having to learn childcare on the job, which proved to be difficult for most of the men. Many young fathers turned out to feel more restricted by domestic routines than they imagined, unwilling – as their women partners usually saw it – to give up street life for home life and become more reliable partners in childcare. Men generally tend to think that they receive too little credit for what they do in the domestic sphere. This difference in perspective between the sexes on the amount of domestic work each does is not unique to young inner-city couples, but appears throughout social classes and lifestyles. What is particular to this group, however, is the centrality of street life. Such young men are used to coming and going as they pleased. Without establishing a reliable domestic or often work routine, such men quickly become auxiliary figures, turning up when they please, rather than co-parents. They drift apart from and finally lose contact with their children and their partners, who are disappointed and angry at the injustice of the men's failure to be supportive, and the situation breaks down.

The policy implications of such findings are particularly significant if viewed through the lens of a developmental perspective (see chapter four). A striking feature of these young men's lives is the lack of any supports to enable them to make successful developmental transitions into fatherhood. Policies and practices need to reverse this trend by addressing vulnerable young men's definitions of themselves in terms of active participation as future fathers (Furstenberg, 1995). Youth work, and work with young men in general – in schools and so on – needs to include a concept of responsible fatherhood in the definition of masculinity adopted in intervention.

In the USA, the National Urban League has endeavoured to reach out to vulnerable young men through its 'Male Responsibility Project'. In this project, young men are encouraged to delay fatherhood and concentrate on their educational and work roles. If they do contribute to an unplanned pregnancy and birth, they are expected to give priority to their father identity and assume responsibility for their children (Marsiglio, 1995, p. 92). The intervention programme attempts to support them in doing just that. Rather than postponing intervention or adopting a hands-off approach to men's involvement with their children, it is far better that we adopt practices that help fathers adjust to their new role transitions immediately. This prevents the increased difficulties that arise from providing fathers with ample time to establish a pattern of paternal irresponsibility and, most important of all, prevents children experiencing the agony of feeling abandoned by absent fathers. It is also crucial to ensure that men do not retreat from fatherhood responsibilities because they are presently limited in their ability to contribute financially to their child's support. It is the interpersonal and emotional aspects of fathering, as well as responsibilities connected with providing financial support, that must be emphasised.

Conclusion

> *'Yet in spite of this contemporary interest and signs of widespread support for an enlarged father role, the pace of change has been slow.'*
>
> Pleck (1987)

This chapter has shown that various forms of State intervention in families, particularly by health care, family care and childcare professionals, have a significant impact on fathers by shaping and reinforcing the existing parenting roles of mothers and fathers. Our analysis reveals that fathers tend to be largely ignored or avoided by State social services. These services still tend to assume that it is mothers who will take responsibility for childcare and, by making this assumption, they help to ensure that fathers do not. The State's health and social services have made little effort to get men directly involved in fatherhood – a neglect which plays into men's traditional reluctance to define themselves in terms of nurturing and caring roles. The result is an almost total absence of supports for fathers from all social backgrounds.

At every point in the analysis presented in this book, we have confronted the absence of a concept of men as active carers. From work structures, to the law, to the perspectives of health and social services professionals, men are barely visible as fathers. One of the reasons why professional caring services avoid fathers is that there is little or no concept of men's vulnerability, either in society generally or in the professional caring community specifically. This has much to do with how dominant forms of 'masculinity' are constructed and perceived in Irish society, not least by men and male-dominated institutions themselves. It has been necessary here, therefore, to start deconstructing the myth of the invulnerable man and father and to set out an agenda for intervention which can provide the kinds of supports fathers, as well as mothers, need if they are to become good parents.

There is a great deal of uncertainty among professionals about how to approach men and work with them. The experience tends to be mutual, however: just as professionals avoid men, many fathers tend to resist engaging with welfare practitioners, regarding such encounters as 'women's business'. In practice, many men are not available due to work and other commitments during the hours when services are being delivered. One of the consequences of the neglect of fathers by State services is that the resourcefulness of fathers to protect and promote the welfare of children in vulnerable family situations is rarely considered, let alone promoted by State intervention. While child sexual abuse tends to gain more media attention, child 'neglect' is still the most commonly reported problem investigated by health boards, and this clearly involves mothers as much as fathers, if not more so. Thus, public policy faces a major challenge in re-focusing practice from its primary concern with the ability of mothers 'to protect' their children and to start working with fathers so that they, too, can become more involved in the parenting process. Of equal concern is the neglect by the State of developing services aimed at rendering abusive fathers safe. It is essential that mandated treatment programmes are developed for convicted sex offenders and wife batterers to fill this gap in services and State accountability.

It was noted in chapter five that men are virtually absent from childcare and related services. The under-involvement of fathers in parenting and support services is underpinned by perceptions of the 'feminised' nature of child rearing. Within the health care system, men's roles are largely restricted to childcare 'managers'. This confers administrative power but carries limited involvement in terms of day-to-day childcare practice.

We are arguing that the gender bias in State services towards families creates a situation that does not encourage fathers to get involved with their children. We are also arguing that the professional community must become fully aware of its guiding assumptions and practices around gender roles. It needs to *re-imagine* and reshape its relationship to fathers and mothers if it is to genuinely allow for the empowerment of men, as well as women, to become active parents. The main implication to emerge from this analysis is that professionals involved in support services for families need to re-examine their practices from the perspective of fathers. These professionals include public health nurses, social workers, General Practitioners and childcare workers. In our view, professionals need to become aware of their assumptions about men and masculinity and how this leads to practices that exclude fathers. Equally, professionals need to be supported through training programmes on how to work effectively with fathers.

This chapter has considered a range of intervention strategies with fathers – from the need to develop universal state services, such as public health nursing, in ways that are more inclusive of both genders and 'father-friendly', to meeting the needs of vulnerable fathers who are suffering from problems, such as depression, through various types of clinical work, to the particular kinds of authoritative work that needs to go on with abusive fathers. In this chapter and elsewhere in the book (particularly chapters one and two) we examined the role that men's groups can play in helping men to find support from each other. We have emphasised the needs of socially excluded men, and we repeat here our endorsement of the support being given to men's groups by the Department of Social, Community and Family Affairs and suggest its expansion.

Our analysis has revealed that some young fathers are especially vulnerable because of their exclusion from the labour market as well as from parenting, either because of their own choice and circumstances or their partner's choice and circumstances. We see a need to devise programmes for these young men to help them make the transition to manhood and fatherhood. Our suspicion is that some of these young men may themselves have had poor fathering experiences and could benefit greatly from a well resourced programme – a New Opportunities Programme for Men – to explore their experiences, both past and present. Programmes like this have been tried elsewhere and could be adapted to Irish circumstances. The emergence of the Intervention Project in Single Sex Boys Schools by the Department of Education and Science for use in second level schools is a welcome and exciting devel-opment which deserves the fullest support in the light of the analysis presented in this book.

To conclude, then, in this book we have examined changing fathers in the sense of mapping out historical changes in fathers' roles as these find expression in the experience of fatherhood in contemporary Ireland. In doing this, we have declared our own commitment to the ideal of fathers being active in parenting their children and have documented the changes which, we believe, are needed to facilitate active, 'good' fathering. We have argued throughout that, as far as possible, it is desirable for fathers to be actively involved parents in the conviction that involved fathering brings benefits to the father as much as to the child and the mother. Fatherhood is an opportunity and a gift that no father should allow to pass him by. We hope that the analysis offered here, and the kinds of initiatives set out in this book, can contribute to the ongoing process of changing fathers for the benefit of children, women and men themselves.

Bibliography

Abramovitch, H. (1997), 'Images of the 'Father' in Psychology and Religion', in Lamb, M., (Editor), *The Role of the Father in Child Development*, Third Edition, New York: John Wiley and Sons, pp. 19–32.

Ackerman-Ross, S., and Khanna (1989), 'The Relationship of High Quality Day Care to Middle Class 3-Year Olds' Language Performance' in *Early Childhood Research Quarterly*, Volume 4, pp. 97–166.

Albiston, C., Maccoby, E., and Mnookin, R. (1990), 'Does Joint Legal Custody Matter?' *Stanford Law and Policy Review*, Volume 2, pp. 167–179.

AMEN (Abused Men) (1998), publicity leaflet.

Andrews, P. (1994), 'A Separated Dad is Still a Dad', Tuesday 1 November, *The Irish Times*.

Arensberg, C.A., and Kimball, S.J. (1942), *Family and Community in Ireland*, Harvard: Harvard University Press.

Arthurs, H., Ferguson, H., and Grace, E. (1995), 'Celibacy, Secrecy and the Lives of Men', *Doctrine and Life*, Volume 45, pp. 459–468.

Auden, W.H. Quoted in Hillman, J. (1996), *The Soul's Code: In Search of Character and Calling*, New York: Random House, p. xi.

Bacik, I., Kelly, A., O'Connell, M., and Sinclair, H. (1997), 'Crime and Poverty in Dublin: An Analysis of the Association between Community Deprivation, District Court Appearance and Sentence Severity', *Irish Criminal Law Journal*, Volume 7, Number 2, pp. 104–133.

Barker, R. W. (1994), *Lone Fathers and Masculinity*, Aldershot: Avesbury.

Barnes, E. (1995), 'Democracy and the Criminal Law', Paper given to the *Second Annual Burren Law School*, Ballyvaughan, 1.4.95.

Bateson, M. (1990), 'My Mother and My Father', Wilmer, H., (Editor), *Mother Father*, Illinois: Chiron Publications.

Belsey, C., and Moore, J., (Eds), (1989), *The Feminist Reader*, London: Macmillan.

Benvenuto, B., Kennedy, R. (1986), *Jacques Lacan: An Introduction*, New York: St Martin's Press.

Bergstrand, G. (1995), 'A Theological Approach to Masculinity and Equality', in *Men on Men: Eight Swedish Men's Personal*

Views on Equality, Masculinity and Parenthood. A Contribution by the Swedish government to the Fourth World Conference on Women in Beijing 1995. Sweden: Ministry of Health and Social Affairs, pp. 74–91.

Bertoia, C., E., and Drakich, J. (1995), "The Fathers' Rights Movement: Contradictions in Rhetoric and Practice', in W. Marsiglio (Editor), *Fatherhood: Contemporary Theory, Research, and Social Policy*, London: Sage.

Bjornberg, U., (Ed.), (1992), *European Parents in the 1990s: Contradictions and Comparisons*, New Brunswick and London: Transaction Publishers.

Bly, R., 1990, 'Father and Son' in Wilmer, H., (Ed.), *Mother Father*, Illinois: Chiron Publications, pp. 3–20.

Bly, R. (1990), *Iron John*, Reading, Mass: Addison-Wesley.

Bly, R. (1992), 'My Father's Wedding 1924' in Bly, R., Hillman, J., and Meade, M., (Editors), *The Rag and Bone Shop of the Heart: Poems for Men*, New York: HarperCollins Publishers.

Bowlby, J. (1969, 1973, 1980), *Attachment and Loss,* Vol. 1,2,3. Hogarth Press.

Bradshaw J., and Miller, J. (1991), *Lone Parents in the UK*, London: HMSO.

Brannen J., and Moss, P. (1991*), Managing Mothers: Dual Earner Households After Maternity Leave*, London: Macmillan.

Brannon, R. (1976), 'The male sex role – and what it's done for us lately' in Brannon, R., and David, D., (Eds), *The Forty-nine Percent Majority*, Reading, MA: Addison-Wesley.

Brazelton, TB., and Cramer, BG. (1991), *The Earliest Relationship*, London: Karnac.Buckley, H. (1997), 'Child Protection in Ireland' in Harder, M., and Pringle, K., (Editors), *Protecting Children in Europe: Towards A New Millennium*, Aalborg University Press.

Burgess, A., and Ruxton, S. (1996), *Men and Their Children: Proposals for Public Policy*, London: Institute for Public Policy Research.

Burgess, A. (1997), *Fatherhood Reclaimed: The Making of the Modern Father*, London: Vermillion.

Byrne, A. and Leonard, M. (1997), *Women and Irish Society: a Socilolgical Reader*, Belfast: Beyond the Pale Publications.

Carlsen, S. (1993), 'New Scandinavian Experiences' in *Fathers in Families of Tomorrow*, Report from the Conference held in Copenhagen, 17–18 June 1993, Copenhagen: The Ministry of Social Affairs.

Carr, A. (1998), 'Fathers in Therapy: Lessons from research', *Feedback, Journal of the Family Therapy Association of Ireland*, Volume 8, Number 1.

Carlsson, I. (1995), 'Why is Sweden devoting substantial efforts and money to an anthology on men in its preparations for the World Conference on Women?' in *Men on Men: Eight Swedish Men's Personal Views on Equality, Masculinity and Parenthood. A Contribution by the Swedish government to the Fourth World Conference on Women in Beijing 1995.* Sweden: Ministry of Health and Social Affairs, pp. 7–8.

Clatterbaugh, K. (1997), *Contemporary Perspectives on Masculinity: Men, Women and Politics in Modern Society*, Colorado: Westview Press.

Cohen, T. E. (1993), 'What do Fathers Provide?', in Hood, J. C., (Ed.), *Men, Work and Family*, Newbury Park, CA: Sage.

Colgan McCarthy, I. (ed.), (1996), *Irish Family Studies: Selected Papers*, Dublin: Family Studies Centre, University College Dublin.

Colman, A., and Colman, L. (1988), *The Father: Mythology and Changing Roles*, Illinois: Chiron Publications.

Coltrane, S. (1989), 'Household Labour and the Routine Production of Gender', *Social Problems*, Volume 36, pp. 473–490.

Coltrane, S, and Hickman, N. (1992), 'The rhetoric of rights and needs: Moral discourse in the reform of child custody and child support laws', *Social Problems*, 39(4), pp. 401–420.

Commission on the Family (1996), *Strengthening Families for Life: Interim Report to the Minister for Social Welfare*, Dublin: Commission on the Family, Department of Social Welfare.

Commission on the Family (1997), *Submission to the All-Party Oireachtas Committee on the Constitution*, 25 March, Dublin: Commission on the Family, Department of Social Welfare.

Connell, R. W. (1995), *Masculinities*, Cambridge: Polity.

Constitution Review Group (1996), *Report of the Constitution Review Group*, Dublin: the Stationery Office.

Cork and Ross Family Centre (1995), *Domestic Violence Treatment Programme: Treatment for Violent Men*, Cork and Ross Male Violence Project, 34 Paul Street, Cork.

Council for Social Welfare (1991), *The Rights of the Child: Irish Perspectives on the UN Convention*, Dublin: Council for Social Welfare.

Council of Churches for Britain and Ireland (1997), *Unemployment and the Future of Work: An Enquiry for the*

Changing Fathers?

Churches, London: Council of Churches for Britain and Ireland.

Council of Europe (1995), *'Ireland'* in Conference of European Ministers Responsible for Family Affairs, Twenty Fourth Session, Helsinki, Finland, 26–28 June, Strasbourg: Council of Europe.

Cousins, M. (1997), *Review of Scheme of Grants to Locally-Based Men's Groups*, October, Dublin: Department of Social, Community and Family Affairs.

Coverman, S., and Sheley, J. (1986), 'Change in Men's Housework and Childcare Time, 1965–1975', *Journal of Marriage and the Family*, Volume 48, pp. 413–422.

Cowan, C. and P. (1988), 'Working with Men Becoming Fathers: The Impact of a Couples Group Intervention', in Bronstein P., and Cowan C. and P. (Eds.), *Fatherhood Today*, New York: John Wiley and Sons.

Coward, R. (1983), *Patriarchal Precedents*, London: Routledge and Keegan Paul.

Crouter, A., Perry-Jenkins, M., Huston, T., McHale, S. (1987), 'Processes Underlying Father Involvement in Dual-earner and Single-Earner Families', *Developmental Psychology*, Volume 23, pp. 431–440.

Daly, K. J. (1995), 'Reshaping Fatherhood: Finding the Models', in Marsiglio, W., (Ed.), *Fatherhood: Contemporary Theory, Research, and Social Policy*, London: Sage.

Deane, M. (1994), *The Legacy of Locasta – A Maternal Metaphor*, Unpublished.

Department of Education and Science (1998), *Objectives of Intervention Project in Single Sex Boys Schools.*

Department of Enterprise and Employment (1996), *Growing and Sharing Our Employment: Strategy paper on the Labour Market*, Dublin: Stationery Office.

Department of Health (1993), *Report on Vital Statistics, 1990, April*, Compiled by the Central Statistics Office, Dublin: Stationery Office.

Department of Health (1995), *Notification of Reporting of Suspected Cases of Child Abuse between Health Boards and Gardaí*, Dublin: Department of Health.

Department of Health and Social Security (1995), *Child Protection: Messages from Research*, London: HMSO.

DeVault, M. (1991), *Feeding the Family*, Chicago: University of Chicago Press.

Dobash, R. and Dobash, R. (1996), 'The costs of violence against women', *Paper presented to the Task Force on*

236

Violence Against Women Conference, Kiliney, Dublin, November 1996.

Doherty, D. (1996), 'Childcare and Protection: Protecting the Children – Supporting their Service Providers', in Ferguson, H., and McNamara, T., (Editors), *Protecting Irish Children: Investigation, Protection and Welfare*, special edition of *Administration*, Volume 44, Number 2, pp. 102–113.

Drage Piechowski, L. (1992), 'Mental Health and Women's Multiple Roles in Families in Society', *The Journal of Contemporary Human Sciences*, March, pp. 131–138.

Drew, E., Emerek, R., and Mahon, E. (1995), 'Families, Labour Markets and Gender Roles', *A Report on a European Research Workshop*, Dublin: European Foundation for the Improvement of Living and Working Conditions.

Dromey M., and Doherty, M. (1992), 'Fathers' Involvement with their Non-Marital Children', *Workshop Conference Paper Presented to the Conference: Surviving Childhood Adversity*, Trinity College Dublin, Dublin: Treoir: Federation of Services for Unmarried Parents and their Children.

Eekelaar, J., and Clive, E. (1977), *Custody After Divorce*, Oxford: Centre for Socio-Legal Studies.

Employment Equality Agency (1996), *Introducing Family-Friendly Initiatives in the Workplace*, Researched and Written by Hugh Fisher, Dublin: Employment Equality Agency.

Erikson, E. (1963), *Childhood and Society*, Toronto: Norton.

EU Directive on Parental Leave (1996), 'Council Directive 96/34/EC of 3 June 1996 on the framework agreement on parental leave concluded by UNICE, CEEP and ETUC', *Official Journal of the European Communities, No I 145/4, 19.6.96*, Luxembourg: Office for Official Publications of the European Communities.

Eurostat (1997), Statistics in Focus: population and Social Conditions, Number 5 / 97, Family Responsibilities – How Are They Shared in European Households?, Luxembourg: Office for Official Publications of the European Communities.

Eurostat (1996), *Labour Force Survey: Results 1995*, Luxembourg: Office for Official Publications of the European Communities.

Eurobarometer 39.0 (1993), *Europeans and the Family: Results of an Opinion Survey*, December, Brussels: Commission of the European Communities, Directorate General V for Employment, Industrial Relations and Social Affairs.

European Commission Network on Childcare (1990), *Men as Carers for Children*, Brussels: European Commission Network on Childcare.

European Commission Network on Childcare (1993), *Men as Carers: Report of an International Seminar in Ravenna, Italy, 21–22 May*, Brussels: European Commission Network on Childcare.

European Court of Human Rights (1994), 'Judgement in the Case of Keegan v. Ireland', Strasbourg: European Court of Human Rights.

Fahey, T., and Lyons, M. (1995), *Marital Breakdown and Family Law in Ireland*, Oak Tree Press in association with The Economic and Social Research Institute.

Farrington, D.P., and Morris, A. (1983), 'Sex, Sentencing and Reconviction', *British Journal of Criminology*, Volume 23, pp. 229–248.

Featherstone, B., and Holloway, W. (Eds.), (1997), *Motherhood and Ambivalence*, London: Routledge.

Ferguson, H. (1996a), 'Men's Issues and Changing Experiences of Masculinity in Ireland', in McCarthy, D., and Lewis R., (Eds.), *Man And Now: Changing Perspectives*, Cork: Togher Family Centre.

Ferguson, H. (1996b), 'Child Abuse as a Social Problem and the Development of the Child Protection System in the Republic of Ireland', in Ferguson, H., and McNamara, T., (Eds.), *Protecting Irish Children: Investigation, Protection and Welfare*, Special Edition of *Administration*, Volume 44, Number 2.

Ferguson, H. (1997a), 'Understanding Men and Masculinities', *Proceedings of the Men and Intimacy Conference*, published by St Catherineís Community Services Centre, Carlow.

Ferguson, H. (1997b), 'Woman Protection, Child Protection and the Implications of the Domestic Violence Act 1996 for Health Boards'. *A paper based on the findings of a research study commissioned by the Mid-Western Health Board*, Department of Applied Social Studies, University College Cork.

Ferguson, H. (1997c), 'Vicious circle: domestic violence and the law', *Gazette: Journal of the Law Society of Ireland*, Vol. 91, no. 3.

Ferguson, H. (1998), 'Working with men and masculinities', *Feedback, Journal of the Family Therapy Association of Ireland*, Volume 8, Number 1.

Ferguson, H., and Kenny, P., (Eds.), (1995), *On Behalf of the Child: Child Welfare, Child Protection and the Childcare Act 1991*, Dublin: A. & A. Farmar.

Ferguson, H., and Synott, P. (1995), 'Intervention into Domestic Violence in Ireland: Developing Policy and Practice with Men who Batter', *Administration*, Volume 43, Number 3.

Ferri, E., and Smith, K. (1996), *Parenting in the 1990s*, London: Family Policy Studies Centre.

Finkelhor, D. (1986), 'Abusers: A Review of the Research', in D. Finkelhor and associates, *A Sourcebook on Child Sexual Abuse*, London: Sage.

Flower, P, and MacCannell, J. (1986), *Figuring Lacan: Criticism and the Cultural Unconscious*, London and Sydney: Croom Helm.

Folbre, N. (1994), *Who Pays for the Kids? Gender and the Structures of Constraint*, London: Routledge.

French, S. (1993), 'Introduction', in French, S., (Ed.), *Fatherhood*, London: Virago Press, pp. 1–8.

French, S. (1995), 'The Fallen Idol' in Moss, P., (Ed.), *Father Figures: Fathers in the Families of the 1990s*, Edinburgh: HMSO, pp. 1–6.

Freud, S. (1954), *The Interpretation of Dreams*, Standard Edition, London: Hogarth Press, Volumes 3, 4.

Freud, S. (1966), *Standard Edition of the Complete Psychological Works of Sigmund Freud*, The Hogarth Press and the Institute of Psychoanalysis: London.

Freud, S. (1977), *On Sexuality*, Vol. 7, Penguin Books.

Freud, S. (1977), 'The Infantile Genital Organisation: An Interpolation into the Theory of Sexuality' (1923), *On Sexuality*, Penguin Books.

Freud, S. (1977), 'The Dissolution of the Oedipus Complex' (1924) *On Sexuality*, Penguin Books.

Freud, S. (1977), 'Some Psychical Consequences of the Anatomical Distinction Between the Sexes', (1925) *On Sexuality*, Penguin Books.

Freud, S. (1977), 'Female Sexuality', (1931) *On Sexuality*, Penguin Books.

Freud, S. (1984), 'A Note on the Unconscious in Psychoanalysis' (1912), *P.F.L. Vol. 11*, London: Pelican Books.

Freud, S. (1977), *Case Histories II P.F.L. vol. 9*, Penguin Books, (first published 1924).

Furstenberg, F., and Cherlin, A. (1991*), Divided Families: What Happens to Children When Parents Part?*, Cambridge: Harvard University Press.

Furstenberg, F., and Nord, C. (1987), 'Parenting Apart', *Journal of Marriage and the Family*, Volume 47, pp. 893–904.

Furstenberg, F. (1995), 'Fathering in the Inner City: Paternal Participation and Public Policy', in Marsiglio, W., (Ed.), *Fatherhood: Contemporary Theory, Research, and Social Policy*, London: Sage.

Fynes, B., Morrissey, T., Roche, W., Whelan, B., Williams, J. (1996), *Flexible Working Lives: The Changing Nature of Working Time Arrangements in Ireland*, Dublin: Oak Tree Press in association with Graduate School of Business, University College Dublin.

Gallagher, C. (1986), The Function of the Father in the Family: Psychoanalytic Notes. *Studies* (Summer).

Gallop, J. (1982), *Feminism and Psychoanalysis*, Macmillan.

Gallop, J. (1985), *Reading Lacan*, New York: Cornell.

Geiran, V. (1996), Treatment of Sex Offenders in Ireland – The Development of Policy and Practice, in Ferguson, H., and McNamara, T., (Eds.), *Protecting Irish Children: Investigation, Protection and Welfare*, Special Edition of *Administration*, Volume 44, Number 2.

Gershuny, J., and Robinson, J. (1991), 'The Household Division of Labour: Multinational Comparisons of Change', in *The Changing Use of Time: Report from an International Workshop*, Dublin: European Foundation for the Improvement of Living and Working Conditions, pp. 152–183.

Gerson, K. (1993), *No Man's Land: Men's Changing Commitments to Family and Work*, New York: Basic Books.

Gibson, J. (1992), 'Non-Custodial Fathers and Access patterns' in *Research Report*, Family Court of Australia.

Giddens, A. (1991), *Modernity and Self-Identity*, Cambridge: Polity.

Giddens, A. (1992), *The Transformation of Intimacy*, Cambridge: Polity.

Giddens, A. (1994), *Beyond Left and Right*, Cambridge: Polity.

Glueck, S., and Glueck, E. (1950), *Unravelling Juvenile Delinquency*, Harvard: Harvard University Press.

Government of Ireland (1996), *Partnership 2000 for Inclusion, Employment and Competitiveness*, Dublin: The Stationery Office.

Government of Ireland (1997), *Growing Our Employment – Sharing Our Growth: A Comprehensive Policy for Enterprise and Jobs*, May, Dublin: The Stationery Office.

Greenberger, E., and O'Neill, R. (1990), 'Parents' Concerns about their Child's Development: Implications for Fathers' and Mothers' Well-Being and Attitudes Towards Work', in *Journal of Marriage and the Family*, Volume 52, pp. 621–635.

Griswold, R. L. (1993), *Fatherhood in America: A History*, New York: Basic Books.

Hanley, D. (1995), 'The Sweet Sorrow of Reconciled Partings' in Hyde, T., (Ed.), *Fathers and Sons*, Dublin: Wolfhound Press, pp. 111–112.

Hannan, D.F. (1973), 'Changes in Family Relationship Patterns', *Social Studies: Irish Journal of Sociology*, Volume 23, Number 6, December, pp. 559–563.

Hannan, D.F., and Katsiaouni, L.A. (1977), *Traditional Families? From Culturally Prescribed to Negotiated Roles in Farm Families*, Paper Number 87, January, Dublin: Economic and Social Research Institute.

Hannan, D., and O'Riain, S. (1993), *Pathways to Adulthood in Ireland: Causes and Consequences of Success and Failure in Transitions Amongst Irish Youth*, Paper Number 161, December, Dublin: The Economic and Social Research Institute.

Hawkins, A., Christiansen, S.L., Pond Sargent, K., and Hill, E.J. (1995), 'Rethinking Fathers Involvement in Childcare: A Developmental Perspective', in Marsiglio, W., (Ed.), *Fatherhood: Contemporary Theory, Research, and Social Policy*, London: Sage.

Hawkins A., and Roberts, T-A. (1992), 'Designing a Primary Intervention to Help Dual-Earner Couples Share Housework and Childcare' in *Family Relations*, Volume 41, pp. 169–177.

Hillman, J. (1996), *The Soul's Code: In Search of Character and Calling*, New York: Random House.

Hillman, J. (1994), *We've Had a Hundred Years of Psychotherapy and the World's Getting Worse*, New York: Random House.

Hochschild, A. R., with Manning A. (1989), *The Second Shift: Working Parents and the Revolution at Home*, New York: Viking.

Hogan, F. (1998), 'Soulful Storytelling with Men: An invitation to intimacy', *Feedback, Journal of the Family Therapy Association of Ireland*, Volume 8, Number 1.

Hooper, C., A. (1992), *Mothers Surviving Child Sexual Abuse*, London: Routledge.

Hornsby-Smith, M., and Whelan, C., (1994), 'Religious and Moral Values', in Whelan, C., (Ed.), *Values and Social Change in Ireland*, Dublin: Gill and Macmillan, pp. 7–44.

Hyde, T. (Ed.), (1996), *Fathers and Sons*, Dublin: Wolfhound.

Inglis, T. (1987), *Moral Monopoly: The Catholic Chruch in Modern Irish Society*, Dublin: Gill and Macmillan.

Ireland (1997), *Labour Force Survey 1996*, January, Dublin: Stationery Office.

Ishii-Kuntz, M. (1995), 'Paternal Involvement and Perception toward Fathers' Roles: A comparison between Japan and the United States', in Marsiglio, W., (Ed.), *Fatherhood: Contemporary Theory, Research, and Social Policy*, London: Sage.

Ishii-Kuntz, M., and Coltrane, S. (1992), 'Predicting the Sharing of Household Labour: Are Parenting and Housework Distinct?', *Sociological Perspectives*, Volume 35, pp. 629–647.

Jackson, B. (1984), *Fatherhood*, London: Allen and Unwin.

Jensen, A-M. (1993), 'Fathers and Children – the Paradox of Closeness and Distance' in *Fathers in Families of Tomorrow*, Report from the Conference held in Copenhagen, 17–18 June 1993, Copenhagen: The Ministry of Social Affairs.

Jump, T. and Haas, L. (1987), Fathers in transition, in M.S. Kimmel, *Changing Men*, London: Sage.

Jung, C. (1961), 'The Significance of the Father in the Destiny of the Individual', *Collected Works*, Volume 4, pp. 301–323, London: Routledge and Kegan Paul. First published in 1909 and revised in 1949.

Jung, C. (1994). Quoted in Ellenberger, H., *The Discovery of the Unconscious: The History and Evolution of Dynamic Psychiatry*, London: Fontana Press. Jung's quotation was first published in 1942.

Kagan, J. (1990), 'The Power and Limitations of parents', in Wilmer, H., (Editor), *Mother Father*, Illinois: Chiron Publications, pp. 69–88.

Keen, S. (1991), *Fire in the Belly: On Being a Man*, New York: Bantam Books.

Kelleher and Associates and O'Connor, M. (1995), *Making the Links*, Dublin: Women's Aid.

Kelleher, M., (1996), Suicide and the Irish, Cork: Mercier Press.

Kelleher, M., et al., (1997), Implications of Regional Differences in Suidice Rates in Ireland, *Irish Medical Journal*.

Kelly, N. (1995), 'Father's Legacy' in Hyde, T., (Ed.), *Fathers and Sons*, Dublin: Wolfhound Press, p. 156.

Kempeneers, M., and Lelievre, E. (1992), *Work and the Family in the Twelve EC States*, Eurobarometer Number 34, Eurostat, Luxembourg: Office for the Official Publications of the European Community.

Kieran, P. (1997), '"They Never Told Me it Would be This Difficult": Making Life Easier for Men', *Proceedings of the Men and Intimacy Conference*, published by St Catherine's Community Services Centre, Carlow.

Kiernan, K. (1992), 'Men and Women at Work and at Home', in Jowell, R., et al (Eds.), *British Social Attitudes: the Ninth Report*, Dartmouth: SCPR.

Kiely, G. (1996), 'Fathers in Families' in Colgan McCarthy, I., (Ed.), *Irish Family Studies: Selected Papers*, University College Dublin, pp. 147–158.

Kimmel, M. (1994), 'Masculinity as Homophobia: Fear, Shame, and Silence in the Construction of Gender Identity', in Brod, H., and Kaufman, M., (Eds.), *Theorising Masculinities*, London: Sage.

Kimmel, M. (Ed,), (1995), *The Politics of Manhood*, Philadelphia: Temple University Press.

Koch-Nielsen (1987), *New Family Patterns: Divorces in Denmark*, Booklet Number 23, Copenhagen: The Danish Institute for Social Research.

Kolvin, I., Miller, F., Scott, D., Gatzanis, S., Fleeting, M. (1990), *Continuities of Deprivation, ESRC / DHSS Studies in Deprivation and Disadvantage Number 15*, London: Avebury.

Kraemer, S. (1995), 'Parenting Yesterday, Today and Tomorrow, in Utting, D., (Editor), *Families and Parenting Conference Report: Proceedings of a Conference held in London, 26 September 1995*, London: Family Policy Studies Centre.

Lacan, J. (1977), *Ecrits: A selection*, Tavistock, Routledge.

Lacan, J. (1951), 'Intervention on Transference', in Mitchell, J., and Rose, J., (Eds.) 1982, *Feminine Sexuality*, London: Macmillan.

Lacan, J. (1958), *The Family*, Unpublished, Translated by Cormac Gallagher.

Lacan, J. (1953), The Neurotics Individual Myth, *Psych Quat*, 1979 Trs. Evans.

Lacan, J. (1973), *The Four Fundamental Concepts* (Le Seminaire de Jacques Lacan, Paris) 1979, London: Penguin.

Lamb, M. (1986), *The Fathers Role*, New York: John Wiley and Sons.

Lamb, M. (1997), 'Fathers and Child Development: An Introductory Overview and Guide', in Lamb, M., (Ed.), *The Role of the Father in Child Development*, Third Edition, New York: John Wiley and Sons, pp. 1–18.

Laplanche, J., and Pontalis, J.B. (1988), *The Language of Psychoanalysis*, Karnac Books.

Law Reform Commission (1982), *Report on Illegitimacy*, Dublin: Law Reform Commission.

Law Reform Commission (1996), *Family Courts*, Dublin: Law Reform Commission.

Leonard, H. (1995), 'The Stroke of a Pen' in Hyde, T., (Ed.), *Fathers and Sons*, Dublin: Wolfhound Press, pp. 36–38.

Leupnitz, D. (1986), 'A Comparison of Maternal, Paternal and Joint Custody', *Journal of Divorce*, Volume 9, Number 3, pp. 1–12.

Lewis, C. (1986), *Becoming a Father*, Milton Keynes: Open University Press.

Lewis, C., et al (1982), 'Father Participation through Childhood and its Relation to Career Aspirations of Delinquency' in, N., and McGuire, J., (Eds.) *Fathers: Psychological Perspectives*, London: Junction Books.

Lewis, C. (1993), 'Mother's and Fathers' Roles: Similar or Different?', in *Fathers in Families of Tomorrow, Report from the Conference held in Copenhagen, 17–18 June 1993*, Copenhagen: The Ministry of Social Affairs.

Lewis, C., and O'Brien, M. (1987), 'Constraints on Fathers: Research, Theory and Clinical Practice', in Lewis, C., and O'Brien, M., (Eds.), *Reassessing Fatherhood*, London: Sage, pp. 1–22.

Lord Chancellor's Department (1998), *Court Procedures for the Determination of Paternity and The Law on Parental Responsibility for Unmarried Fathers, Consultation Paper*, March, London: Lord Chancellor's Department.

Louv, R. (1994), *Reinventing Fatherhood*, Vienna: United Nations.

Lowe, N. (1982), 'The Legal Status of Fathers – Past and Present' in McKee, L., and O'Brien, M., (Eds.), *The Father Figure*.

Lyons, A., and Hunt, P. (1988), 'The Effects of Gender on Sentencing: A Case Study of the Dublin Metropolitan Area District Court', in Tomlinson, M., Varley, T., and McCullagh, C., (Eds.), *Whose Law and Order? Aspects of Crime and*

Social Control in Irish Society, Belfast: The Sociological Association of Ireland, pp. 129–142.

Maccoby E.E., Depner, C., and Mnookin, R.H. (1990), 'Co-Parenting in the Second Year after Divorce', *Journal of Marriage and the Family*, Volume 52, pp. 141–155.

Maccoby E.E., and Mnookin, R.H. (1992), *Dividing the Child: Social and Legal Dilemmas of Custody*, Cambridge Massachusetts: Harvard University Press.

Mandela, N. (1994), *Long Walk to Freedom: The Autobiography of Nelson Mandela*, London: Little Brown.

Marks, E., de Courtivron, I. (Ed) (1981), *New French Feminisms*, Schocken Books.

Marsiglio, W. (1995), 'Fathers' Diverse Life Course Patterns and Roles', in Marsiglio W., (Ed.), *Fatherhood: Contemporary Theory, Research, and Social Policy*, London: Sage.

McCarthy, D., and Lewis, R. (1996), *Man And Now: Changing Perspectives*, Cork: Togher Family Centre.

McCashin, A. (1993), *Lone Parents in the Republic of Ireland: Enumeration, Description and Implications for Social Security*, Broadsheet Series, Paper Number 29, September, Dublin: The Economic and Social Research Institute.

McCashin, A. (1996), *Lone Mothers in Ireland: A Local Study*, Dublin: Oak Tree Press in association with the Combat Poverty Agency.

McCullagh, C. (1996), *Crime in Ireland: A Sociological Introduction*, Cork: Cork University Press.

McGrath, K. (1992), 'Inter-Agency Co-operation in the Provision of Group Therapy for Adolescent Sex Offenders and Their Parents', *Unpublished paper presented to the Ninth International Conference on Child Abuse and Neglect*, Chicago IL, 2 September.

McGrath, K. (1996), 'Intervening in Child Sexual Abuse in Ireland: Towards Victim-Centred Policies and Practices', in Ferguson, H., and McNamara, T., (Editors), *Protecting Irish Children: Investigation, Protection and Welfare*, Special Edition of *Administration*, Volume 44, Number 2.

McGuinness, C. (1993), *Report of the Kilkenny Incest Investigation*, Dublin: Stationery Office.

McKeown, K. (1997a), 'Marriage: A Male Perspective' Paper presented to a conference on *Love, Marriage and Divorce: A Male Perspective organised by Marriage and Relationship Counselling Services and held in the Royal College of Surgeons*, Dublin 2, Saturday, 1 November.

McKeown, K. (1997b), 'Vocation Re-Defined' in McKeown K., and Arthurs, H., (Editors), *Soul Searching: Personal Stories of the Search for Meaning in Modern Ireland*, Dublin: Columba Press, pp. 91–97.

McKeown, K., and Gilligan, R. (1991), 'Child Sexual Abuse in the Eastern Health Board Region of Ireland in 1988: An Analysis of 512 Confirmed Cases', in *The Economic and Social Review*, Volume 22, Number 2, January, pp.101–134.

McKeown, K., Gilligan, R., Brannick, T., McGuane, B., Riordan, S. (1993), *Child Sexual Abuse in the Eastern Health Board Region, Ireland, 1988: A Statistical Analysis of all Suspected and Confirmed Cases of Child Sexual Abuse Known to the Social Work Teams in the Community Care Areas of the Eastern Health Board which were Open at any time in 1988*. Dublin: Eastern Health Board.

McKeown, K. and Fitzgerald, G. (1997), *Developing Childcare Services in Disadvantaged Areas: Evaluation of the Pilot Childcare Initiative (1994–1995)*, Dublin: Area Development Management Ltd.

McLoyd, V. (1989), 'Socialisation and Development in a Changing Economy: The Effects of Paternal Job and Income Loss on Children' *American Psychologist*, Volume 44, pp. 293–302.

McNeely, D. (1996), *Mercury Rising: Women, Evil and the Trickster Gods*, Connecticut: Spring Publications.

McRae, S. (1997), 'Household and Labour Market Change: Implications for the Growth of Inequality in Britain', *British Journal of Sociology*, Volume 48, Number 3, September, pp. 384–405.

Meade, M. (1993), *Men and the Water of Life: Initiation and the Tempering of Life*, New York: HarperSanFrancisco.

Mendel, S. (1995), *The Male Survior*, London: Sage.

Milotte, M. (1997), *Banished Babies*, Dublin: New Island Books.

Millar, J., and Warman, A. (1996), *Family Obligations in Europe*, London: Family Policy Studies Centre.

Milner, J. (1993), 'Avoiding Violent Men: The Gendered Nature of Child Protection Policy and Practice', in Ferguson, H., Gilligan, R., and Torode, R., (Eds.), *Surviving Childhood Adversity: Issues for Policy and Practice*, Dublin: Social Studies Press.

Milner, J. (1996), 'Men's Resistance to Social Workers', in Fawcett, B., Featherstone, B., Hearn, J., and Toft, C., (Eds.), *Violence and Gender Relations: Theories and Interventions*, London: Sage.

Mintel International Group Ltd. (1994), *Men 2000*, London: Mintel International Group Ltd.

Mitchell, J. (1974), *Psychoanalysis and Feminism*, Penguin Books.

Mitchell, J., Rose, J. (1982), *Jacques Lacan and the Ecole Freudienne: Female Sexuality*, London: Macmillan

Moore, R., and Gilette, D. (1990), *King, Warrior, Magician, Lover: Rediscovering the Archetypes of the Mature Masculine*, New York: HarperCollins Publishers.

Morgan, P. (1966), *Who Needs Parents? The Effects of Childcare and Early Education on Children in Britain and the USA*, London: the IEA Health and Welfare Unit.

Moss, P. (1992), 'Foreword' to Ruxton, S., 'What's he doing at the family centre?': *The dilemmas of men who care for children, A Research Report*, London: National Children's Home.

Moss, P. (1993), 'Strategies to Promote Fathers' Involvement in the Care and Upbringing of their Children: Placing Leave Arrangements in a Wider Context', in *Fathers in Families of Tomorrow, Report from the Conference held in Copenhagen, 17–18 June 1993*, Copenhagen: The Ministry of Social Affairs.

Muller, J. P. and Richardson, W.J. (1982), *Lacan and Language: A Readers Guide to Ecrits*, New York: International Universities Press, Inc.

Murphy, M. (1996), 'From Prevention to "Family Support" and Beyond: Promoting the Welfare of Irish Children', in Ferguson, H., and McNamara T., (Eds.), *Protecting Irish Children: Investigation, Protection and Welfare*, special edition of *Administration*, Volume 44, Number 2.

National Economic and Social Council (1996), *Strategy into the 21st Century, Report Number 99*, Dublin: National Economic and Social Council.

National Task Force on Suicide, (1998), Report, January, Dublin: Stationery Office.

Newburn, T., and Stanko, B. (1994), *Just Boys Doing Business? Masculinities and Crime*, London: Sage.

Nickel H., and Kocher, N. (1987), 'West Germany and German Speaking Countries' in Lamb, M.E., (Ed.), *The Father's Role: Cross Cultural Comparisons*, Hillsdale NJ: Lawrence Erlbaum.

Nolan, B., and Farrell, B. (1990), *Child Poverty in Ireland*, Dublin: Combat Poverty Agency.

O'Brien, M., and Jones, D. (1996), 'Fathers Through the Eyes of Their Children', in Bjrnberg U., and Kollind, A-K., (Eds.), *Men's Family Relations*, Stockholm: Almqvist and Wiksell International.

O'Connor, C. (1996), 'Integrating feminist and psychological systemic approaches in working with men who are violent towards their partners: The Cork Domestic Violence Project', *Feedback*, Vol. 7, no. 1.

O'Connor, C. (1997), 'Men and Intimacy: Fathers and Sons' in *Men and Intimacy Conference Proceedings, Saint Catherine's Community Services Centre and Accord*, Carlow: Saint Catherine's Community Services Centre, pp. 19–33.

O'Hagan, K. (1997), 'The Problem of Engaging Men in Child Protection Work', *British Journal of Social Work*, Volume 27, pp. 25–42.

O'Hara, P. (1997), 'Interfering Women – Farm Mothers and the Reproduction of Family Farming', *The Economic and Social Review*, April, Volume 28, Number 2, pp. 135–156.

Olds, S., (1992), 'Saturn' in Bly, R., Hillman, J., and Meade, M., (Eds.), *The Rag and Bone Shop of the Heart: Poems for Men*, New York: HarperCollins Publishers, p. 128.

O'Mahony, P. (1997), *Mountjoy Prisoners: A Sociological and Criminological Profile*, Dublin: Stationery Office.

Ottosen (1996), 'Relationships Between Non-Resident Fathers and Their Children in Denmark' in Bjrnberg U., and Kollind, A-K., (Eds.), *Men's Family Relations*, Stockholm: Almqvist and Wiksell International.

Owen, M., and Cox, M. (1988), 'The Transition to Parenthood', in Gottfried, A., Gottfried, A., and Bathurst, K., (Eds.), *Maternal Employment, Family Environment and Children's Development: Infancy Through the School Years*, Plenum Press.

Parental Equality (1997), *The Custody Crisis: A Submission to the Minister for Equality and Law Reform*, February, Dundalk: Parental Equality.

Pleck, E., and Pleck, J. (1997), 'Fatherhood Ideals in the United States: Historical Dimensions', in Lamb, M., (Ed.), *The Role of the Father in Child Development*, Third Edition, New York: John Wiley and Sons, pp. 33–48.

Pleck, J. (1997), 'Paternal Involvement: Levels, Sources and Consequences', in Lamb, M., (Ed.), *The Role of the Father in Child Development*, Third Edition, New York: John Wiley and Sons, pp. 66–103.

Pleck, J. (1993), 'Are "family-supportive" employer policies relevant to men?', in Hood, J. C., (Ed.), *Men, Work and Family*, Newbury Park, CA: Sage.

Pleck, J. (1987), 'American fathering in historical perspective', in M. Kimmel (ed), *Changing Men*: London: Sage.

Polikoff, N. (1983), 'Gender and child-custody determinants: Exploding the myths', in Diamond, I., (Ed.), *Families, politics and public policy: A feminist dialogue on women and the state*, New York: Longman.

Pruett, K. (1983), 'Infants of Primary Nurturing Fathers', *Psychoanalytic Study of the Child*, Volume 38, pp. 257–277.

Pruett, K. (1985), 'Children of the fathermothers: Infants of Primary Nurturing Fathers' in Call, J., Galenson, E., Tyson, R., (Eds.), *Frontiers of Infant Psychiatry*, Volume 2, New York: Basic Books, pp. 375–380.

Pruzan, V. (1993), 'The Modern Family – A New Generation of Parents?', in *Fathers in Families of Tomorrow, Report from the Conference held in Copenhagen, 17–18 June 1993*, Copenhagen: The Ministry of Social Affairs.

Radin, N. (1982), 'Primary Care-giving and Role-Sharing Fathers', in Lamb, M., (Ed.), *Non-traditional Families: Parenting and Child Development*, pp. 173–204, Hillsdale, NJ: Erlbaum.

Radin, N. (1994), 'Primary Care-giving Fathers in Intact Families', in Gottfried, A., and Gottfried, A., (Eds.), *Redefining Families: Implications for Children's Development*, New York: Plenum, pp. 11–54.

Real, T. (1997), *I Don't Want to Talk About It: Overcoming The Secret Legacy of Male Depression*, New York: Scribner; Dublin: Gill and Macmillan.

Richards, M. (1982), 'Post-Divorce Arrangements for Children: A Psychological Perspective', *Journal of Social Welfare Law*, pp. 133–151.

Richardson, V. (1991), 'Decision-Making by Unmarried Mothers, *The Irish Journal of Psychology*, Volume 12, Number 2, pp. 165–181.

Richardson, V. (1995), 'Reconciliation of Family Life and Working Life', in Colgan McCarthy, I., (Editor), *Irish Family Studies: Selected Papers*, University College Dublin, pp. 127–146.

Roberts, C. (1996), 'The Place of Marriage in a Changing Society', *Presentation to the Lord Chancellor's Conference: Supporting Marriage into the Next Century, 3 April, Working Paper Number 2*, London: Family Policy Studies Centre.

Robins, L. (1966), *Deviant Children Growing Up*, New York: Robert E., Krieger.

Robinson, M. (1995), *Family Transformation Through Divorce and Re-Marriage*, London: Routledge (Quoted in *The Irish Times*, Tuesday 28 March 1995).

Rooney, D. (1994), *Dora, Desire and the Oedipus Complex.* Unpublished.

Rutter, M. (1994), *Clinical Implications of Attachment Concepts, Retrospect and Prospect*, Bowlby Memorial Lecturer.

Ruxton, S. (1992), 'What's he doing at the family centre?': *The dilemmas of men who care for children, A Research Report*, London: National Children's Home.

Rylands, J. (1995), *A Study of Parenting Programmes in Ireland: Exploration of Needs and Current Provision*, Dublin: National Children's Centre/Department of Health.

Ryce-Menuhin, J. (1996), *Naked and Erect: Male Sexuality and Feeling*, Illinois: Chiron Publications.

Saint Catherine's Community Services Centre and Accord (1997), *Men and Intimacy, Conference Proceedings*, Carlow: Saint Catherine's Community Services Centre and Accord.

Sanik, M. (1981), 'Division of Household Work: A Decade Comparison, 1967–1977', *Home Economics Journal*, Volume 10, pp. 175–180.

Sandqvist, K. (1987), 'Swedish Family Policy and the Attempt to Change Paternal Roles, in Lewis, C., and O'Brien, M., (Eds.), *Reassessing Fatherhood*, London: Sage, pp. 144–160.

Sandqvist, K. (1992), 'Sweden's Sex-Role Scheme and the Attempt to Change Paternal Roles', in Lewis, S., and Israeli, D., and Hootsmans, H., (Eds.), *Dual-Earner Families: International Perspectives*, London: Sage, pp. 80–98.

Schneiderman, S. (1986), *Returning to Freud, Clinical Psychoanalysis in the School of Lacan*, Ed. S Schneiderman, New York: Yale University Press.

Schultheis, F. (1993), 'Perspectives: Towards Socio-Political Recognition of Paternity in the Countries of the Community' in *Fathers in Families of Tomorrow, Report from the Conference held in Copenhagen, 17–18 June 1993*, Copenhagen: The Ministry of Social Affairs, pp. 230–237.

Second Commission on the Status of Women (1993), *Report to Government*, January, Dublin: Stationery Office.

Segal, L. (1990), *Slow Motion: Changing masculinities, Changing men*, London: Virago.

Seidler, V. J. (1997), *Man Enough: Emodying Masculinities*, London: Sage.

Seltzer, J. (1991), 'Relationships Between Fathers and Children Who Live Apart', *Journal of Marriage and the Family*, Volume 53, pp. 79–102.

Shiel, D. (1995), 'My Father' in Hyde, T., (Ed.), *Fathers and Sons*, Dublin: Wolfhound Press, pp. 157–169.

Silber, J. (1990), 'The Myth of the Hero' in Wilmer, H., (Ed.), *Mother Father*, Illinois: Chiron Publications, pp. 129–160.

Skynner, R. (1995), *Family Matters: A Guide to Healthier and Happier Relationships*, London: Methuen.

Smith, R. (1995), 'Loss, Grief and Unemployment', *Inside Out*, Autumn.

Smith, R. (1996), 'The Life of a Men's Group', in McCarthy, D., and Lewis, R., (Eds.), *Man And Now: Changing Perspectives*, Cork: Togher Family Centre.

Social Europe (1994), *The European Union and the Family, 1/94*, Brussels: Directorate-General for Employment, Industrial Relations and Social Affairs, European Commission.

Sternberg, K. J. (1997), 'Fathers: the Missing Parents in Research on Family Violence' in Lamb ME., (Ed.), *The Role of the Father in Child Development*, New York: Wiley.

Stitt, S., and Macklin, A. (1997), 'Changing Gender Balances in the 'Culture' of Domestic Violence', *Paper presented to the Sociological Association of Ireland Conference*, Westport, Mayo, May 1997.

Swedin, G. (1995), 'Modern Swedish Fatherhood: Challenges Which Offer Great Opportunities' in *Men on Men: Eight Swedish Men's Personal Views on Equality, Masculinity and Parenthood. A Contribution by the Swedish government to the Fourth World Conference on Women in Beijing 1995.* Sweden: Ministry of Health and Social Affairs, pp. 112–131.

Task Force on Violence Against Women (1997), *Report*, Office of the Tánaiste, Dublin: Stationery Office.

Tolson, A. (1977), *The Limits to Masculinity*, London: Tavistock.

Utting, D., Bright, J., and Henricson, C. (1993), *Crime and the Family: Improving Child rearing and Preventing Delinquency, Occasional paper 16*, London: Family Policy Studies Centre.

Volling, B., and Belsky, J. (1991), 'Multiple Determinants of Father Involvement During Infancy in Dual-Earner and Single-Earner Families', *Journal of Marriage and the Family*, Volume 53, pp. 461–474.

Wadsworth, M. (1979), *The Roots of Delinquency*, London: Martin Robertson.

Wallerstein, J., and Kelly, J. (1980), *Surviving the Break-up*, New York: Basic Books.

Walzer, S. (1996), Thinking About the Baby: Gender and Divisions of Infant Care, *Social Problems*, Volume 43, Number 2.

Weitzman, L. (1985), *The divorce revolution: The unexpected social and economic consequences for women and children in America*, New York: Free Press.

West, D. (1982), *Delinquency: Its Roots, Careers and Prospects*, London: Heineman.

West, D., and Farrington, D. (1973), *Who Becomes Delinquent*, London: Heinemann.

Wheelock, J. (1991*), Husbands at Home: The Domestic Economy in a Post-Industrial Society*, London: Routledge.

Whelan C., and Fahey, T. (1994), 'Marriage and the Family', in Whelan, C., (Ed.), *Values and Social Change in Ireland*, Dublin: Gill and Macmillan, pp. 45–81.

Whelan, C., Hannan, D., and Creighton, S. (1991), *Unemployment, Poverty and Psychological Distress*, Dublin: The Economic and Social Research Institute.

Wilmer, H., (Ed.), (1990), *Mother Father*, Illinois: Chiron Publications.

Wilson, J., and Neckerman, K. (1986), 'Poverty and Family Structure: The Widening Gap Between Evidence and Public Policy Issues', in Danzinger, S., and Weinberg, D., (Eds.), *Fighting Poverty*, Cambridge, MA: Harvard university Press.

Winnicott, D. (1964), *The Child, the Family and the Outside World*: London: Penguin Books.

Zorza, J. (1992), 'Friendly Parent Provisions in Custody Determinations', *Clearing House Review*, US: National Centre on Women and Family Law Inc.

INDEX